SEVEN BLANK PAGES

From Ruin to Radiance:
A Solo Travel Memoir of Courage,
Awakening, and Reinvention

BY

WHITNEY JOY

Disclaimer: This book is memoir. It reflects the author's present recollections of experiences over time. Some names and characteristics have been changed, some events have been compressed, and some dialogue has been recreated.

Seven Blank Pages
Copyright © 2025 by Rune Publishing

ISBN: 979-8-9999005-0-0 (Paperback) | 979-8-9999005-1-7 (eBook)

First Printing Edition 2025
For more information, visit www.whitneyjoy.com

"Whitney Joy doesn't just tell her story—she immerses you in it until her courage becomes contagious. As a Broadway producer, I recognize the rare alchemy at work here: a story that entertains, inspires, and invites us to confront our own blank pages. This is the kind of authentic storytelling that proves reinvention is not only possible—it's essential."

—Marisa Sechrest, 4x Tony Award-Nominated Broadway Producer

"As a storytelling coach, I've seen how truth can rewire a life. This book is proof. Whitney turns *Seven Blank Pages* into a living guidebook for courage and reclamation, reminding us that the most important story you'll ever tell is the one you *choose* to live.

Whitney writes fully, fiercely, and with the kind of vulnerability that can crack you open to claim your life. It feels like sitting across from a friend who refuses to let you settle for the life you've outgrown.

This is not a comeback story… it is a becoming story. For those who dare to admit, *There's something more for me."*

—Colleen Schell, Founder FABx: Storytelling for Coaches and Leaders

"The legacy of visionary leadership begins at the trembling edge, where truth first breaks the surface and the soul begins to receive beyond listening. In this luminous memoir, Whitney shows us what is possible for each of us, as she gracefully and bravely invites us into those exact moments in her own life... moments where awareness blooms with universal intelligence and soul purpose, so that miracles can begin their quiet ascent. *Seven Blank Pages* is a must-read for those remembering that the sacred journey begins with curiosity and the courage to keep listening."

—Tammy L Michelle Scarlett, Founder, White Lotus Global Initiative & Harmonic Legacy Institute

"Intelligently colorful, authentically captivating and provokingly honest...*Seven Blank Pages* is a master class in vulnerability, surrender and resilience. The stages of Whitney's transformation from illusion to self-acceptance are relevant and relatable to any soul experiencing life as a human."

—Mark Laisure, Co-Founder, Life Changes Network

"*Seven Blank Pages* is an energizing account and an inspiring journey in search of the self. The experiences Joy relates are likely to prompt both wanderlust and reflection, and her worldwide bounce-back shows that, with the right mindset, it is possible to accomplish pretty much anything."

—Independent Book Review

"*Seven Blank Page*s is deep, real, and raw in the most beautiful sense. Whitney doesn't just tell a story—she takes you into the layers of it all: the feminine, the ways society shapes us, the spiritual threads we're often too busy to notice—woven together so beautifully you can't help but feel it in your bones.

The lessons in these pages are exactly what you didn't know you needed. They're a reminder that the universe is teaching us every single day—and that we must take the risks to dive deeper into those lessons of who we really are.

This book is a mirror. It shows you how your inner world and outer world are constantly reflecting one another—and how most of us are too caught up in the noise, the rules, and the *shoulds* to hear the truth of our own soul.

Reading it feels like giving yourself permission to choose freedom, follow desire, and drop the expectations. It's the kind of book that leaves you both wide open and more grounded than ever."

—Renae Fieck, Bestselling Author, Feminine Leadership Coach, Occupational Therapist

"*Seven Blank Pages* is not just a memoir—it's a portal into what becomes possible when you ditch the script and surrender to the magic of the Divine. It's the kind of book that grabs you by the heart and stamps your proverbial passport with a sign from the Universe that reads: "Trust me, I got you."

Whitney has given us a masterpiece that reads like a love letter to the tender ache of reinvention. Each page pulses with poetry. Each chapter hums with the curiosity of a woman remembering herself—moving in rhythm between far-off love affairs, fractured identities, and the reclamation of her soul.

As a woman who's undergone multiple reinventions, I saw myself in every page. *Seven Blank Pages* is for the woman standing on the edge of a new beginning, pen in hand—terrified and exhilarated—wondering if she's allowed to rewrite her life. (Hint: You are.)"

—Kimberly Spencer, Bestselling Author of
Make Every Podcast Want You

"Whitney's words carried me back to my own threshold moments, the ones where life cracks open and you step forward without a map. Her journey reminded me that even in seasons of loss and uncertainty, the self we are becoming is quietly taking shape. *Seven Blank Pages* is a compass for the soul, guiding us toward the courage to begin again."

—Syama Bunten, Co-Founder, Wealth Catalyst

"It is not just a travel story. It's a meditation on risk, resilience, and the search for meaning. Each chapter feels like both a leap into the unknown and a homecoming to the self. The writing is vivid and alive… It's for readers who crave adventure and honesty more than tidy answers. And it's for anyone willing to believe, even just a little, that magic might still be possible. FIVE Stars"

—Literary Titan (Gold Book Award Winner)

"*Seven Blank Pages* is not merely a travel memoir, nor is it just a collection of pivotal life events. It is a sacred unveiling. A reminder that we are not defined by our past, our titles, or even our pain— but by our willingness to rediscover who we truly are.

Whitney has walked through fire, not to be burned, but to be reborn. And in this book, she invites you to witness that rebirth— not as a perfectly polished phoenix, but as a woman committed to living courageously, honestly, and with a heart wide open.

Her words are not only beautifully crafted but energetically potent. With poetic grit and spiritual grace, she shows us what it means to choose presence over performance, meaning over achievement, and connection over control.

Treat this book not as a passive read but as a sacred activation. Let it stir the questions you've been too afraid to ask.

—Anil Gupta, The Love Doctor

"*SEVEN BLANK PAGES*, an *EAT, PRAY, LOVE* for seekers who want to live a life of magic and authenticity, is a sexy, honest, and beautiful ride around the world and back again. When you turn the last page, you'll be inspired, enlivened, and enriched."

—Estelle Laure, Author, Literary Agent

"What distinguishes this memoir from the many "escape through travel" narratives is its balance between external adventure and internal reckoning. The book's gentle insistence is that meaning isn't found, but embodied, through small moments of courage and surrender. Readers are not invited to marvel at exotic destinations but instead recognize themselves in Joy's struggle to let go of the familiar. The writing is direct and emotionally open, allowing the lessons on synchronicity, manifestation, and empowerment to feel lived rather than prescribed. Comparisons to Elizabeth Gilbert's Eat, Pray, Love are inevitable, but Joy's work transcends such facile comparisons by emphasizing the applicability of her journey to the reader's own life.."

—Kirkus Reviews (starred review)

To all those standing on the edge.

FORWARD:

I STILL REMEMBER the first time Whitney Joy walked into our Mystery School circle on a starry night in the Colorado Rockies. It was the fall of 2023—the fires were lit, the air crisp with fresh snow blanketing the log cabin path—and she carried a blend of curiosity, wisdom, and spirit about her. It was an invitation-only Future Innovation of Health and AI Summit for audacious entrepreneurs, and I was demonstrating the power of quantum healing as she eagerly witnessed the spontaneous resolution of pain and suffering in multiple group volunteers.

Whitney soon stepped forward—eyes bright, heart blazing—and asked whether I could help her little boy, who lay fevered and sleepless with a stubborn virus. She held him in her arms as I laid my hands upon his tiny frame. Minutes later, his vitals began to slide back into coherence, his symptoms started to resolve, and he drifted into his first peaceful rest in days.

Immediately, we were immersed in a discussion about coherence, soul resonance, and the mathematics of consciousness—concepts that usually surface only in my postgraduate intensives. I knew then that she wasn't merely curious; she was already in a committed free fall on her journey of awakening, actively building wings along the way as she uncovered and remembered the universal wisdom within. The wisdom that would write the very pages you now hold.

For more than two decades, my work in Human Intelligence has been to blend rigorous biological and psychosocial foundations with the subtle quantum phenomena of energy and intention—helping people remember the encoded genius alive in every one of their cells, and the reality that their existence spans far beyond the limitations of the human body, mind, or even the dimensions of time and space. I have had the honour of advising governments, the United Nations, and Fortune 500 visionaries—yet it is encounters like the one with Whitney and her son that keep my compass true. In her, I witnessed a rare fusion of radical vulnerability and unrelenting courage: the alchemy required for genuine and exponential transformation.

That alchemy pours through every line of *Seven Blank Pages*. Yes, this is a travel memoir that spans Parisian rooftops, Swiss chalets, and Andaman catamarans—but geography is the least of what moves here. Each destination becomes a chrysalis in which old identities dissolve and a more luminous version of the self emerges. Rather than presenting a polished, post-trauma success story, Whitney invites us into the raw geometry of becoming: the midnight tremors of doubt, the electric clarity of intuition, the quiet miracle of choosing to show up for life instead of hiding from it. In doing so, she affirms a truth I teach in every program: beginnings are sacred. They set the template for what follows; they tell the universe how serious we are about our own evolution. I experienced my own awakening in my early twenties when I was diagnosed with a terminal disease. It changed me—who I am, how I see the world, and what I choose to spend my life doing.

Read carefully, and you will find more than postcard prose. You will find primers on listening to the body's electromagnetic whispers, on stripping inherited beliefs from your personal operating system, on wielding imagination as a force of conscious creation.

You will taste the physics of gratitude in a Sicilian tomato, feel shadow work crack open under the Thai moonlight, and watch manifestation land—in real time—as encounters are orchestrated from a mix of emotion and instinct. These moments are not literary ornaments meant to captivate your attention; they are field notes for anyone ready to activate their innate capabilities.

Why does this matter now? Because the collective storyline is fraying. We live in an era of escalating noise—data, dogma, dopamine—and the antidote is not more information but deeper remembrance. Whitney's narrative offers exactly that: a mirror that says, "Your intuition is still intact. Your dreams are still writable. Your passport is never too full for miracles."

In my laboratory and in my healing circles, I have watched neuroscience confirm what mystics have whispered for millennia: when a single human being chooses authenticity over autopilot, the resonance field around them recalibrates. Families shift. Companies innovate. Communities heal. One woman's seven pages become seven billion possibilities for humanity.

So, dear reader, before you dive into chapter one, pause. Feel the subtle ripple that has already begun simply because you are holding this book. Ask yourself what territory inside you longs to be mapped next. Perhaps you will recognise your own halfwritten desires in Whitney's New Zealand dawns or Jaipur sunsets; perhaps you will glimpse your own unexplored capacities—telepathy, lucid creation, cellular regeneration—that you once dismissed as fantasy.

Either way, treat these pages as invitations, not endpoints. Highlight them. Argue with them. Meditate on them. Use them as kindling for the question that changes everything: *What is possible if I just say yes?*

It is my privilege, as Whitney's mentor and fellow traveller in the art of conscious evolution, to assure you that the journey ahead is worth every moment. Turn the page with an open heart and a scientist's curiosity. The adventure that follows may upend your coordinates—but it will return you, unmistakably, to your truest self, somewhere along this most profound and powerful experience that we call life.

—Professor Matt Riemann, Health Futurist,
Founder & CEO Shae Group

PROLOGUE:

JULY 2016

"9,500 FEET," THE PILOT called out over the humming Cessna engines. "Get ready." The airplane was set to circle once more, and then we'd jump.

Clouds painted a soft crowd of characters in the sky as morning light sliced across the desert horizon. The view above the rocky canyons, sandy riverbanks, and secret waterfalls was breathtaking. Circling to elevation provided a meditative, quiet space; the higher we went, the lighter I felt. I was alarmingly calm. Even though—like a mega-powered magnet—I would soon plummet to the ground, in that moment, I was free.

One thing I loved about skydiving was that there was no pressure to *do* anything. I was not in control at all. I had to put full faith in another human not to kill us both. Weirdly, even though this was my first jump, that allowed me to relax. Once I decided to go, I was hooked for the ride—there was no escaping. This was in stark contrast to most of my life, since I'd always been in the driver's seat. The liberation from being in charge was intoxicating, and amidst the sound of the crew's chatter above the whirling wind, my soul surrendered.

"So, what are we celebrating today?" my twenty-something, dreadlocked and tan skydiving instructor asked.

"Divorce," I said with a soft smile. My 120 pound, five foot three frame felt firmly attached to his, though the ride jostled us a bit.

"Congratulations?" he said as we climbed to ten thousand feet. "Whose?" He looked from me to the only other jumper.

My gaze shifted from the clouds to lock with the green eyes I'd fallen in love with so many years before.

"Ours," he said.

Silence followed. "Well… that's a first," my instructor finally replied. "Hey man, is it too early to ask her out?"

Laughter cut the tension in the small passenger cabin like the ripcord that would soon end our freefall towards Earth. It was time. We moved to open the door, and I stepped out on the wing, feeling as if doing that alone was as momentous as the moon landing.

"Ready?" my instructor asked as my heart held still.

I wasn't calm anymore. Now, I felt *everything*. A lifetime of adrenaline sports and recent emotional turmoil came steamrolling up from my toes and into my throat, sucking the air from my lungs. I felt the perfectionistic pressure I'd been holding in since I was a child; I felt my heart break for what was; I felt the betrayal of my career; and I felt the utter loneliness of being on my own for the first time at thirty years old.

"Set?" Like a film strip, memories of my world travels, family, tear-soaked pillows, impossible conversations, and pivotal life changes flooded me.

There was no *go*. We jumped, heads down, diving toward the ground. In an instant, everything leapt out of my body and exploded like a firework of white light. Physically detached from the earth and spiritually free from the heavy constraints of change, loss, and expectation, I finally let go. I don't even remember if I screamed; I didn't feel as if I was in my body at all. I was somewhere lost in time, experiencing everything and nothing simultaneously. It was bliss.

Then he pulled our ripcord and we shot up vertically, beginning the float. It was silent and peaceful. I started laughing, and so did my instructor—we whooped and hollered with freedom and joy. Looking down past my toes, I saw the surface of the world; I was instantly part of its rhythm again, and suddenly motivated to hit the ground running.

I am here, I heard my soul say. *I am here to live, to create, to begin again.*

As we descended, gliding beneath the cliffs and around emerald treetops, I craved more time. More flight time, but also more time to show up for my life. I didn't yet know where to begin, but beneath the questions pulsed a quiet certainty: I was ready to remember.

I thanked the crew as I looked back up at the sky. My ex-best friend and lover was still airborne. Two days earlier, we'd walked hand in hand into the courthouse to officially file for divorce. After completing the mandatory paperwork while tears streamed down my cheeks, we set off for Moab, Utah, to camp together for the weekend. It was impossible to explain or understand how two people with so much love for each other knew separating was the best path forward.

Symbolically, this dive represented a crossover as I departed from my meticulously curated life and plummeted into the unknown of the next. I didn't know where my life was going, but I knew it was time to jump.

IT WAS A Thursday evening in August 2015, and a predictable summer shower had just passed through the Rocky Mountains. Rain lingered on aspen leaves, and clouds somersaulted over the ridgeline towards the east. I lived in Vail, Colorado—the ultimate outdoor enthusiast's playground—and was the Director of Global Events for Framebridge Jewelers—the most upscale jewelry store in the area. That morning, I'd woken up in a tent, cozy in Merino wool pajamas after finishing a rafting trip under the full moon at 3 a.m.. Now I was at work wearing a silk dress, one hundred mm stilettos, and the same necklace Celine Dion wore at the 1998 Oscars when she won Best Original Song for "My Heart Will Go On."

The Heart of the Ocean. Yes, the actual necklace from *Titanic*.

The chain, studded with 103 diamonds, draped my collar bones, and the 171-carat, vibrant blue sapphire pendant rested only a few inches above my heart. Prisms of light escaped each facet as I rotated, and the gemstones whispered with mystery. The power of its frequency was palpable to everyone in the vicinity.

I love my job, I thought, trying to remember to breathe. Staring in the platinum-lined, dimly lit oval bathroom mirror prior to the evening's festivities, I thought to myself, *I am so happy.* I shivered with it. *I am so grateful to be in this moment. In the other room is the man I love, I'm at a job I love, and I'm living a life I love.*

The jewelry store was on Gore Creek Drive near the finest residences and hotels. Normally, it welcomed customers with matching marble pillars, sparkling jewelry showcases, a watch parlor featuring the world's finest timepieces, and the first custom Patek Philippe Bar, where we never charged for serving the finest of pours.

But tonight, my thirty-three-point checklist had transformed the space into an intimate reception venue. I'd moved the lounge furniture to create space for a temporary stage and gold audience chairs, installed a custom ice sculpture to dispense our signature drink, and created a makeshift kitchen around the jewelers' benches in the backroom for our private chef. Luxurious velvet drapes covered the spotlit wall cases, flowers flanked the mahogany displays, the bar glittered with hand-cut crystal glassware, guests sipped Dom Perignon, and smiling servers laced the crowd, offering platters of caviar and crème fraiche on flowered sweet potato canapés or dark chocolate truffles. Light gleamed through the statement chandelier as romantic string music filled the air. Guests couldn't help but be enveloped in sensory magic.

The event was called "Heirlooms and Treasure" and explored the inherent potential in investment and rarity. I was about to walk directly into the spotlight with my long blonde hair tucked into a neat low bun, accessorized by this one-of-a-kind necklace for the night.

Having grown up on a farm, the exhilaration of wearing a $10 million necklace was a far cry from the feeling of running in for the night at the sound of my grandmama's dinner bell.

When I was sixteen, my first job had been at a locally owned jewelry store in downtown La Crosse, Wisconsin. I didn't want to own the pieces, although a discount was always nice—no, the jewels brought out a deeper curiosity in me. I was fascinated with where gemstones came from and how something so small could affect so much. They adorned royal crowns and religious artifacts and had even instigated wars. Some claimed they possessed healing powers. I always loved that gemstones were entwined with influence and history, but I never thought I would be *wearing* one of those immaculate pieces.

I was overflowing with joy in a delicious state of childish enthusiasm. What a lucky girl I was to be there. It was work, yes, but it was also play. With a slow breath, a final touch of lipstick, and a wink in the mirror, I exited the elegant bathroom and headed towards the walk-in vault to meet Hans, a sturdy-framed, unassumingly dressed, off-duty local detective, who was my bodyguard for the evening.

"Ah, there she is," greeted Mr. Framebridge in his customary bowtie and small, wire rimmed glasses. He had been a wonderful role model to me; as a fifth-generation jeweler, he'd inherited his legacy, yes, but he'd also charted his own path. His love of the outdoors had taken him into wilds all around the world, and he had stories for days: tales of teaching Hollywood stars how to fly-fish during expeditions in Alaska, pulling snakes out of grass huts in Africa, or even hiding diamonds in his shoes while crossing borders in Europe to evade their confiscation, even though his ownership of the gems was one hundred percent legal. All the while, he ran one of the most prestigious, privately owned luxury stores in the United States. I'd spent time with his family in Greenwich, Connecticut—the location of our flagship store—and respected his approach to life.

"I think we both know this is the minimum number of diamonds I can wear," I joked, trying to shadow my excitement. He smiled, and I looked at Hans.

"Pleasure to meet you," Hans said as he extended his hand.

"Likewise. And thank you for sharing your discerning eye with us tonight," I said. "Don't worry, these shoes may look unsteady, but I assure you I'll embrace my inner running back if someone goes for the necklace." We all laughed.

This wasn't my first time having a bodyguard, as armed security was a mandatory element when I hosted events off-site. I curated strategic partnerships with brands like Bentley and the Yankees and sponsored events like the Aspen Food and Wine Festival or film premiers. But tonight was next level—tonight, I was half Duchess of Cambridge, half Beyoncé.

"Shall we?" Mr. Framebridge ushered us toward the stage's draped entrance.

WHEN THE EVENING'S discussion concluded and we wrapped a mini paparazzi session for the one-of-a-kind necklace, I headed for the bar, where my husband was chatting with the bartender. He sat on the last stool with two glasses of champagne and an intoxicating, boyish grin. Even after a decade of being in love, the sight of him still sent butterflies swirling in my stomach. He looked like he'd popped off the cover of *GQ*: his suit was draped perfectly over his athletic build and layers of brown hair swept over his vibrant green eyes.

Both of us hailed from the same small town in Wisconsin and had met at a mutual friend's wedding when he was twenty-three and I nineteen. We'd gone to the same high school, but hadn't attended at the same time due to our age gap, and my family's sixth-generation farm was only fifteen minutes from his parents' house near the Mississippi River. He was charismatic, deeply kind, giftedly athletic, honest to the core, and fascinated with *me*. His interest had caught me off-guard, since he'd had many suitors and I didn't consider myself a standout. I matched him athletically, but was also stubbornly career-driven and brought a feminine energy to his Peter Pan lifestyle. Nevertheless, our overlapping childhoods made us feel like we'd known each other forever. At the time, he had already been living in Colorado, pursuing a professional snowboarding career, and I'd left university a year later to join him.

As a married couple, we embodied the adrenaline lifestyle: he continued to build his portfolio as a sponsored athlete while I excelled in my luxury career. My job financially provided for our life, and his kept us pushing our limits.

"After this," he said as he took in my necklace, "I'll never know what to get you for Christmas!" We stole a kiss. His touch was home to me: comfort, love, passion, and adventure, all in a single point of connection.

"The bar is set, babe. And it is *high*," I laughed, turning to face the room after clinking our flutes. Hans was still by my side, and I introduced them.

"Have a moment to sit?" my husband motioned to both of us.

"I wish," I said, rolling my eyes and dropping my shoulders. "I need to keep this alluring masterpiece on the move." I touched the sapphire, which had taken millions of years, under intense heat and pressure in the depths of the earth, to form.

"The duty to sparkle must feel relentless," he said, sneaking in another kiss.

"Thank you for my life water," I said flirtatiously, raising my champagne. "You know what? Come with me. Let's do the rounds—everyone will love to see you."

"Absolutely," he said with a slight nod. With my husband on my arm and muscle-clad Hans two steps behind, I felt carefree and confident, like I was being escorted by the Secret Service, or on a job in *Ocean's Eleven*. My heart was singing an aria of happiness as the Heart of the Ocean danced above it, tuning in and turning up the vibration.

I was as proud of having my husband on my arm as he was of having me on his. We balanced each other: I supported his snow-boarding career by being on the first chair of the morning with him as he prepared for backcountry competitions, armed with cameras, snacks, and weather reports. He returned the love by dressing up, embracing small talk, and attending the elaborate events I planned. He was somewhat of a town celebrity, and his talent and genuinely gregarious attitude made him a natural people magnet. I was the odd one in Vail—the one with a "real job" in a valley of seasonal positions. We worked as a team in all things, and our relationship thrived because of it.

Between extreme sports and luxury, there was never a dull moment. Vail, famously known as "Little Switzerland" for its snow-capped peaks and white and brown scalloped chalet buildings, hosted a slew of events, from World Cup races to mountain games and triathlons. Framebridge was well-known for offering exquisite estate collections, the world's finest timepieces, and premier custom jewelry. Recently, we'd handled the ruby and sapphire suites liquidated by a Saudi Arabian palace after the tragic loss of their matriarch. Something interesting was always afoot at Framebridge.

"Hello, hello, dear Whitney," said Dr. Barry Grundland, who had been a client for three seasons. I was fond of his visits, and his profession in cell-level healing also fascinated me. He was a pioneer. "How are you, my friend?"

"Fabulous," I replied, framing the necklace. "Do you remember my better half?" I sashayed to the side. My husband had been dealing with herniated discs from a lifetime of hard landings off jumps or logs, and Dr. Grundland had prescribed guided meditations, exercises, and supplements to aid his healing.

"Of course," he said with a warm, wise grin. His bright white hair accented a tan face and youthful body. "How are you feeling?"

"Flexible and solid, thanks to you. I've avoided going under the knife so far and am living without my days being controlled by aches and pains." He went on to explain that he had been visualizing his breath going to the herniations as "oxygen warriors with the power to self-heal," which had been surprisingly effective.

"Thrilling, isn't it? What the body is capable of?" Dr. Grundland genuinely cared, and I always loved hearing what he had to say. "I'd be interested to learn more about your experience. Follow up with my team, and they'll guide you to the next steps in the journey."

"I can't thank you enough." With a sincere smile, my husband added, "But I'm confident you aren't here for patient follow-ups. I'll leave you two to it." He nodded to the tanzanite rings that Jeannine, Framebridge's sales associate and my best friend, had out on the counter. Jeannine was a true professional at work, rode her mountain bike like the devil, was as loyal as a sibling, and genuinely radiated love from every limb. Her athletic body was a result of her active lifestyle, and her long brown hair mixed with strikingly light blue eyes kept her dating docket jam-packed. I'd started a spreadsheet to keep the gentlemen straight. We lived vicariously through each other, trading experiences of my rooted companionship and her diverse encounters.

In short, I loved her.

"Is there anything I can get you two from the bar?" my husband asked. "Jeannine, do you want anything?" We all shook our heads, and he took his leave. I swiftly assumed my position behind the case.

We were both transplants; Jeannine from Maryland, and I from Wisconsin. We'd met at a bachelorette party—I'd told her I was into gemology, she said she'd always had an affinity for rocks, and the rest had been history. She'd started working at the store two months later.

Now, Dr. Grundland had one ring in each hand, gently pressed between his thumbs and pointer fingers, which he rotated back and forth to take in their full architecture and uniqueness. After a moment of contemplation, he held one forward. "I believe this one speaks to me and will connect most with her."

He raised the ring—a beauty set in platinum with a halo of diamonds—towards me.

"It does seem to sing with light, doesn't it?" I agreed, noticing the dispersion between the stones—gems radiate a language of their own, an esoteric song of light and frequency. "It has an aura of violet promise."

"I agree, it's the one." He nodded, loosening his scarf. Job done.

"Do you want any of the details? Carat weights, quality?" Jeannine asked.

"No, thank you. My heart clearly favors this one," he affirmed, pointing to his selection.

"I wish I dared to follow my intuition like that," I said, in awe and more than a little jealous of his self-trust.

"I've learned that's the only way to freedom. You must trust what's inside," he replied, with a twinkle in his eye. "You have a philosopher's soul, Whitney."

"A philosopher?" I said, teasing. "Because I speak crystal?"

"Because you are in it for the adventure of the stone," he said, as if it were obvious.

"Aren't we all?" I smiled.

"Excuse me, Whitney. Mr. Framebridge requests your presence," Hans said, as guests continued to swirl throughout the room.

"Of course. Barry, as you know, you're in good hands with Jeannine."

"Absolutely. Thank you, dear." He touched my arm, holding me back for a moment. "But remember—it isn't about the treasure, it's about the journey."

Still processing his comments, I walked away. Tiny hairs stood on my arms as I repeated *the adventure of the stone*. I did seek out stones whenever I traveled—finding a tsavorite in Tanzania, for instance, after climbing Kilimanjaro. But surely the journey he was referring to culminated with more than a memento.

"Whitney!" Mr. Framebridge exclaimed as I walked up. He was with the Beckers, another wonderful set of clients. "Let's get a close-up of that masterpiece."

"May I try it on?" Mrs. Becker inquired. Her sharp bob exposed a long neck on top of a petite frame.

"I'm sorry, but no. I'm not allowed to pass it around this evening. As you can imagine, it would get a lot of action."

"How about a picture, then?"

"Of course." I stepped beside her and away from Hans. "Make sure not to outshine the necklace though, will you, Mrs. Becker?" I smiled.

After the pictures were taken, I resumed my place near Mr. Framebridge on the opposite side of the case. "So, what are we shopping for today?"

"A new watch for me," Mr. Becker proclaimed, standing a little straighter. He was only a smidge taller than his spouse and boasted a rounder belly.

"You don't need a new watch, dear. You have your father's." Mrs. Becker was always polished in a smart outfit and gold necklaces, and tonight was no exception. She wore a slim, matching cherry red ski set with a layered gold herringbone chain and tennis necklace.

"I love this watch," he interrupted, gently caressing the classic Cartier Tank on his wrist, "but sometimes it's time for a change."

"If you want change, get a new suit. Or a car. Some things— things you have a relationship with—shouldn't change," she said.

"I understand I can embrace change in many ways, sweetheart, but I feel as though I'd like to showcase another side of my personality with a new watch. Something to mix it up a bit... highlight another facet of your dynamic husband," he added, with a kiss that finally won her over.

"Well, at least you've picked out something different. Overall, I like the Rolex. Especially with the rubber strap. It'll be appropriate for when we're on the water."

"Exactly. Let's wrap it up."

"Smart choice," Mr. Framebridge affirmed. He always approved of balancing tradition and purpose while embracing variety.

"I can't wait to see pictures of your new watch sailing the open seas with you," I said, excusing myself to keep the Heart of the Ocean circulating.

As I smiled while other guests took pictures of the necklace, I couldn't help but ruminate on the ideas of change and intuition. Micro impermanence is constant. But big change? Choices about the directions your life takes? Surely Dr. Grundland couldn't just follow his intuition for those. Surely, in those instances, the mind took precedence over gut feelings, and contemplation trumped emotion.

Either way, I didn't need any big life changes.

I'd stay right where I was, thank you very much.

A WEEK LATER found Jeannine and I reaching the summit of La Plata Peak, at 14,360 feet above sea level. "Whoo-hoo," I cheered to Jeannine, who was only a pace behind. We were finishing a three-and-a-half-hour ascent that had covered 3,600 feet of elevation gain over 3.75 miles. The hike had taken us through dense pine forests, over steep ravines, winding through meadows, and around lakes edging up into scree fields filled with jagged switchbacks, false summits, and rocky ledges. La Plata, deep in the Sawatch Mountain Range, is known for a few very different routes to the top. This was my third time gracing the summit, and every time had been unique.

Whenever I reached the peak of a mountain, I felt like a whole new world opened. My perspective shifted the moment I took in the secrets of the other side—suddenly, I'd better understand where I'd been, while hearing the call to go further into the distance. My nervous system calmed when I was hiking. My mind cleared, and even though my muscles might fatigue and my breath might grow labored, I was in flow.

My love for hiking started when I was eight years old and summited Mt. Elbert, the highest peak in Colorado and the second highest in the United States (second only to Mt. Whitney), with my parents and older brother during a family vacation. My dad had to carry me a bit during the final ascent, but as soon as I'd seen my mom at the top with her arms open wide, I *ran* to her. Everyone on the summit had cheered, and I'd felt the rush of success after hard work. It had been my first taste of adrenaline-laced victory, and by the time I had reached my mom, I was hooked.

Ever since then, exploring the mountains had been my church and my playground. Exquisite views held spiritual significance for me, bordering on the sacred—they inspired me to think and feel in diverse ways, captured my heart, and reinforced my relationship with nature.

As Jeannine joined me, a similar holiness came over both of us.

"Yeah, girl," she said. "The effort is always worth it."

"Thanks for leaving your bike in the garage for a day and coming with me," I said as I passed out sandwiches, trail mix, and fresh fruit. We settled on some nearby rocks to rest. Her summer addiction was mountain biking, and she was damn good at it. Sponsored, she regularly did twenty-four-hour races, town races, and even empowered others by co-founding Sacred Cycle, which helped victims of sexual abuse find confidence and independence on the trail.

"When I hike, I feel my body's efforts, like biking. But being less technical, I'm able to embrace the blissful stillness of it." She was completely right. "Plus, I haven't hiked La Plata since your fundraising climb a few years ago."

That was the second time I'd climbed it. I'd been with my husband for the first time, and it held special significance for us as our first peak together. Since then, we'd climbed over fifty mountains side by side.

"I loved that event," I said. "The sponsor photos still pop up on Facebook memories. They get me every time." While working for the jewelry store, I also created Bucket Events, a company that hosted fundraisers for nonprofits.

"It's not every day you have a helicopter circling a 14,000-foot summit with a photographer hanging out of it," Jeannine chuckled as we looked in the direction of where the helicopter had soared, still envisioning the telephoto lenses capturing all our cheering faces.

"A hundred people climbed together in support of alternative psychological therapies. It always amazes me what we can do with our hearts in the right places." This was another thing my family had taught me from early on: my mom still operated an Equine Facilitated Mental Health Program on our farm, and fundraising was a way I could contribute from afar.

"Also amazing: the live music, silent auction, and BBQ feast at the end." Jeannine always knew how to keep it real. "Are you going to organize The Group Summit Challenge again?"

"No, three years in a row was enough." I meant it. The final year had been an especially pressured event, during which I struggled to stay focused while my mom was going through breast cancer treatment. Thank God she had entered remission a few months after. It had been a scary and intense experience for all of us, and I needed to step away, at least for now. "I'm going to keep the LLC going to support other nonprofits, and I'm volunteering as a chaperone for Children's Global Alliance next spring so I can help with their events on the side."

"If only you could do something interesting with your life," Jeannine said, sighing. "You have a full plate, my friend."

"Look who's talking. Anyway, I like today's route better. The southwest trail is quieter than the northwest—almost like a secret."

"Some trips are better en masse; some are meant to be solo," she shrugged, finishing her sandwich. Birds flew in and out of pale columns of sunlight that peeked through the clouds near us. The sight reminded me of the religious posters hanging in my grandparents' house. The view should have been captioned, "Angel Wings from Heaven Above."

"Cheers to options," I said, hoisting my camelback of water towards the sky.

"Speaking of. I've been comparing ideas for the spring offseason—what's your plan?"

"What makes you think I have one?" I challenged.

"You?! Not have a plan?" She laughed. "Yeah, that'll be the day."

"Fine, fine. Ecuador. I think we want to climb Cotopaxi. It's relatively affordable and at the same elevation as Kili, but it's ice. We're talking full gear, with a guide only."

"You want technical?" She grimaced. "All that ice?"

"No. Not really. It scares me, to be honest." I laughed, only half joking. Living the resort town life, my husband and I made traveling a priority during the off-season. Neither of us had grown up traveling internationally, and we were committed to exploration in our adult lives. In fact, our wedding in Isla Mujeres, Mexico, had been the first time many of my family members had cause to get a passport.

"They say everything you want is on the other side of fear. But come on—maybe we just need a cabana with a slushy drink and a straw for a few days. How about a resort vacation or city shopping trip?"

"With how I've been trying to save lately, that would scare my bank account," I said.

Shopping and hotels were much more expensive than camping and hiking. My husband and I had had our ups and downs financially, and right now we were just heading back into the black. Some people had nice things or new cars. We booked trips, choosing to spend every penny above our basic expenses on travel. Although, opportunity to travel alone was a privilege, and I deeply respected that.

Once upon a time, when we were working eighty-hour weeks and still on a ramen noodle budget, I could only dream of a vacation. But one random evening, I walked into our local bar, The Dusty Boot, grabbed a beer, and was handed a raffle ticket. Not ten minutes later, I won a trip for two to Hawaii. I must have manifested it out of thin air—my heart was truly craving an adventure, and I got one. I had been hanging on by an emotional thread: working all hours, handling the bills, recovering from yet another ski-induced knee surgery, and still remaining unshakably positive. That trip to Hawaii had given me the reset I needed to keep going—much like my first big hike got me addicted to hiking, that trip made me fall in love with traveling.

"I don't know that I need shopping or cabanas," I mused, "but I've been called towards internal exploration rather than the gear-oriented kind lately."

"Why don't you sign up for another yoga retreat?" she asked.

"The one I went to in Panama was nice." *Really* nice. We had slept in tents on an island so small you could traverse it in twenty minutes. It had been liberating to dive into spirituality, meditation, and yoga for a week, completely disconnected from technology and the modern world—even if sand flies had mercilessly attacked us at sunset, and our *delicious* dinner had been prepared in a three-sided wooden shack.

"Not today, but maybe tomorrow," I said, as I did to many questions I couldn't quite answer. "What about you? What options are you considering?" I watched the birds flying in and out of the light with nothing but mountain peaks in the distance.

"Staycation. Or a staycation."

I gave her a side eye. Such a wide range of options.

"I'm going to Switzerland to race the Swiss Epic next fall," she said. "So I have to save."

"Amazing! Congratulations!" This was a big deal.

"No congrats yet, I need to make it there first." She would need to meet the qualifications to compete, which included race records, sponsors, equipment, and more.

"I would love to see your tired and muddy face cross that finish line," I said, imagining the celebratory scene.

"So would I!" She laughed.

"Well, the race is what, a little over a year away? So no need to finalize anything just yet." The wind was picking up, and clouds were moving faster now. An afternoon storm was on the way. "For now, let's get packed up and head down. You can explain your whole plan along the way."

We linked arms, standing together—grounding and absorbing the unwavering power of the mountains—and took one last look at the majestic view. I felt like part of the wild up there—I felt free. Even though we were at the top, I felt there was nowhere to go but up.

Hopping from rock to rock until we reached the trail again, we began the trek back to my Wrangler, which waited at the trailhead with cold beverages and camping gear. I was looking forward to dinner, when we would dine on open fire delicacies of grilled pork loin with pineapples, jalapeños and onions, roasted potatoes and carrots, s'mores, and a little whiskey. An evening under the stars and a cozy sleeping bag were my love language. Until then, we had a long descent ahead of us, which gave me plenty of time to think.

My life had always involved sport. From six years old on, I played competitive fast-pitch softball and ski raced—both disciplines that usually culminated in national competitions. I had also played volleyball, basketball, and ran track to cross-train and maintain fitness throughout the year.

Being a petite and relatively shy girl, I had been consistently underestimated and always felt like I had something to prove. Once, I was whitewater rafting in Nepal on class four rapids, and our guide had been thrown out of the back of the boat. I had been placed closest to him because he figured I wasn't as capable as the beefcake men in the front. But once we were captain-less, those scrappers just cowered, holding their oars close to their chests. I knew we'd be overboard, launched against jagged rocks, if we didn't start navigating the boulders and current. So I'd stood up, started steering, and directed from the back, gladiator style, yelling, "Right side paddle! Left side back! All paddle forward! Paddle! Paddle! Paddle!"

After a bit, we had gotten through the cliff section and safely into an eddy below. I guess being underestimated worked out for us all.

Thinking of Nepal made me smile, and I looked up to tell Jeannine the story.

Crack! Pop!

Instantly, I was on the ground, head spinning.

"Whitney! Are you okay? Oh my god, what happened?" Jeannine gasped as she squatted down next to me. I looked back, trying to sort the injury and source the pain. This section of the trail was soft dirt, level and clear of debris. What had I tripped over? My ankle throbbed. When I located the offender, anger saturated my pain. It was a stupid shoelace.

"Ooooouch," I breathed, holding my faint head in my hands.

"Do you think it's broken?" We both took in the sight of my limp right foot.

"Judging by the sound of the snap I just heard, yeah."

"I think I rolled it almost to the ground."

"Damn girl, do you think you can walk?"

"Of course." I hesitated. "I'm sure it's okay." We still had two miles to the Jeep.

"Let's take it one step at a time. We'll get you to the stream by the trailhead and take your boot off to see what we're dealing with."

"Let me quiet my breathing," I said, my face grimacing, "and then we'll go."

We sat in silence. Joyful birds chirped, tree tops swayed, and I thought to myself, *What an idiot. Did I really just trip myself and break an ankle? What the fuck—I don't have time for this crap.* After my anger raged some more, I calmed down enough to continue. I had to hike out.

Jeannine grabbed my elbow, and I slowly stood up. One step. Solid. Interesting. Another. Another.

"*Fuck* me—yeah, that hurts. But if I keep my foot really flat, it seems to be okay."

I knew it was going to suck, and suck it did. But an hour later, I took off my bursting boot and stuck an enormously swollen, black and blue ankle into ice-cold mountain water.

"Colors like that usually mean it's a bone," Jeannine informed me, as if I didn't know.

"I guess our campfire date will have to wait. Let's get back to town." We were a thirty-minute drive from cell service and another hour from Vail.

"Do you want me to take you straight to the hospital?" she asked.

"No, take me home." It was a Friday night, which meant I could only be seen in the ER, and I didn't want to spend the money. It was essential to save money by being extra frugal while living in an expensive place like Vail. "I already know it's broken, which might mean surgery. If not, it's a no-weight waiting game, so I might as well go home to elevate and ice all weekend. I'll call the doctor on Monday." I could handle the pain and be practical about my care.

I rode in the back of the Jeep with my foot on the ceiling and tried to keep from speculating about what this injury might derail. Between now and the new year, I had fourteen events to host for work, eight of which were in Greenwich, Connecticut—plus a family reunion in Wisconsin, one out-of-town snowboard competition, and we had planned to finally close on our house and start remodeling... all before we had guests coming to celebrate my thirtieth birthday in January. Crutches and a cast would be a problem.

FOR THE REST of August and September, I was on crutches, nursing my fractured and sprained ankle. Surgery wasn't necessary because the doctor figured if the bone didn't move during the hike out, it wasn't going to at all. By early October, I was approved to use a knee-high walking boot. One evening after dinner, my husband and I cuddled up in front of the fire in our cozy living room. This was a regular occurrence for us, and we melted into the casual intimacy of it. Photo albums, board games, books, and pictures all held their space amongst the travel décor and comfy furniture surrounding us.

In a decade of living in the mountains, our home address had changed several times. When I was twenty-one, we'd bought our first house, but after the real estate crash in 2007, we had been way upside down and ended up renting throughout the years, even doing live-in caretaking in Beaver Creek. Being ski-in, ski-out had been more than an adequate exchange for watching the owners' home while they were away.

By 2015, we had finally secured a long-term rent-to-own agreement, positioning ourselves on the brink of homeownership again as soon as we secured the necessary down payment. Our townhouse featured two floors atop an oversized one-car garage, with picture windows and a front deck offering unobstructed views of the mountains we loved so much. Our backyard oasis, nestled beneath towering pines, enclosed a small, terraced garden and an inviting flagstone patio, accented by pallet furniture we'd built ourselves. Our house, a space we had come to cherish deeply, was more than just a residence—it was an anchor to our future, a sanctuary that might one day echo with the laughter of our children. The thought filled me with an immense sense of pride and boundless optimism.

Despite being eager to make the space our own once our names were on the title, my time out of commission forced me to slow down. Naturally, there were fewer outdoor excursions and social engagements. Though my husband was always ready with nourishing food and fresh icepacks, he wasn't exactly thrilled about trading his usual role of patient for that of caregiver. Beyond the temporary shift in our dynamic, two deeper tensions began to surface: my work and his passion for snowboarding. Normally, these were the pillars of our foundation, but now friction was beginning to arise. Despite his quiet protests, my job continued to pull me east to host events, and even after tragic avalanches killed a number of our friends, he still ventured into the backcountry, chasing fresh snow.

Over the past three years, we'd attended more funerals than weddings, and a heaviness had settled into my heart, alongside frantic visions of rescue teams tracking faint, blinking red lights to buried beacon signals, their efforts a desperate race against time. This scene had now played out tragically on more than eight occasions, each concluding not with the triumphant rescue of the courageous and highly skilled athletes, but with the harrowing recovery of a body.

The most haunting memory was when I had to call a good friend of mine to deliver the news that her husband was never coming home. I can still remember the frequency of her cries, hearing her body fall to the floor, and listening to questions I didn't have answers for, both our hearts shattering into pieces with every word. Nothing would compare to her emotion in that moment. Nothing. But something in me had also died that day, and I started to disassociate with the acceptance of the risks my husband took on a regular basis. He forged ahead, and I… well, I downshifted.

The change in our domestic rhythm, alongside the quiet undercurrent of resentment growing between us, had begun to cast a shadow over many of our conversations. He held his breath each time he looked at the calendar, seeing the dates blocked off when I'd be away. And my pulse quickened every time I pictured him launching off a mountain peak, dropping into a rocky chute, or carving through cliffs and open fields of snow. The new energy between us felt eerie.

"Can't someone else host the events in Greenwich?" my husband asked as we cuddled. I served him a flat look. "How long are you gone this time?" As the fire crackled and the ice waned in our drinks, both of us grew quiet.

"I have three events next week: a charity fashion show, a Ferrari/Panerai launch, and the Greenwich Film Festival VIP pre-party."

"Wow, busy," he said, shifting his weight to lean back on his arms in our puddle of pillows on the ground. "I bet you're excited to be off crutches while you're running a marathon at each party."

"Set-up and tear-down will certainly be easier." Although I had an incredible team for support, my nature was to be the first and last one on site. No task was too mundane for me to execute, crutches or not. "I'm going to stay with Heather for a night after everything, so I'll be home next Monday," I added, realizing he wouldn't be thrilled to hear I was staying longer than necessary.

As I stretched out on the blankets, I rolled over towards him, knowing the closer I got to him, the more likely my clothes would be off, our dialogue cut short. Even if a chill had filtered into our communication, there was still plenty of heat between the sheets.

"Are you going into the backcountry this week?" I asked, already knowing the answer.

"The conditions look solid, don't they?" he said, referring to the snowpack, weather, and avalanche report. Typically, we both approached these discussions with a sense of optimism. But pre-season snow had inspired him to take out his snowboard gear extra early this year, and my heart was not ready for another winter of endless days waiting for him to make it home.

"Um, I don't know," I said, as he moved around me to grab another pillow. "I didn't look." I fumbled with my words and continued, "But listen to your intuition. It's more important than any piece of gear out there."

If he was going to continually test this fate, he needed to trust himself and nature when making these decisions. As much as I needed him to need me, I couldn't be the voice in his head granting the go-ahead—it was too much responsibility. I could only imagine how I would feel if I made the wrong decision, and he was hurt... or worse.

"I'm going with a great crew. The forecast is bluebird, so we'll get some decent footage." Some of the rewards for venturing beyond the safety of groomed runs and into the man-powered lines were, of course, the video and photos captured for sponsors and publication. He was massaging my shoulders now, and my head was getting heavy. The tension between us was present, but kind. We both understood the other's dilemma.

He leaned in for a kiss and left his strong arms around my shoulders, his flirtatious eyes locking with mine. Little brown specks dotted them like kiwi seeds.

"I'm going to be fine."

Yes, he probably would be. But would I?

Each time he left for the mountain, I felt a piece of our connection, our partnership, our "us" erode. Outwardly, I maintained a facade of calm resolve, projecting unwavering support for his pursuits. I loved him. I didn't blame him for following his calling. His pure love of the sport and commitment to it were things I deeply respected about him. Snowboarding wasn't just a pastime or even a professional pursuit; it was his oxygen.

Yet, out of self-preservation, I was shutting down. Little by little, I tried to create space between my input and his choice. It hurt too much; it was too much pressure. Could I live with myself if I agreed it was good to go, and he didn't come home?

I wondered if his feelings about my career growth mirrored this frustration. I knew he was proud of me every time I was promoted, and certainly supportive if my documentary—about sourcing diamonds directly from the mine in Botswana, Africa—was approved, especially since he was slated to come along. But did he think I was constantly choosing work over him? Was he disconnecting so that choice didn't hurt?

"Good luck with everything this week. I know you'll kill it, especially sporting that sexy Velcro walking boot," he said, pulling me onto his bare chest, kissing my forehead. He lingered, waiting for permission as his fingers traced my collarbones, around my breasts, then jumping off towards my hips. "I miss you a lot when you're gone. Do you know that?"

"I do." Extending the last word, I encouraged him to keep talking and exploring my body.

"I'm proud of you."

"And I, you."

As I nuzzled into him, I remembered something: "Oh, please deposit your check this week."

He looked confused before nodding his head in understanding. "Okay, no problem."

"No, really, it needs to be there for the downpayment verification."

"It's on the counter, I think, and ready to go."

The kisses started to build and stole my focus—after so many years, our attraction for each other hadn't wavered. But I didn't feel like the same girl he'd fallen in love with. *Who was that person?* I had started to wonder, feeling more and more disassociated.

Navigating the inevitable sadness and depressive funk resulting from attending so many funerals had been difficult enough. But needing to heal my own busted ankle had inspired me to really dive in, and I'd visited energy healers, and started meditating and reading books like *The Buddha Walks into a Bar* by Lordo Rinzler, *Celestine Prophecy* by James Redfield, and *The Alchemist* by Paulo Coelho. The books intrigued me—they ignited my fascination around what the human being is capable of and what we're connected to. But no matter what I tried, nothing really soothed the emotional turbulence.

Over the past few years, I'd invited my husband on these self-discovery endeavors, diving into the workings of grief, energy, the universe, and our place in it. But he hadn't subscribed. His coping mechanism for managing survivor's guilt seemed to be shutting out the past and numbing a bit of the present. And as much as I was trying to make everything okay for both of us, we were still individuals. So who was I to judge how he handled these tragic and complex feelings?

I determined that while he was off pursuing his dream, I'd focus on work, love him in the moment so as not to fear the next, and twist my wedding rings—the natural yellow sapphire and diamonds set in yellow gold—willing him to come home safely.

GLINTS OF LIGHT reflected off snowflakes like diamonds in the November sun. A pavé of fresh powder promised magical skiing conditions on opening day at Beaver Creek Ski Resort. We leapfrogged down the mountain, slaloming through widespread aspen groves and arching through fresh fields of virgin snow. My skin tingled with cold snow as it whirled around my cheeks, and my body relished the familiar exercise. *Swoosh, swoosh, swoosh*—like floating on clouds, the silence was electric.

As I neared the end of the run and skied towards the lift line, I saw so many familiar faces. Opening day brought out all the regulars; it was a social scene, vibrant with high-fives, new gear, and reconnecting conversations ending in après plans.

"Whew! What a season starter, eh, babe?" my husband said, pulling me in for a hug.

Grateful that my ankle felt solid, I said, "I think I'm good to go." I tapped my pole on the outside of my boot.

"And how's the knee?" I'd had three surgeries on my left knee over the years.

"Sturdy." I smiled. "Your back?"

"Still attached," he hollered, bending backwards for emphasis.

"Listen to you two," interrupted one of our friends, as we unbuckled our boots and got ready for the chairlift, "seeing if all your Mr. and Mrs. Potato Head parts are still intact."

"There's Barbie and Ken of the mountains!" chimed in another we hadn't seen since last spring. They both wore bright, patterned coats, matching pants, and reflective goggles. It was difficult to recognize people in new kits, but you could always tell a friend by their riding style and stance. These two were pros.

"Brain Bleeds at The Boot?" he called as we all traversed the lift lines. A Brain Bleed was a special kind of tequila shot used for initiation into a local-only crew.

"I think my eyes are all set, maybe later," I quipped. After snorting the salt and drinking the liquor, the lime gets squirted into your eyes. "You two going to make it to the Burton Open this year?" our friend inquired.

"Will we?" my husband asked, looking at me.

"You will, I won't," I replied, not fully turning around. "Someone has to work," I said, pushing forward in the lift line, laughing. "Will we see you at my birthday party on January 8th?"

"We were at your twenty-first, wouldn't miss your thirtieth," both our friends confirmed.

"I'll never forget my ride to the restaurant on my birthday eve!" They were both snowcat drivers and groomed the mountain at night. One of them had picked my husband and me up at the base of the mountain in that gigantic machine, taken us over the jumps in the terrain park, up the steepest trail, and finally down a long traverse to a members-only club for dinner, where another friend was the executive chef. Being a local really had its perks.

"Whitney!" I heard a little voice call out from the ski school line.

"Bodhi!" I squealed back. "Look at you, my man! Having fun?"

"Yeah! We're going so fast today! Learning how to tuck, no turns!" my five-year-old chosen nephew informed me. His bright blonde hair popped out from under his helmet, and he seemed as if he'd topple over any second in his older brother's puffy jacket.

"Wow! You're almost ready to start racing with me in the gates, then, eh?"

"No, no. I want to snowboard next. Go off the big jumps."

"Then you will, Bo. You can do anything," I called out as the next chair whisked us away and up the hill. I'd been in the hospital with his mom the day he was born. Home—there were so many layers of home in Colorado. After a decade of life in the valley, we'd curated an incredible and diverse circle of family. We were auntie and uncle to children who were rapidly growing up, and couldn't go into a restaurant, hotel, or shop without running into someone we knew.

When we traveled during the off-seasons, there was always an unmistakable pull guiding us back home—a quiet, steady current. I was at peace there, cradled by a marriage rooted in love and a community that felt like an extension of family. Yet somewhere beyond the familiar, a new energy stirred, calling to me from a place I couldn't yet name. Perhaps it was the residual pulse of time spent near New York City, or maybe the ideas seeded by the books I had been devouring that had awakened something dormant within me. Whatever the cause, the internal sanctuary I once counted on and the certainty of home no longer felt untouched.

"Feels good to be back at it, doesn't it?" my husband asked as we settled in for the fifteen-minute ride up.

"So much so," I replied. I was happy to be on the mountain after my injury, and to be seeing friendly faces after a long summer.

"I couldn't imagine living anywhere else. This is it for me," he said, gazing at the ridgeline in the distance. I believed him, and smiled. But I couldn't respond—I couldn't get out an authentic, agreeable reply. My throat was tight, and I squinted in the opposite direction. This was our life, I knew that. But the thought of never doing anything else made it hard for me to breathe. I grabbed his hand with a tight squeeze and centered myself on the chairlift, flying up the mountainside past towering pines. I closed my eyes and relaxed into the morning sunlight. In that exact time and space, surrounded by health, love, and possibility, we were perfect.

AIRPORTS. I FOUND myself in airports every other week. Newark to Denver, Denver to Newark. Departures, arrivals; arrivals, departures. The trips and parties blurred together, but I was finally wrapping up my time out east for the year, having just hosted Framebridge's annual holiday party in Greenwich in mid-December. Per tradition, I was ending the visit by spending an evening out with Heather.

The air was crisp and cool, with holiday lights shimmering from every storefront, casting a fleeting, almost wistful glow. As my chauffeured town car wound through the towering silhouettes of New York's skyline, I felt like a part of its ambitious energy. A sense of being grounded in a world of immense opportunity grew within me. I relished conversations with colleagues and friends about founding companies, investing, and politics—dialogues fueled by vision and momentum. What would it be like to be a resident here? I imagined morning walks to coffee shops tucked between brownstones, spontaneous Broadway nights, and lunch meetings in bustling restaurants. I couldn't help but wonder—indeed, I *had* to wonder, as I had just been offered a promotion that would require relocating to New York—about this long-held dream I had set aside in exchange for another life. The opportunity thrilled me and quietly broke my heart.

"My Heather!" I squealed with delight, jumping into her arms. Another midwestern daughter, Heather and I had been friends since we were teenagers—we'd bonded in school over horseback riding, DECA (a business club), and during the bi-annual class trip to Spain. She was now a badass female entrepreneur in the tech space, living in the center of commerce. Within our friendship, we filled unofficial roles: she was my professional advisor, and I was her relationship coach. Over the years, we'd offered each other pivotal advice, shoulders to cry on, and countless glasses of champagne.

"My Whitney. How was your week? Are we celebrating or commiserating?" she asked, two glasses of bubbles already gracing our dimly lit corner table in a speak-easy style pop-up, tucked below a flagship restaurant in the meatpacking district.

I could count on her to pick a hot new place, and I loved the variety. She was always fashionably dressed in outfits that complemented her sharply cut blonde hair, including stilettos, a chic handbag, and evening-red lips. I, too, loved a dramatic red pout and brought out my Dior Rouge whenever the festivities called for it.

"Celebrating, always. It was fabulous—busy, but really fun. We had almost three hundred people at the holiday party this year, and I had a total blank canvas of a new location." I'd literally painted murals on the walls, designed the lighting from scratch, and transformed an entire 10,000 square foot former Restoration Hardware into a temporary luxury jewelry store for a Bing Crosby-themed Christmas event. "I missed seeing you there, though."

"I know! But it's not like I could pass up the L'Oréal Women in Entrepreneurship awards." She beamed, as she should. She'd been a panelist and had accepted an award at the prestigious event. Heather's life revolved around her business; it had to, since the company was rapidly expanding in terms of employees, customers, and patents. I admired her tenacity, especially because I knew being the founder and CEO wasn't always easy. She had to persevere through fundraising rounds and questionable markets, all while paying herself significantly less than her talents would yield on the free market. But she was creating her dream life, and her drive was palpable.

"Your social posts from the awards were incredible—I'm so happy for you. And I'm excited for what's to come for me here." My eyes and body adjusted to the atmosphere as I contemplated my last conversation with my boss. *We'd love for you to continue growing our event portfolio and strategic partnerships. But, for efficiency, the position should be based out of headquarters.*

"How did event season wrap?" she asked.

"The events have been smooth and pivotal on multiple layers. The relationships we're building yield a deeper ROI." I'd save the promotion news for the next round of drinks. "More importantly, how are *you*? Ms. Freshly New Fiancéd Fiancé," I said, grabbing her left hand to ogle the gorgeous ring her partner had designed, which I'd helped him procure.

I hadn't always been Director of Global Events. Throughout my tenure, I had also been in sales, custom jewelry, management, and buying. Heather's fiancé was a very talented graphic designer and left no detail to chance. His integrity followed him to both the boxing ring and the closet; he was in incredible shape and always well-dressed. The engagement ring was a unique, meaningful piece that they'd both cherish forever.

"Amazing." The diamond sent reflections skipping around the shadowy walls as she told me about his romantic city stairway proposal. "We're so excited to jump into wedding planning. It's going to be in Italy to pay homage to my roots, but we're not sure where exactly. Tuscany-ish."

"I see tall cypress trees and a classic yellow, countryside villa already... I'm in. Knowing you two, it'll be amazing no matter where you decide to become Mr. and Mrs."

"Well, I hope you're coming. I can't get married without my maid of honor."

"*What*? Oh my god, yes!" We giggled, hugging each other and rocking back and forth. "My Heather, I'd be honored. No pun intended. Wow, thank you."

"Of course. If it wasn't for you, we might not even be together."

"Oh, don't give me so much credit. You two would have found a way—what's meant to be will be." I had one hundred percent faith in these two and their love. They were in sync with visible goals like professional endeavors, travels, and real estate, but deeper than that, their mutual respect, love, and curiosity were what sealed the bond.

"True, but when I needed to hear a hard truth, you didn't sugarcoat it." There had been a moment during the early days of their relationship when I'd told her she was acting like a schoolgirl instead of the boss that she was. "You called me out. And it helped us avoid a major bump in the road. That's one of the reasons I love our friendship—we can call bullshit when we see it."

"Cheers to that."

"Speaking of..."

"Oh dear, now I'm in for it. Bartender, another round, please," I joked, waving my hand up and around. Our waiter, a twee distracted, seemed to have abandoned our corner.

"Seriously, though, what's going on? You keep saying you're okay, but you're like a muted version of yourself or something."

"Muted?"

"Confused or sad, quiet. You haven't seemed like my positive-bubble-of-constant-future-plans-and-ambition-girl lately."

"Come on. My Supergirl cape is just in the laundry," I said, referencing a magnet my mom had given me last year for my birthday. "Seriously, though, I'm not on mute—healing from a broken bone takes time, the house is on hold until spring, work is the priority, and all of it is just a buffer to other things I don't have time to focus on." I paused.

"What other things?"

"Well," I started, feeling unsure, "something might be off." Despite my confession, I wasn't sure I wanted to open this door. I wasn't sure what was even behind this door. Did I even know I had a door? "Maybe at home... or with me." I lingered on each word so that my mind could catch up with what I might be saying. I couldn't hold back from Heather. "At home, I feel like we're settling into a co-dependency. It's like we're both losing ourselves by trying to make the other happy. He looks to me to make every decision: vacations, bills, social calendar... and seems to be cut off from his internal compass, questioning his own decisions and jumping between jobs. He works hard, but it isn't consistent, and I'm growing resentful of carrying the financial burden. But I don't seem to be able to separate myself from his happiness. Maybe I don't even know myself anymore. We're both shutting down but digging in at the same time. Does that make any sense?"

She took a breath. "It probably just means there are things to look at and deal with. You guys have been together since you were teenagers, and I don't think you've ever fought once. It's fair to think you might have a hard time seeing where you end and he begins. Don't be afraid to have problems."

"I'm not afraid." It was different receiving relationship advice; I was usually in the seat with the clipboard. As if to convince myself, I repeated, "I'm not afraid, Heather, it's just that I can only do so many things at once. I'm tired of carrying it all." My head started to spin like a wind-up toy, and my palms were getting warm.

"Okay, okay. I understand your focus is divided right now..."

"I was offered a promotion today," I cut her off.

"Wait, what? Why didn't you open with that? Congrats!" She pushed back into our plush booth for support.

"Someone called me infinitely interesting, and I almost had an affair on the spot." I ignored her and cocked my head to the other side like an angry parrot.

"An affair?" She laughed. "That's dramatic. You've never looked at another man."

"And... my husband... he didn't deposit a crucial check when he promised me he would."

"I'm really not following..."

"When I found out, I wasn't even mad. I was *indifferent*... and I've never felt so... so hollow." Just thinking about it, my chest caved and my lungs emptied.

"Wait, wait, let's just slow down a bit, babe," she said, sitting up straighter.

"And he could have died twice last year."

"Now stop," she commanded. "These are big things you're saying, and you're going to need to explain them, Whitney. I want to *help*."

Not realizing I was crying, I just looked at her, stunned. I never broke. I never let go or lost control, especially not over my emotions or with intimate information. I paused to warp time, to give myself a chance to retrace what I had said. But instead of finding clarity, I sensed nothing but fear.

"I'm sorry. You're right," I said, blinking my eyes to regain composure. "It's just... been building for a long time, I guess. Shit, maybe I've been in full denial." I wiped the smudged makeup from my cheeks with a cocktail napkin, clearing a foggy mirror of truth.

"Go back. Let's start with the promotion. That's a huge opportunity."

"I have to say no," I said, shaking my head. "It means relocating out here, which would never work." Where would he work, or snowboard? How could our life morph into a city pace?

"Do you have time to think about it?"

"Yes. It would happen after the winter season ends, so next spring."

"Good. This is a critical choice to design the next phase of your life. I know you love Colorado, but you moved there when you were nineteen, and you've always wanted to live in other places." She was right. I never planned to be in Colorado so long. "Don't try to take care of everyone else right now. We all love your husband, and the two of you together, but be *honest* with yourself while you figure this out."

"I've always said I could handle anything in life as long as I'm with him. That our marriage was the one thing I couldn't live without." I stared into my nearly empty glass of bubbles, my cheeks now dry from the unexpected saltwater facial.

"And that's how one should feel," she said, as she must have been thinking of her own pending nuptials. "So, let's get to that discussion."

"This is going to sound," I sighed, "nuts. It's like it doesn't even make sense."

"This all sounds nuts. So just keep going."

"When I got home from a work trip last month, his payroll check was on the counter. He promised me he'd deposit it at the beginning of the week." It was for the down payment. Even though his checks didn't cover the bills, they helped keep our finances flowing, and I'd been trying to get him to be more accountable for domestic things. "But instead of taking care of it, it was left there for me to handle, and late. Normally, no big deal, right? It's a small thing; he'll remember next time… But it was the straw that broke the camel's back. I looked at him and said, 'I don't even care anymore, I'm not upset, and that feels worse than anything.'" Which it did. I was gutted by the void of emotion. It was a lonely and foreign feeling. "And then I went upstairs into my office and noticed a sterling silver angel my grandmama gave me years ago, hanging in the window. There's an Eleanor Roosevelt quote on it that says, 'You must do the thing you think you cannot do.' And a confident voice inside announced: *Leave your marriage.* Almost like a command. And I fell to the ground crying."

Heather just watched me as everyone else around us faded into a blur. "I've never thought that in my life, Heather. Never. He's the one steady I *need.* But now, I can't unring that bell, and I'm scared. Honestly, I'm scared of what's to come. It's like I flipped a switch— hence, even the *idea* of someone else."

"Wow. It sounds like things have been cracking under the surface for longer than you're admitting, or maybe longer than you even realize. It's obviously time to start really looking at your concerns and addressing them with him out loud."

"And twice last season, I directly asked him not to go snowboarding that day." The requests hadn't been rooted in rationality; rather, an intuitive sense of foreboding had gripped me, whispering warnings that something was wrong. "And on both occasions, he returned home with tales that justified my fears. By all rights, he shouldn't have survived either day."

"Wait, what? What do you mean?" Heather's world wasn't as filled with physical risk as mine.

"Before he left for the mountain, he asked for my thoughts on the plan, and I said it didn't feel right. But he didn't listen. The first time he tangoed with death, he was riding down an open face, and the snowpack cracked and broke, many layers below his feet. A seventy-five-foot-wide avalanche started steamrolling down the mountain. He was swept away and cartwheeled with the icy boulders more than two hundred feet down the slope. He was lucky as hell that he ended up on top of the debris instead of underneath the snowpack."

He was *insanely* lucky, which I realized after we sat on the couch, huddled together, watching the GoPro footage he'd captured on his helmet. He'd surfaced above the tidal wave of snow and emerged into sunshine before plunging again into darkness, frame after frame. When we were done watching, he looked at me without saying a word. My breath had caught, and my heart paused thinking of the dodged consequences. I had searched his face and then the room for support but only found remnants of freshly smoked joints. Another reminder of our misalignment.

"The second time I asked him not to go, he only returned home because of the riding order." I told her the story of how he had gotten cemented upside down in a tree well—again, he had come home with a hollow look in his eyes, knowing I had been right to warn him not to go. Both times, he'd held me tight, thinking about his narrow escape, knowing he would go out again. Both times, my internal world had raged with unreleased emotion as a tornado of hormones and anxious energy swirled.

"Damn, Whitney." With tears in her eyes, Heather said, "That's intense. That isn't normal to have to deal with."

The panic of those memories sent my mind racing with renewed worry. My heart had been existing in a low vibrational state of silent fear that I, too, would be on the other end of a life-changing phone call. I had been in continuous fight or flight mode, and it was as if I couldn't hold it steady any longer. I was destined to break.

"Maybe I was shutting down little by little, and then the check debacle just flipped the switch." Saying this all out loud was as eye-opening for me as it was for her. "Maybe that's why I seem quiet in general—I don't know what to feel about the future, what I want, or who I am, so I've stayed mute. Until now." My body shivered with the release of saying it out loud. I was also getting nauseous.

"I'm here for you, in every way—for anything," she said, with what felt like her whole heart. "What would feel best to talk about first?"

"None of it." With an exasperated pointer finger, I circled my blotchy face and said, "Time for a quick restroom refresh. I'll grab another round, and when I get back, tell me *all* about Shoppable. I want way more than water cooler details."

"No," she countered. "When you're back, we're still dealing with this. You can't avoid it anymore."

She was right. But it was petrifying to acknowledge how I felt. If something really was wrong in my marriage, I absolutely knew I wouldn't survive. My whole identity was woven together with his— losing him would be losing a part of myself.

A few hours later, Heather and I ended the night with loving hugs and a look that said, *No matter what, I'm with you.*

BY APRIL, I was sitting cross-legged on the floor, dwarfed by a life-size game of moving box Tetris as I packed our final things. My thirtieth birthday party in January was the last time my community of friends had all been together, and my husband and I were still an "us." Now there were three piles: his, hers, and donate. The thought brought back a quiver of tears. Today, our mountain life and our fairytale romance were over. Even with the turbulent ripples, no one totally understood our separation. We didn't completely understand it, either—but it was real, and it was happening. I was here, with nothing but the screeching and tearing of packing tape.

Un-showered and in my pajamas, I made it to the third shelf of our ceiling-high bookcase with tears still welling up. It was time to pack the photo albums. Every year I would sift through snapshots of birthdays, travels, and daily life and arrange the moments into a story. Now they looked like an encyclopedia collection, radiating with frequencies of laughter and love. In a separation, who got the photo albums? Who *wanted* the photo albums? We were going different ways, and the story was changing, but it didn't mean the chapters hadn't been lived. *I'm keeping them,* I decided as I wiped my eyes. I was happy to share the digital versions if he wanted to reprint them.

My body shuddered, my knees weakened, and I reached my left hand to my neck to steady myself. I touched the spot where I still felt his soft kiss, the one he'd left as we'd hugged goodbye that morning. He'd been sleeping on the black leather futon in my office, but the night before, on our last night living under the same roof, I wasn't able to go to our bedroom alone. I couldn't make the right at the top of the stairs and sleep in our perfectly dressed king bed, so I'd taken a left and gone to him instead. He hadn't seemed surprised to see me peeking in the doorway, holding my pillow and blanket, looking at him with a look that said, *I've loved you for as long as I can remember, and you know me better than anyone in the world.* A look that made him feel, *I still love you and always will.* A sincere and humble look that also said, *I'm sorry. I'm so deeply sorry for my part in all of this, and most importantly, I'm sorry for hurting you.* He hadn't been surprised, because he'd looked at me the same way. Without saying a word, he'd raised his covers, inviting me into his arms, and we had fallen into each other.

We'd slept on the floor together. Neither the bed, where a happily married couple used to sleep, nor the futon, representing months of solitude, confusion, and pain, felt right. We'd found each other in between mismatched layers of blankets and pillows on the carpet. In between names and meaning. In between lives. Stripped of expectation and hope, filled with raw emotion and fixated on nothing but the present moment, our bodies still knew how to love.

Standing in our living room now, my tears were flowing like pinballs off my cheeks and my shoulders caved in to protect my broken heart. Looking around at the empty walls, I still saw them filled with pictures from our wedding and family holidays. Seeing the room empty made my vision come alive with scenes of entertaining friends with delicious meals in the dining room and countless nights cuddling on the couch in front of the fire, watching movies. To me, the space wasn't cold or silent with generic cardboard boxes. It was still overflowing with the energy of our married life—everything warm and familiar and routine. I closed my eyes to deny the reality of the set change, but all I heard was a relentless drumbeat in the back of my mind, echoing *ending* on repeat. I was learning that heartbreak was a thousand slices of love, cutting over and over and over again as I clung to good times and retraced what had gone wrong.

Sealing up the last box of albums, I noticed something sticking out of the one titled "Honeymoon 2010." Careful not to fully open the page, I slid the small rectangle out and saw it was a playing card from *Cards Against Humanity*. Smiling, I turned it over to see one of my favorite cards: Mother Fucking Sorcerer. I couldn't contain my laughter, which rang through the room. I hugged the card to my chest for a few silent minutes as I appreciated the comic relief. Once

I finally loosened my grip, I decided to tuck it into my wallet for future access to these secret powers of humor.

Finally, I stood to get an aerial view of my Tetris city, then turned on my heels to do a quick once-over upstairs. I got a glimpse of myself in the staircase mirror and let out another laugh at my reflection; I'd found a plastic princess crown with pink and blue crystals while cleaning out the games and used it to hold back my ratty, tear-soaked hair. I shook my head. Seeing my red, puffy cheeks streaked with tears, and tired, weary eyes, I couldn't help but be thankful for my eyelashes. The elegant and long hairs stood as vigilant guardians, cradling my blue eyes like a ceremonial headdress adorns a priestess. They had boosted my confidence for as long as I could remember, and in that moment of intense turmoil, they grounded me with gratitude.

Finally reaching the master bathroom at the top of the stairs, I looked around for forgotten items. And then I saw it: in an instant, my stomach churned with the ultimate reminder of why we were going our separate ways. He'd left his wedding ring marooned by the sink. The custom, black Damascus steel sphere sat on the cool white porcelain with a simple, way-too-familiar message: "You take care of it."

Instead of taking responsibility and dealing with what needed to be done, he'd left it for me to handle. No, I wouldn't throw this away for him or choose how to alleviate the pain from the broken promises it represented. I was done making both sides of the decision. Seemingly small actions had caused ripples that had become waves which, left untended, fed tsunamis. Over time, there had been so many of them that we were surfing to opposite shores to survive the storm.

He may have abandoned his ring, but I wasn't leaving mine. My yellow sapphire engagement ring was coming with me. So were my tsavorite and platinum ring, my thick yellow gold wedding band etched like tree bark, and my classic diamond eternity band. They were the special, sparkly, and glamorous parts of my identity. Together with my gold watch, which was a wedding gift from him (also coming with me), and mascara on my long lashes, they balanced the grit and gear with a little bit of sass and class. They were essential elements for my sense of self.

I stood up straighter, raised my throbbing head and pushed my weary shoulders back, and let out a long exhale as I went back downstairs. Aside from a few things in storage, our furniture, kitchen items, and housewares had been donated or given away. I fully believed in giving; where energy goes, energy flows, and these items were meant for another life now. I had full faith that when I needed a set of kitchen knives or a popcorn maker, another would be available.

The only thing we specifically split up was our gear. An altar to the Colorado outdoors, gear adorned all sides of our oversized garage and was cared for with the same appreciation and attention as my jewelry. Skis, snowboards, stand-up paddleboards, hiking, rafting, biking, and camping kits were mutually divided. The rest of our house was left for me to deal with.

A few hours later, I had stopped crying, redone my makeup, packed the crown, loaded the final boxes, locked the door, and climbed into the Jeep. As I drove away, I snuck a peek in the rearview mirror and felt the image of a happy life punch like a stamp in my memory. The image disappeared as I said out loud, "With courage and grace, I salute the past, and about-face."

I can hold this together, I thought. *I can rebuild and keep going. I will.* I breathed into my cells as if to cement it into reality: *I will.*

"CHAMPAGNE FOR EVERY occasion," I announced, walking in with two cold bottles. From rainy days to mountain summits, the flirty drink was always a welcome element in my world. For the moment, I left my boxes, sadness, and to-do list in the car. "Hey, roomie," Jeannine called from upstairs. "I have our spread ready." She was referring to our traditional dinner: antipasto, crudité, nuts, grapes, and chocolates.

"Cheers to a tragedy of choices. Welcome to failure," I said, opening the champagne and sitting next to her on the classic plaid mountain sofa.

"You are not a failure. This is life, and you two are making the hard choice," Jeannine offered.

"There is no easy choice," I said. "There are a thousand reasons to separate or to stay together, and none of them are easy. It hurts, it's messy. Your mind wallows clinging to the past and races with anxiety about the future, all but denying the present because, well, it's just too painful."

"Cheers to *that*, then. The pain hurts because you truly loved."

I drank to that. Looking out at the aspens through her two-story wall of windows, I asked, "You know the best example of love I've ever seen?"

"Who?"

"My grandparents. My mom's parents."

"Aw, Grandmama. Of course," Jeannine had gotten to know her when she road-tripped with me to Wisconsin one summer, surprising my family by spending a week working on the farm as they opened the back forty. Learning how to bake a rhubarb-raspberry pie with Grandmama's secret recipe had been a highlight of the trip.

"One summer, my grandmama broke her leg—she had a full cast, up to her hip. A few weeks later, it was a hundred-plus degree day and humid, but she saw the weeds getting unruly in her garden and was absolutely determined to free her flowers from the intruders. So, my grandpa put her in the red Radio Flyer wagon we cruised around in as children and pulled her row by row until her duty was done. He would go forward one step at a time while she leaned over the side, weeding her way through the blooms. It was the ultimate display of love. The best example of partnership I've ever seen."

"I love that. Not a story you hear anymore."

"I wonder what she would think of the situation I'm in now. They were happily married for seventy years before Grandpa passed away." Separating is foreign to my family, but I know in my heart she'd still love me. She'd sit and chat with me and hold my hand for as long as I needed. She had a way of knowing what would help—a wisdom of love—and I hoped to make her proud again.

"She'd still love you and, yes, she would be proud of you." Had I spoken that out loud, or was this proof of how well Jeannine knew me? "Come on, you guys have gone about breaking up as graciously as anyone I've ever seen. She'd see that, too," Jeannine continued. "My parents would be the same if I were in your position. Honestly, I couldn't comprehend break-ups until my thirties, when I started to see some of my friends going through it. Only then did I see the complexities and emotion around it, especially how it affects so many people outside of the couple in question." She said softly, "Even though I haven't been married, my opinions aren't so innocent or narrow anymore."

"We keep saying, 'With love and respect.' I don't have any ill will towards him. I just want what's best for both of us. Do you know what he said this morning?"

"What?"

"He wants to officially file for *divorce* right away."

She stopped mid-bite and looked at me. "I thought you were going to wait and see how living apart went?"

"Me, too, but he said, 'Why are you fighting for something you don't want? Just because you can't admit it didn't work. There's no reason to wait, we need to file.'"

"Ouch." We both sat back on the couch. "What did you say?"

"My mind went blank. It's like I shut down when the truth needs to come out. I don't want to get divorced. But I know we can't stay married. How can I have it both ways? I know it's over, but I'm so afraid to say it. Eventually, that reality sunk in, and I agreed to file."

"Damn. So, tonight isn't just the first night out of the house, it's the first night *alone* as well?"

Hopeless and afraid, I looked at her in silence, then dropped my gaze to my legs folded beneath me. I covered my face, trying to mask the ache etched into it, and drew a long, deliberate breath.

"Yup... house, gone. Husband, gone." And then I raised my eyes to meet hers, adding in a whisper, "But there is a force behind all of this. Something I can't explain, like an invisible cord pulling me into a future I can't see." I didn't understand it, but I was following it.

She paused, slicing another piece of cheese and gently refilling the bowl of olives. "That's kind of sad, though," she said softly. "Something pulling you away from so much happiness."

"Happiness... yeah, I did what was expected: went to school, fell in love, built a career and a home. And look at me now. As it crumbles all around me... Bonafide superhero."

"At least time is on your side—you're only thirty."

"Time—what a funny thing. This return to Saturn is really making me dance out on her rings of change, isn't she? Well, I don't want any more change, thank you very much. I'm going to sit my spinning, solo ass down and reground by focusing on work. Framebridge is all I have, and Manhattan is calling. I think my time gracing your loft will be short-lived. I'm going to reignite my relocation conversation and move out east."

Four months earlier, I had turned down the promotion that might have launched my career to the next level. Relocating to headquarters, embedded in the pulse of the industry, would have expanded my professional horizon in every direction. Synchronicities had been urging me eastward: serendipitous invitations, unexpected real estate opportunities, even the lyrics of songs on my morning commute seemed to conspire in favor of the move. But accepting it would have sealed the fate of our already-fragile marriage, and I hadn't been ready to be the one to drive in that final nail. We ended up six feet under anyway, but I would have never forgiven myself had the job decided that for us. Now, with nothing left to hold me back, I was free to dive in, headfirst.

"Why don't you take some time off?" She rested, satiated, and sipped her drink.

"I did. Besides my meeting with our CFO tomorrow, I'm off the rest of the week to prep for my volunteer trip in Nicaragua." I was going on a ten-day trip as the lead chaperone of a group of high schoolers, helping at a school for children with special needs.

"I mean for an extended period of time," Jeannine said, expanding her hands far away from her body. "Like a sabbatical or something. You've been working straight for over a decade, and you need time to recalibrate."

"And do what? Just cry all the time? Miss him? Change my mind? No, downtime isn't the next step. Work is."

"Right. I'm talking to the woman who skis all day after knowingly blowing out her knee and hikes two miles down a mountain after breaking her ankle," she muttered as she cleared our plates.

"Don't judge me," I said, getting up to help her. My legs tingled with blood flow and emotion after holding me on the couch for so long.

"Fine, fine," she softened as we put the food back into the refrigerator.

The main floor of the house was above the garage and had two bedrooms, where Jeannine stayed. This level featured a beautiful view down the valley. There was a bathroom, kitchen, dining room, and fireplace, all part of an open floor plan. A patio welcomed the world outside, and the upstairs contained a large storage closet and an open loft with a clothing rack, a mattress on the floor, a small desk, and a full-length mirror, which was my free room for now. Home.

"Well, my blonde Buddha," she said, using the nickname she'd given me years ago because of my intuitive hits and random sessions of advice I gave strangers. But the nickname didn't feel appropriate given the context, and I shot her a look. "We have an early morning."

"Thank you, my friend. Thank you for everything," I said, hugging her before we went to our separate sleeping quarters. "And sorry we didn't talk about your new boyfriend." Ugh, I'd forgotten. "I want all the details tomorrow. Is the spreadsheet officially down to one line?"

She laughed, "It's hot and heavy, but nothing's official. And don't apologize—tonight was about way more than a guy I met a few weeks ago. I love you, lady."

"Love you more."

The loft had a classroom-sized world map hanging on the ceiling above the mattress, and I found myself unable to fall asleep. I tossed and turned in my new cocoon of fresh blankets, looking at the map all the while. I visually traced the places I'd been, noted those I hadn't, and let myself be distracted from my sadness.

A sabbatical—why not? Who wouldn't love that? But no, not now. I quickly corrected my imagination. *Now I need to focus on salvation.* After Nicaragua, it was back to work with 110 percent commitment. *The travel can wait, and the playtime will need to wait, too. I need to earn it first.*

THE NEXT DAY, I woke up determined to recalibrate my depressed energy into something positive and productive, so on the way to my work meeting, I swung into a gas station to buy a lottery ticket. I didn't necessarily buy tickets to win the lottery, although that outcome would have been thrilling. I bought them to kick off manifesting something specific, to invite in the same energy that had graced me when I'd won the Hawaii trip. It was my way of supporting a desire by taking clear action. I'd set an intention, buy the ticket as a symbol, and release it into the ether—then I'd trust the universe to conspire and send results my way. It was a strategy that had worked for me many times.

My intention today was for my career to surprise me. One option was to resurrect the promotion conversation. Or maybe the answer lay with a pending contract I had with a production team for the documentary in Botswana. It had a $250,000 budget and was due to be signed any time—that would be an amazing project to immerse myself in. It was also possible I'd finally get to hire support staff; if I did, I'd be able to expand our schedule of events *while* overseeing the documentary *and* have the bandwidth to strategize for the future instead of operating quarter to quarter. No matter what, work would be a great distraction as I recalibrated my unpredictable emotional state.

Careful not to succumb to heartbreak this early in the day, I pushed my emotions down and carefully tucked away the lottery ticket next to the Mother Fucking Sorcerer card in my wallet, feeling confident they'd plot away. A solid pairing.

Driving down the highway toward Edwards, a town just twenty minutes west of Vail, where our corporate offices were, I noticed the snowcapped mountains shining brightly in the early morning sunshine. You never knew what nature would be like in April—you could be bringing out ski gear and skinning over a few feet of fresh snow, the trees and animals still hibernating, or you could be dusting off your bike for a day on dry dirt with wildflowers popping up along the trail. Today was a mix of both: lingering, slushy snow piles melted into streams lined with budding aspens with leaves not yet big enough for shade. The duality was not lost on me. As winter resisted its annual retreat, the new life of spring refused to wait. The next fifteen minutes of my drive west were calm and quiet. The fifteen minutes after were not. The Bookworm Café was lively with coffee enthusiasts, chatty friends, open laptops, and a few rogue children. I sat across from my direct boss, the CFO of Framebridge, at a small, square, wooden table, eager to hear what he had to say. As I leaned into the conversation, he slid a sealed manila envelope across the table.

I looked down and froze. Surely this wasn't... this couldn't be... not on my first day out of... and then I heard his words.

"Whitney, this isn't performance-based. We're simply reorganizing and eliminating your position. You're welcome to reapply in any location." His voice floated on as the breath left my lungs. "Or, there is a severance offer and agreement in this envelope you're welcome to review."

The world went into slow motion like one of those action movies in which a bomb detonates or a car plunges underwater. My body managed short, robotic movements as my tongue unglued itself. I somehow found enough composure to quietly thank him for ten years of support and camaraderie. And I meant it. But I left the bookstore in zombie mode. The knots in my stomach told me driving wasn't a good idea. Besides, I didn't have anywhere to go—I felt completely untethered. Lost in a way I had never been lost before, I meandered down the street to a back staircase toward the Eagle River. I found a lonely bench and collapsed onto it, staring at the water, the unopened manila envelope by my side.

The last golden thread holding the tapestry of my purposefully woven life had been severed in an instant. Every cell in my body felt the unraveling—it was as if I were about to disappear.

As reality started to sink in, my eyes shifted back and forth, not registering anything but searching my consciousness for changes to make or actions to take. Something, anything, to fix this. I loved my job. After working and growing with Framebridge throughout my entire twenties, they felt like family to me. I was jolted. There was still so much to do. This couldn't be. They'd ended it, ripped off the Band-Aid with no respect for the tiny hairs attached and no consideration for the wound it would leave exposed, as if it never mattered. What would I do without this role? Who was I without this title?

I let out a deep breath while my lips quivered. I didn't have the one person I called first anymore. The automatic number I would have dialed led to the person who once lent unconditional support and reassurance: my person. My husband. He was gone, too. Our final embrace wasn't even a full day before, and I knew that his pain was as fresh as mine. Calling him with this news would be selfish.

I imagined what he'd say, though. *What? No. They love you. You mixed up their traditional vibe and were just establishing the bridge to the next generation. Plus, you've done like every role over the past decade. Laying you off doesn't seem fair.*

But there was no one to talk to, and nowhere to go. Crumpling into myself on the hard bench, I missed my home—my safe haven— where I could shut out the world and be alone. I longed for privacy to scream, or cry, or both. I wished to disappear into my favorite couch and pour an endless glass of wine into my go-to stemless cup—all of which I had donated to Goodwill. I looked up into the trees for guidance, but was met with silence. My hopeless stare shifted back to the water.

I could no longer suppress the wellspring of emotion. I'd been experiencing a constant stream of tears these days, and once again they rolled down my cheeks, mirroring the flow of the river beside me. Everything: husband, home, *and* job. The pillars of my existence had been bulldozed in twenty-four hours. I wished I could rouse from this dream, but the waking universe, it seemed, had its own sense of timing.

Face buried in my hands, arms and legs crossed, my whole body tensed, trying to protect myself from my own unraveling—desperate to hold me together. I cried, thinking, *I'm no longer a devoted wife, a responsible homeowner-to-be, nor the employee of a bougie jewelry empire. No longer a future mother, kitchen renovator, event producer, or an accomplished member of society on any front.*

A new question loomed, suspended in time and space: *who am I?* The question was haunting—it echoed into oblivion with a hollow gravity. The defining facets of my societal identity had dissolved, leaving me with a blank page.

I found no script and no goals to direct my next steps. Blank.

In this stillness, I could think of nothing but watching the water. It flowed to its ultimate destination without instruction—what a feeling of freedom that must be. No choices to make.

And then, almost as if the wind whispered it, my spirit said *go.* Suddenly, I was filled with the desire to embrace the nothingness. To drive west, leave Colorado, and escape the shambles of my life—ignore it all and go.

My tears slowed, and I found myself laughing at the idea of this potential odyssey of self-discovery. Ten minutes into an identity crisis, and I was teetering on the brink of madness. The "screw it" mindset was unfamiliar territory; one I was reluctant to tread. Whatever I do, I do it to perfection—how could I acquiesce or *let go* to perfection? What would that even look like? No, surrendering wasn't my style. I reached for the manila envelope, bracing myself for whatever my severance held inside, silently vowing to take control of the chaos. But something stayed my hand, and I pulled back as if the envelope would have burned me. What was even left to fix?

My eyes bulged, and I thumped back into the bench and huffed out an exasperated breath into the chilly air. For the first time, I found myself genuinely at a loss. I felt stunned, hopeless, and yet charged with angry desire. I was paralyzed by paradoxical emotions, and I truly didn't know what to do.

"THIS IS BULLSHIT!" I yelled at my computer screen. "I don't want to be job searching. I want the job I created, the career I manifested and molded for over a decade. Give it back to me!" I pleaded with the universe: "Fucking rewind the clock and I'll accept the promotion last year and move out east. There is nothing here, nothing in Colorado worth keeping me in this valley of relentless memories."

I had survived the initial week of losses by throwing myself into the only thing I could—my volunteer trip at the school in Nicaragua. Remaining laser-focused on the children and on the mission to care for, build, and educate their local community had been a worthy distraction. In this state of emptiness, I couldn't help myself, but I could help others. It had also been an important reminder of my privilege—that I'd had a job and a house to lose in the first place.

But stateside again and void of purpose, I barricaded myself in the loft. Jeannine, still employed with Framebridge, had informed me that people had been laid off throughout the company due to a restructuring inspired by outside counsel. When I said no to the relocation, it had raised the question as to whether my position could be divided based on location. I was happy that Jeannine was still there, although she was uneasy, unsure of how the changes would affect her down the line. She was delicate with me at home and careful around the subject, but always available to vent or brainstorm.

She also picked up groceries and alcohol for us because I was adamant about avoiding any place I might run into someone to whom I would need to *explain* things. I couldn't bear the potential barrage of questions: "Wait, you're getting divorced? Where are you living? How's work?" So I remained un-showered and in my pajamas, surfing LinkedIn and Craigslist while laying on her sofa, daydreaming at the world map above my mattress, or talking to the trees outside the windows, all the while succumbing to the anger and denial boiling in my veins.

You are welcome to reapply, the words from my ex-boss echoed in my brain. Maybe it was my pride, or ego, but hell no. After years of hard work advancing through those positions, I wasn't going back to square one. Nope. I was going to show them. Reaching out to all my external contacts around Greenwich and Manhattan, I was sure there was an opportunity for a skillset like mine. I could still move to New York and continue this trajectory if I wanted to.

While I fed my professional resentment, the energy also expanded into romantic bitterness. My anger that I had to navigate this alone overshadowed my heartbreak from losing my best friend—besides, denial was easier. No, I wasn't going to contact my ex. And no, going to the courthouse to pick up paperwork, talk to lawyers, and prepare to file for divorce wasn't my priority, either. I had handled everything practical for us since we met, and I was done caring. He could lead the charge, if he was so motivated. Legally married or divorced? Who cared? I didn't. I was on my own. Fuck paperwork.

I had my savings, thank the Lord and Gods above—that had been a mission for the past few years. I was collecting four months of severance, and I took out a personal loan the day I had been laid off as a precautionary measure. I didn't have a plan for it, but from previous experiences I knew that if I needed cash in the future, a loan wouldn't be possible without income and a consistent work history to back it up.

What do I want? I wondered. I was such a brat to be sitting here in my pity party, but that awareness didn't make my depressive reality any less painful. I was just pissed off and needed to let the anger run its course. *All* my belief systems had been shattered—work hard, trust you are valued, love will prevail. I was confused. What I'd been taught to do for a good life had backfired.

I shut my computer down and made myself another margarita, having concluded nothing would get sorted that day. During the tumultuous time in which my husband and I had begun our separation, we were both careful to never have a conversation under the influence of alcohol. It wasn't worth it. But that wasn't an issue anymore—might as well sit and sulk next to my unpacked cardboard boxes, get thoroughly tipsy by myself, and laugh about this shit show.

FOUR MONTHS LATER, it was August again, and I was in Wisconsin. It had been a year since I'd broken my ankle, and nothing in my life looked the same. After a brief yoga session, I walked the horse trails at my family's farm, acutely aware that my morning zen routine had become more of a frustrated reflection session than a spiritual practice. I was there for my seven-month-old goddaughter's baptism. I was tired, still cranky, and more lost than ever; still living on Jeannine's couch and exploring leads in Manhattan but paralyzed at the thought of making any decisions.

Farmland isn't like the peaks in Colorado. It offers a different embrace, the kind that wraps you in a hug as the breeze comes through oaks, maples, and pines, winding down the bluffs to find our horse barn, goat pastures, and the original farmhouse. The energy of the stones that form the basement cellar is powerful—they radiate perseverance and acceptance, like the feeling after an honest day's work feeding animals, making fresh bread, and tending the garden. You feel a part of the land's world, the rhythm and cycle of life. The barn boards creak from years of flexing, and the oak trees sway in the wind, having grown from saplings to towering landmarks in the sky. Meandering through the old hay wagon routes and secret pathways to our childhood forts always invokes a sense of belonging and peace—two things I certainly hadn't felt much of after my life unraveled.

I slowly picked wildflowers along the trail, thinking, *There is magic in this native landscape.* One hundred and seventy-six years ago, when my mother's family settled here, they'd built a dairy farm. I was the sixth generation to grow up on the land, and when I was eight years old, my parents had converted it into a horse ranch. In the winter, we'd go sledding, in the spring we'd splash in the creek, chase fireflies around the bonfire all summer, and jump into piles of leaves in the fall. A perfect representation of the seasons changing, one graciously yielding to the next. Nature is in a constant state of change. Some call it transition, but when you inspect that transition more closely, it's full of a thousand micro changes. Why couldn't I be like that?

"Good morning, sunshine," my mom chirped as she neared me on the trail. She'd just finished the morning rounds, feeding the horses and goats as our dog trotted beside her.

My parents are opposites. Mom is a quiet, redheaded hippy psychologist country girl, and my dad is a left-brained economics major from the city with a MacGyver mindset who believes you can fix anything with duct tape and engineering creativity. From church to the teepee, Mom is my spiritual inspiration, and Dad is my example of adaptability and versatility in a variety of social situations. Both are loyal to family roots and traditional pathways to success: in their eyes, school, marriage, family, and staying close to home all make an upstanding neighbor and citizen.

I knew security from an early age—material and emotional. I always had a closet full of back-to-school clothes and enjoyed an annual family vacation. My schedule had been jammed with competitive sports to piano lessons, show choir, and time with friends; giggly Friday nights at the roller-skating rink or county fairs while we whispered about boys by the cotton candy stand transitioned into bonfire parties in cornfields and secret hillside spots for steamy make-out sessions.

But what had been unique or unusual in my Midwest upbringing was that I'd grown up exposed to very opposite lifestyles. Living on the farm, I'd known where my food came from, what it felt like to spend a day wearing jeans in the summer baling hay, and that helping your neighbor was as important as keeping the animals secure. But since my father was a professional pilot, I had also been exposed to considerable wealth and life outside the county line: I was comfortable occasionally jumping in the private jet to tag along on his work trips. My dad and I had embraced our own activities—day trips shopping in New York, fishing weekends in Canada, or last-minute Spring Break skiing in Colorado—while the businessmen conducted their meetings. I had been ecstatic every time I was lucky enough to sit in the right seat of the cockpit and in awe of the otherworldly panorama views, wishing only to go up further into space. So, from a very young age, I learned a core truth, unbeknownst to me: that life is full of extremes, and we need them to exist. Nothing will ever truly be equal, and that's okay.

The appreciation of opposing perspectives from my childhood also helped me foster an "anything is possible" mentality. This ingrained conviction—not just a fleeting notion, but a deep-seated certainty—served as a guiding light throughout my life and shaped my early career. Empowered by this mindset at nineteen, I had the confidence to move away, lean into my dreams, and start my own event company. Establishing a side hustle alongside my job at the store had proved to be a pivotal decision—one that eventually led to opportunities to orchestrate events for the store itself, ultimately carving out the role I loved so dearly. The inspiration to form my company had been to help nonprofits and do something good with the skills, resources, and access I had, and honest intention delivered full-circle results. None of this would have come to fruition without the fundamental belief in my capabilities—the audaciousness of "why not?" Despite lacking formal education or extensive experience, my intuition told me that I possessed the ability to succeed, and so I had pressed onward, defying conventional wisdom and forging my own path.

When my mom reached me, I said, "I was just thinking of how I started Bucket Events to raise funds for Horses for Joy. How easy it was when I was passionate about my projects, and everything felt in flow."

"My goodness, you were on fire, my dear. You've always been that way," she said as we continued along the trail together.

"Like you? When you left the school district as a psychologist to be an entrepreneur?"

"Exactly," she said, patting my shoulder. "But eons before that, I had to overcome seasons of being a quiet wallflower on the sidelines with an internal dialog of self-doubt and unworthiness before I decided to fake it until I made it." She picked up and threw random sticks off the trail, clearing debris for the next time the lawnmower came through.

"So, how or when did you decide to kick it into gear?"

"Well, I was an influential course and policy creator in the school system even before I started fighting for alternative therapy awareness. One day I realized I was already walking the path of a pioneer, and that I could transfer my tactics to work with the horses."

"I'm sure you had Dad, Grandma, Grandpa, and others questioning you along the way."

"Of course. And my nature, like yours, is to be an overthinker—getting lost trying to make others happy instead of focusing on myself. But I found my footing here on the farm."

I looked up at her as we wound through the forest and settled on a rock wall covered in soft moss. She continued, "The trees, the seasons, the rhythm of the land… at one point it simply struck me to trust my internal voice like nature trusts it will go on, regardless of whatever weather arrives the next day."

"You had an innate knowing you couldn't ignore anymore?"

"Yes, dear. Something quiet but stronger than any line of external questioning."

"That's what I'm trying to find right now. That quiet voice to listen to. And I've been trying all the things…" I looked up, first at the trees and then again towards her, the words caught in my throat.

"What is it?"

"The fire is out, leaving my inner world alarmingly silent. Worse, I feel I'm even contradicting my own frequency," I said, feeling disconnected from the innate currents that had once guided me. There were no gut instincts to explore, no divine inspiration to chase, only an unsettling void where alignment once lived. "My compass seems to have vanished, and after four months, I can't justify it anymore."

"Why are you trying to justify anything?" It was an interesting question, I thought, as she rose from the rocks. "You know, your grandpa proposed to your grandma right here."

"I didn't know that," I said, looking around the sacred space. The rock pile was perfectly positioned on a corner of the trail, yielding views up the hill to the ridge or down the valley to the farm.

"It's a place to think about choices and commit to one direction or another."

There wasn't anything I could say to that.

"I'm going inside to start breakfast with your father. Come in and eat when you're hungry." She paused to turn around. "You're not just adrenaline sports and your job. Think about what inspired you as a child—if you're going to reinvent yourself, start from scratch. Stop trying to put broken pieces back together." And she left, not waiting for my reply.

"Childhood inspiration, leave the broken pieces behind..." I repeated, like a mantra. Even in my childhood, I had learned to love myself because I always accomplished my goals; from sports to academics, I won. And when I hadn't, I'd stopped trying. I'd slipped in the batting order on my softball team, so I had quit at the end of the season. I hadn't made the varsity show choir, so I had walked away from music. Success had come easily and frequently enough that when it didn't, I didn't know how to face failure within me. *Maybe as a kid, I should have been more of a kid,* I thought. But then again, looking around the woods that surrounded me, I had created mystical worlds in the forests, spun stories, and dreamed of treasure hunts. The thrill of imagination and discovery had always called to me. How was I supposed to chase it as an adult, especially when I wasn't even sure what the treasure was?

I traced light circles in the moss that blanketed the rocks. *I love this moss,* I thought. It was an incredible, soft, healthy, vibrant green, and it grew almost anywhere—on any foundation, thriving in unforgiving conditions. It even had tiny little flowers popping up like Van Gogh's brushstrokes come to life. I used to imagine I lived in a house made of moss, like a character out of the nineties movie *Fern Gully.*

I wished for nothing more than to communicate with myself again—to get a feeling, a message, anything, about how to move forward. I had hoped getting lost in the magic of the moss would help, but the only instructions I heard came from my grumbling tummy. So, after only a few minutes, I decided to go in and get some breakfast.

"HI, SCOM!" MY dad said as I walked into the kitchen, my mom by his side. This was the acronym for Sweet Child of Mine from the Guns N' Roses song—our song. Our house had been built on the foundation of the old dairy barn and the kitchen—complete with brick walls, an antique clawfoot gas stove, large windows overlooking the pasture, and a deep sink—sat just off a spacious wrap-around deck.

"Morning, Dad. Smells good," I said, referring to his famous healthy pancakes and the strong coffee brewing in the corner.

"I did years of R&D on this recipe. It's just about perfect now." Not missing a beat, he added, "You know, my parents always held us to high standards and expected all five of us kids to do the best we could."

"Right into it, are we?" I said under my breath, rolling my eyes. "Yeah, you raised me with the same perfectionistic expectations." He was always correcting my grammar and posture, and pointing out a B+ was not an A. He didn't care as much about the grade, but insisted we do our *best*, which meant an A.

"Well, when my dad returned home from the Airforce, he started his own flying business here in town." I knew this story well enough. But he continued, "At sixteen, all my siblings and I were encouraged to start working there. There weren't a lot of options or much thought around what we wanted to do—flying was inherited. Luckily for me, I love it."

I looked out the window at nothing particular and said, "I don't love anything like you love flying or Mom loves horses." Speaking the words out loud only widened the emptiness they left inside.

"But what you don't know," he flipped the pancakes while my mom grabbed cups for coffee and started setting the table, "is that when I was in my early thirties, I went through a lot of hardship over a short period of time. Not the same, but similar to what you're going through now." I listened more intently as I searched the refrigerator for some berries. "Your mom and I suffered a tragic miscarriage, and then my mother died from lung cancer, and on top of it all, due to increasing interest rates and some poor partnerships, we lost the family business. I was mourning two major losses and forced to figure out my professional life on my own for the first time, and yet still had real responsibilities to take care of."

"I didn't know that happened all at once." I felt a pang of sadness as I looked between them with respect. That must have been a heavy season to navigate.

"I stuck to what I knew, and found a corporate flying opportunity that provided for us. The point is, right now, I think you should stick to what you know and get a handle on your responsibilities again."

He was referring to my lack of income, but Mom came at me from the other side. "Honestly," she said, "many of us still don't understand why your divorce happened, so it's difficult to help."

Without a clear reason for divorce, it seemed impossible to explain the complexities of the heart. She continued, "I mean, you went camping together the weekend you officially filed for divorce. No wonder you're finding it difficult to move on. It's like you're still attached."

It was true. After my initial defiance once I had returned home from volunteering, we'd reconnected and made the divorce official. "We're still friends," I said quietly, thinking back to that weekend in Moab, skydiving, biking, rafting, and camping together. It had been a departure from life as we knew it, as only we would do it. "I understand it's hard on everyone," I said, exhausted. "I'm sorry, don't think I'm not embarrassed and ashamed my marriage didn't work."

"Well, your mother-in-law reached out last week. How should I handle that? I mean, she's a board member for my nonprofit, after all."

I let out a big sigh.

"Mom, you have your own relationship with her. Keep it going or give yourself some space." I couldn't be responsible for how she moved forward.

"You know we love him, Whitney," my dad interjected. "This isn't simple." My parents might have been opposites in many ways, but their approach to my current situation was unified.

"Dad, I know. And it sucks that things are complicated." I felt horrible for hurting everyone. I didn't intend to do it. *There were two of us in the marriage—and in the divorce*, I thought. But it always felt like the blame was on me, because I was the one who started it.

We finally sat down at the kitchen island for breakfast, and I was desperate to change the subject, so I pivoted. "You know what I always tell my volunteer kids?"

"What?" they asked in unison, enjoying warm bites of pancakes.

"Well, we always eat family dinners during the trip and discuss the day. Like clockwork, on the first night after working at the school, they won't eat. They'll pick at their plates and inevitably one will say, 'Why should I eat when the children at the school aren't fortunate enough to have food like this?' After a healthy discussion, asking questions to help them through their answers, my advice always comes back to this: 'Who is served by you wasting the food on your plate? Why not choose to be grateful for it, and consciously use the energy it gives you to be better teachers tomorrow? Kids, you have an opportunity on your plate because of where you live, in the United States, that is a fact. What matters is what you decide to do with it. Don't resent the food in front of you, and don't waste it. Use it wisely, so you can create it for others.'"

"That's wonderful advice," my mom said.

"But my problem is, I don't want the food on my plate right now. I know I should be grateful. But I just can't *see* the future I want to create." I said, eating blueberries one at a time.

"You can't go back," my dad said. "Stop being so picky. Just say yes to *something*."

"Work is the only thing I've focused on since I was sixteen. That, and being in a relationship."

"And look at what you've accomplished," my dad went on. "You're not a quitter, SCOM. You can't avoid this because it isn't fun." Our family believed endeavors should be financially fruitful, not whimsical.

"You can't leave heartbreak behind, Whitney Joy. It will be with you anywhere you go," Mom added.

"Don't you think I know that by now? My heart breaks every single day as I repeat a loop of memories, and *what-ifs*, and *fuck-me*'s. I can't *think* in Vail, or anywhere that is saturated with ashes of an old life." Spicy tears welled up, and my breath shortened. I just needed a break; I needed out of the polarizing, energetic coffin I found myself in. I needed space to breathe.

"Do you remember what you told your oldest uncle when you were six years old?"

I shook my head, looked down, and calmed my tears. Of course I didn't.

"One day, you were sitting on the side of his sailboat, staring down at the water. He asked you what you were doing. You turned to him and said, 'I'm thinking. And then I will be brave.'"

"What did I do after that?"

"Jumped into the river to swim to the island where your brother and cousins were playing."

"I wish I had the same clarity as my six-year-old self. That life was as simple as 'think and be brave.'"

"Maybe it is," he said.

Interrupting the unhelpful dialogue, my mom put her silverware down and asked, "Did you get your goddaughter a baptism gift?"

"I did. A sparkly pink blanket and a rose quartz guardian angel," I said, as I wiped my eyes and started to eat my pancakes. "I bought one of the angels for myself and her older sister as well. This way, the trio will stay connected no matter where they are in the world."

"Very thoughtful," she smiled, taking a sip of her coffee. "What else are you going to do while you're in town?"

"Not much. Hang around here and visit the family. But I'm going out with Steph and Heather tonight, then flying back to Colorado early next week."

"Oh, fun—please tell the girls hello."

We fell into a comfortable silence, allowing the soft hum of NPR on the vintage radio to carry us through the remainder of breakfast. Home, while a place of comfort and healing, also bore the weight of unspoken expectations. Their support was genuine, but so were their subtle pressures, rooted in the ambitions of my childhood. As a sensitive child, I had internalized those well-meaning standards as a personal mandate. But now my heart yearned for a new rhythm.

I PATIENTLY GREETED each and every horse, letting them sniff and size me up. Their snorts and cuddles were a welcome medicine after feeling judged and confused. I dusted off a few saddles in the tack room, grabbed the pitchfork to clear the inside stalls, and then headed to the farmhouse. As I walked through the door on the screen porch, it creaked but swung open with ease. Entering the house felt like stepping back in time. Wallpaper from decades past held steadfast to the walls, metal kitchen utensils still graced the shelves in the walk-in pantry, and the large kitchen table anchored the room, overflowing with memories. Six generations had called it home, although no one had lived there since my grandmama's passing five years earlier.

I sank down at the table to recalibrate, taking deep breaths with my eyes closed. I heard birds rush the feeder outside the window, the soft creak of the windmill turning in the breeze, and felt an invisible embrace wrap around me. I could have sworn I smelled her perfume—the familiar scent of lilies of the valley—though I knew it must have been my imagination. She had been a petite powerhouse at just four foot eleven, leading her church's bell choir, tending greenhouses, running the kitchen, and never missing a single one of her grandchildren's events. I called her my hummingbird.

Grandmama, why did you give me that angel with the Eleanor quote on it? I asked silently, sensing her presence. No answer came. Yet, I heard the quote clearly: *You must do the thing you think you cannot do.*

"I understand now," I whispered to her. I had lived it; I had done the very thing I once thought impossible. In doing so, my actions had forged a bond with those words, transforming them from an abstract idea into a lived truth. The iconic message had become a tangible memory, and its inception in my life felt undeniable. It was personal now, as if the quote was a part of me.

I thought back to the foreshadowing of my divorce: at the time, the idea of leaving my marriage had seemed absurd. It wasn't logic that had guided me—it was a feeling, a knowing buried beneath layers of denial. Perhaps my subconscious had recognized the truth long before my mind would even admit we had problems. We are conditioned to avoid conflict and discomfort, and my brain had re-coiled—*uh oh, pain; no, not going there.* So I had shut it down.

But I didn't want to shut it down anymore. I didn't want to keep trading my knowing for someone else's version of safety.

But what does that mean, tangibly, for what's next? I wondered for the hundredth time. Everyone had an opinion—everyone but me. There had to be something bigger here, some reason why all of it—the collapse, the loneliness, the decision paralysis—had to happen. Next time, I vowed to align with a lighter quote like "take a walk on the wild side," or "laugh it off, we're just meat-covered bones hurling through space on a spinning rock."

I silently thanked my grandmama for her gift, even though I knew there were still layers left to dig through. For now, though, I had to get up, pull myself together, and meet the girls. A night out wasn't going to solve anything, but it might remind me there was still a pulse beating somewhere underneath it all.

DOWNTOWN IS FULL of college bars, intimate concert venues, locally owned bookstores, cafés and even a famous guitar shop. I was meeting Steph and Heather at one of our favorite spots, The Helm—a sports bar with pool tables and happy hour. Neon signs glowed all over the walls, separated by fading posters, flashing TVs, and beer clocks. We used to frequent this place during college to kick off long nights of fun. It was only two blocks from the jewelry store where I had worked and eight blocks from my apartment. Steph and I had been good enough at pool to win a few free drinks, but usually smart enough to walk away before the game got too competitive.

Ponying up to the bar, the three of us hopped up on barstools to order the first round.

"Manhattan is where your people are now," Heather said, hanging her purse on the hook below the counter.

"But I don't have the ambition it takes to survive there. I feel like I'd get swallowed up in the skyscrapers and eaten alive by Louboutins." I checked my face in the mirror behind the bar and, after greeting my tired and pale reflection, wiped under my eyes and fluffed my hair.

"I could think of worse deaths," Steph joked, spinning around on the stool in her short shorts and knee-high black boots. She could easily be confused for Molly Sims, or any other model, with her tall, slender frame and striking features. Though we were two years apart and had gone to separate schools, we had been college roommates. We'd never lived on campus, but our apartment had always been a hotspot. We'd also shared the same two part-time jobs: running a tanning salon and working retail at a jewelry store, though we usually had different shifts, so we could commiserate but didn't totally get sick of each other. I always respected the fact that you could count on her to say it like it is, even bordering on jealous of her confidence and honesty.

"Can't you think of anything but work?" said Steph, pulling her hair into a low ponytail.

I played with the coaster on the lacquered wooden bar as we waited for our mixed drinks. Home was turning out to be a series of uncomfortable conversations with people I loved too much to ignore—or lie to.

"Maybe you should embrace not having a plan *being* your plan. You've always dared to leave behind what's not meant for you anymore. You left uni when Gemology called, you left La Crosse when Colorado called, and now your marriage," Steph said. "So what else are you ready to let go of? Including that dress—it's no longer serving you." She gestured at the black button-up, collared office look I had going on. "We need to purge your closet and christen a new style. Your new clothing mantra needs to be *Fuck Yes, No Less.*"

"My closet? You mean my suitcase." I laughed at the mantra, but it felt like decent advice.

"I don't care what we need to empty, you have to stop focusing on the boring parts of life so damn much. You've *never* been single—focus on that."

"I should just date my way through this crisis?" Dating in Vail was nearly impossible. It was such an intimate valley, and everyone knew me as my ex-husband's wife. "And how did you put it, have 'no plan' be my plan? I can't wait for my first date when I introduce myself and say, 'Hi, nice to meet you. My life just blew up, and I have nothing going for me.'"

"Please, please stop stressing so much about what other people think," Steph said. "Fuck them. No one knows what you went through, and no one has the right to judge how you move forward."

"I agree with that," Heather jumped back in, putting her phone down after answering a pressing email. "Not the part about only focusing on dating, but that you need to stop thinking so much about what others think of you." She added, "All you have to do is start showing up for your life again. Take back control."

"So, your suggestions are to, one, become a working tron. Or, two, a promiscuous menace to society?"

"Don't forget I lived with you in college," Steph said, looking at me sideways. "You have your wild ways, Ms. Goody Two Shoes."

Thinking of my youthful sexual encounters made me blush; I used to be adventurous off the ski slopes, too. Of course, after I met my husband, he had been the only one for a long, long time. But before that, I had a very curious nature and dated a wide variety of people. Was I that girl anymore? I had no idea. It felt like just another thing I'd have to figure out.

Frustrated, I jumped down from my seat, about to head to the pool tables. "Decent pep talk, ladies," I said. "Just to get this straight, I need a cocktail of all my sexy, dark desires mixed with celestial fire, swirled with shopping—yes, shopping—all hermetically sealed into the gold lantern of a new job." I ended with my hands cradling an imaginary lantern for effect.

I finished my drink in one long gulp and sighed, setting the glass on the bar.

"What do you want?" asked a tall, tan, dark-haired, handsome bartender.

"Excuse me?" I said, registering that he wasn't the bartender from earlier. Noticing another man's looks was interesting; his jawline was firm, his eyes soft. My curiosity was more than growing. Out of the corner of my eye, I saw Steph exchange a long look with Heather.

"Do you know what you want?" he politely repeated as he poured a cool beer from the tap for my neighbor, who must have been able to hear us but paid no attention, eyes shielded under a ball cap as he watched the game. I stared at the bartender; I knew full well he was inquiring about my beverage choice, but the question underscored my dilemma with such piercing accuracy, it stuck me. I didn't know what I wanted. Or I couldn't say.

"Would you like another one of the same?" he switched it up, motioning with his gaze to my empty tumbler.

"No. No, thank you, I want something new. I'd like to see the menu."

"It's right there up on the wall," he said, sensing that there was more going on than drinks and still being polite. "I'll be back in a bit." I smiled sheepishly as he left.

"That's what I'm talkin' about," Steph said enthusiastically. "Wait, have you been with anyone since…?"

"The thing is," I challenged, "I can't stand the thought of being in a jewelry store, helping people pick out family heirlooms or celebrate romantic milestones. And my marriage—obviously done. Neither hole can just be filled with another one. I want something new. Different. On all fronts."

"*Rawr*," Steph fake growled.

"Look, I get the allure of the roll-the-dice vibe Steph is rooting for," Heather stated.

"How do you know unlocking desire between the sheets won't unlock a clear purpose again?" Steph was on a roll.

Shifting her weight, Heather continued, "But your severance money is spent, right? A job is your best option. Otherwise, how would you pay for, like, your life?" She was always the pragmatic entrepreneur, which was one of the reasons she was so successful as a CEO.

I shrugged. "Savings?"

"After all you've been through with your finances?" Heather counseled.

"50 Shades of Eat, Pray, Shag." Heather rolled her eyes, but Steph could not be stopped, lightly pounding her fist on the bar to ride her own momentum.

Looking at Steph, I said, "I would one hundred percent not call it that."

"But you want to 'explore?' You're 'curious?'" Steph asked, punctuating her question with air quotes.

"Of course I'm curious. I'm a newly single thirty-year-old who's been with one man for the past decade—I'm just not experienced and have no idea where to start." I was getting a bit angry with both of them. "Dating apps scare me. I'm shy! And of course I remember going through bankruptcy to get out from under a morbidly upside-down house, Heather. It's not something you forget. But I've been working my ass off all the while, supporting another adult for so long that if I choose to spend my savings on myself, that'll be my damn choice."

The bartender circled back.

"I'll have a Tito's martini, shaken, dirty, with olives," I said. He nodded, as if in on my sudden liberation and take-charge-ness. "Three, please."

Heather and Steph looked at each other.

"What? I can't stay in a pity box of indecision."

"True. And a pity box will only lead to Botox," said Steph, which made us all laugh.

"I still think you should move to New York. Commit to that and you'll figure it out once you're officially there. And you can live out your 50 Shades of Whatever in New York."

Steph's eyes light up. "You can do both. But I don't see it happening, realistically. You'd have to say yes to just *you* to make that happen, and you're too Wisconsin, too practical for that."

"This is getting too serious, Oprah one and two. Let's play some pool," I said, fully annoyed. They were only trying to be helpful, each with their own ideas about what my freedom should look like. Although my purpose was cloudy and direction disoriented, my vision for the future didn't agree with either. Still, I was getting more than tired of being subordinate to the master illusionist of fear. I had never let fear control me before—what was I even afraid of? With that, I slid the whole row of olives into my mouth at once.

"Too Wisconsin, my ass," I muttered under my breath, turning on my heel to go grab a cue. It was time to get back in the game.

THE TATTOO NEEDLE revved up again, and the sharp pricks unleashed a rush of hormones, my body's desperate attempt to numb the pain radiating across my left forearm. Thank goodness the work on my ribcage was over. The relentless needling of that tender area had been intense—compared to that, the sensation on my arm felt like a series of mosquito bites.

After my goddaughter's baptism, I had flown back to Colorado. On the flight, my seatmate, a gray-haired, obstinate woman in her seventies, clad in a pastel floral sweatsuit, had offered me unsolicited advice. After announcing that divorce was an ugly, dirty business, she'd insisted I should either remain hidden with my family in Wisconsin until the scandal blew over, or beg my husband to take me back. She was serious; I was floored. It was as if the very concept of a woman living life on her own terms was the modern version of seeing a famished, saber-toothed tiger roaming the ancient plains.

Back at Jeannine's, I had gone to sleep with rage but woken up with a vision. I didn't need a man to define me, or a job—or a permanent address, for that matter. I was struggling with indecision around filling those exact voids because I wasn't *meant* to fill them. *I don't need them,* my inner voice said clearly. *I'm running into a wall trying to fill in blanks on an arbitrary piece of paper because I don't need them.*

I'd sat up in bed, grabbed my journal and a pen from the hotel in Panama, and started drawing, my thoughts finally clear. *Fuck it. I need to go. Buy a one-way ticket and put all my chips on red.*

I'd paused, staring up at the world map plastered across the ceiling. Could I let fate steer me? Could I surrender that completely? It wasn't an original idea; humans had been embarking on hero's journeys since the beginning of time. But this wasn't about originality. This was about authenticity, something that felt one hundred percent true. Goosebumps had rippled down my arms. *It's time to fully dive into this moment and find something besides loss. I'm not a victim.* I sat up a little straighter. *I should stop acting like it.* Victim, my mind had echoed, as I returned my gaze to the sketch. *No, the opposite—I'm bulletproof. People can throw their best shots; it wouldn't matter. My conviction would be like steel.* In my mind's eye, I had seen my spirit rising like some cheesy yellow superhero, cape flapping in the wind. I relaxed my body again. In all seriousness, I knew I didn't want to rebuild. I didn't want to replace. I didn't want to *fix* anything—if I wanted to create the space to discover what was truly meant for me, that meant diving headfirst into the unknown, not avoiding it. And if societal expectations didn't define me, what did? In a twisted way, my seatmate had said exactly what I needed to hear to push me so far out of my comfort zone that I could never return. *Thank you,* I thought. *You made it impossible for me to ignore the call of the wild any longer.*

Although, truthfully, I still had no idea what that meant.

I'd looked down at the paper: my sketch was complete. Ever since my yoga retreat a few years earlier, I'd been searching for the right symbol or saying to embody my personal manifesto. I had deliberated over countless quotes and endless designs, but nothing had fully aligned—until now. The moment I'd woken up that morning, clarity had arrived. The choice had been made. A quote, an acronym, and a constellation: *Fortis Fortuna Adiuvat*, MMRL, and Pleiades—the Seven Sisters. The design wasn't something I chose; it was something I dreamed.

I hadn't had a definitive identity, but I believed those new tattoos would serve as a permanent reminder to stay true to my beliefs, even as they continued to evolve.

So there I sat on the plastic tattoo chair, breathing deeply to calm the rush of adrenaline, trying to focus on anything but the buzzing needle. My skin burned—not just where the artist worked, but everywhere. The tattoos were relatively small, but details take time and I appreciated the precision. More deep breaths... I knew this was right. I was waking up. And I could finally feel the beauty braided into the pain. Something big was coming—I could almost taste it.

LATER THAT EVENING, I sat back at Jeannine's, my fingers grazing the bandages that protected my new ink. "You know how sometimes you know something before you really know?" I asked Jeannine as we sat in my oasis in the loft, snacking on Chinese takeout and sipping Syrah while we pulled oracle cards.

"I think so."

"Like when I saw the Eleanor Roosevelt quote and knew I needed to leave my marriage?" She nodded. "It was soul resonance, an innate knowing. When your higher self sends messages down to your consciousness." She expertly maneuvered chopsticks and sipped wine as I continued, "Well, I finally figured out what to get tattooed. And I believe my higher self told me in a dream last night."

"Okay…"

"When I woke, I felt the ink already needled into my skin." I was nodding. "So I got them done today."

"Show me!" As I began to undo the light bandages, she continued. "You're saying when you stopped chasing something, it found you?"

"Yes. But here's the catch: although *what* to get tattooed was clear, I don't feel like I necessarily understand them yet. Does that make sense?"

"Getting permanent markings on your body, but you don't know *why*? Nope, I'm not with you on that one." This is from a person who got her only tattoo as a teenager and has regretted it ever since. "But they are beautiful. I love the simplicity of the letters in black and stars in blue."

"I know what they mean, like the literal definition. But I feel like I need to remember what they really mean *to me*. I need to live it to remember."

"Okay... but still, Whitney. You seem to be reaching. I have to be honest with you; however you explain it, this all rings pretty desperate."

"That's just it," I said, looking directly at her, "I am desperate. It's time to start trusting some of the crazy that is coming through me."

I told her how I wanted to disappear. Be free. Go wild. Explore. Not have a plan or anything to do—just be. I desired a spherical life. A life that expanded from the athletic and professional and incorporated the girly, carefree, sometimes lazy or wild sides of me.

As humans, our character and interests vary and change like the light radiating through delicately cut gemstones. It's impossible to have simultaneous dispersion, but we must remember to tilt, rock, and roll the stone a bit to appreciate the whole rainbow.

"I want to listen to this Kali card," I said, raising the last oracle card on the table in front of us, "and let it burn."

Seeking wisdom from mythical beings or animal spirits goes back to my childhood with my mother. Her connection with the spiritual world was innate and I was raised believing in otherworldly guides. Tonight, I was pulling cards while asking for partners to walk with me during this turbulent time. I had shuffled and mixed the cards until two chose me: the Goddess Kali popped out of the deck, and the Black Jaguar highlighted itself from a hundred cards we'd sprawled across the table. Kali represents death as a natural and healthy cycle of life, inspiring one to literally let it burn so that new growth can begin. Black Jaguar encourages you to walk confidently into the night and calmly into the unknown, eyes open. I hoped their ideas and symbolism would flank my steps and psyche moving forward.

The synchronicities were stacking up, and I was done resisting. My physical and metaphorical muscles had reached fatigue. The not-so-quiet-anymore voice inside clearly said to walk away. *Go.* Maybe even an ayahuasca retreat was in the future; the medicine had called to me for some time, and I believed it had the potential to facilitate a powerful connection to spirit and cleansing of the past, both of which I needed.

"J, I need to test the saying 'get lost to be found.' I want to experience the ideas in the books I've been reading and be living proof of their theories." Is the universe conspiring to support our highest potential? If other people deliberately manifest their lives and trust their intuition to direct them, could I? "My heart calls out for freedom. Freedom from expectation or definition, and I... I need to let it burn." I tossed the Kali card back down on the table—I had to find out. I had to see what I, without limitation or expectation, was capable of creating and experiencing in this beautiful world. All on my own. My new mantra: no expectation, no limitation.

After deliberate consideration, she said, "Okay, I love it. It sounds empowering. Take off alone and go. But what does that look like?"

"I need different. I need to unplug from everything I know. A full circuit reboot."

"That's the big picture again. What are the details? When you wake up tomorrow, what are you going to change?"

"Okay then. One thing I have to stop is trying to plan." I took a breath. "And I want to be alone, travel alone, make decisions just for me." Another breath. "Pack a bag, book one destination after another based on, I don't know... based on affordable airfare and sunshine in the forecast." I made all this up on the spot, but it felt so right.

"Nice weather is a decent North Star." She was trying to be supportive, but her posture was defensive. "Most people don't leave everything behind in adult life."

"But here's the thing: I don't want to do this for a week, or even several weeks. I need to go and not know where or when I'm coming back." I looked toward the world map for inspiration, but my eyes glazed across the continents and oceans as I whispered, "I have to leave everything." Then I noticed my passport resting on the corner of my small desk and grabbed it, slowly flipping through the pages of memories.

Jeannine rose to grab something from downstairs. "We don't get many chances in life to hit the reset button. This could be your shot," I heard from the kitchen.

"It is. It's the opportunity in all this mess. I want a family someday, and a career again. But right now, I just *don't care.*"

"Well, it sounds pretty bold," she declared, coming back with more wine. "And brave."

"Huh. There you have it, another sign. One of the tattoos I just got is *Fortis Fortuna Adiuvat*: Fortune Favors the Bold. The sign in your dining room that says, 'Why not India?' makes me want to book a ticket to India right now. And I don't even want to go to India." Tears welled up as I continued flipping through the pages of my passport, stamped with countries from so many seasonal adventures, romantic escapes, and volunteer trips... all documenting a great life.

Seeing me, Jeannine said, "There's nothing but love in those pages," as I wiped my face and straightened my shoulders.

"I know. That's what makes it hurt so much more. How could I be here?" I defaulted to internal insecurity.

"Because you're meant to be. That's it, and that's all there is to it—like you said before, you may not understand everything, but you know it's right." She handed me the box of tissues, always at the ready near my mattress on the floor. "India, huh? Why not? Maybe you should go. We both know they have the best sapphires," she said with a sly smile.

Taking a long drink, I let my fingers linger on the final pages of my passport, counting them one at a time: seven blank pages. "That's it. I'm going to travel until these pages are full." My hands were starting to shake. "Eventually, I need to surrender this passport when I change back to my maiden name. But until then, I'm going to fill it with freedom."

"Now I see the idea forming. And seven should be another sign—it's certainly a sacred number."

"Good point! And another one of my tattoos! The Pleiades constellation; the Seven Sisters." An energy healer had told me I was a Pleiadian the other day, and after some research, their message had resonated deeply within me. I also connected with the fact that the constellation was the original navigational beacon for travelers—a lighthouse in the cosmos. "And I like the random idea of using sunshine and affordable airfare as my compass." My mind was catching up now; after months of feeling lost, it was flowing with ideas.

"How far will the money you have get you?"

"Well, it depends on how I spend. If I'm frugal, maybe half a year? If I let my purse strings out, maybe a few weeks." We laughed. "It'll be a total gamble."

"What's the backup plan? The financial plan B if you're stuck halfway around the world and need an emergency evac?"

I told her about the impulsive, semi-kosher personal loan.

"Damn girl. Not one hundred percent legit, but I gotta hand it to you... savvy."

"It's time I start living by choice again instead of existing in default mode. I'm going to end this 'ex-Mrs.' chapter on my terms. To New York when I'm done."

Raising her glass, she said, "Well then. Cheers to your solo, impulsive, vow-of-silence-type odyssey." Jeannine had the right idea. Sort of.

After we clinked our glasses ceremonially, I added, "I mean... not silent, silent. I'd like to meet people and possibly cram a decade of dating into it."

"Wait... *what*? Oh, you little minx—*now* I get it." We howled.

"It's time to mix it all up and mix it all in. A little silence, a little dating. I want to be carefree and have some fun."

I wanted an adult Guest Pass.

"You're going to do this, aren't you? I can see it; your mind is made up."

"I think it's been made up since the day I was laid off." That's why my internal faculty, my intuition, my heart, and my higher self felt as if they'd been on mute the past few months. They'd told me what to do right away. But I hadn't listened—not until now.

"Oh, hells yeah, girl! This is extraordinary. This is so you. I'm a little jealous—well, no, not really, but you know what I mean." She was getting caught up in the moment as well. "Back to the idea of dating. How ready are you? Ready to jump on the horse and barrel race in a competition? Or ready to pet a pony at the fair?" Her analogies were priceless.

"As you know, I've been intimate with other people since the divorce, but it's been limited. I mean, it still feels weird, and I'm always worried they'll want or expect more than I can give. I'm not looking for serious."

"Let's get you cranking, then. You'll need an app," she said, grabbing my phone. "Tinder. You're not looking for serious... it's perfect. And you can update your location and meet people anywhere in the world."

"I feel like an awkward teen or something. I have no idea what to do, or wear, or say. Oh my... if only I had you for advice the whole time." I giggled away my anxiety.

"True—you do need a friend with you." She paused. "Let's name Tinder, and you can talk to it."

We named Tinder Tanya—after Donna's wild and unbridled best friend in *Mamma Mia*—and Jeannine declared, "You're set, then. Seven pages to stamp up and you'll go with Kali, Black Jaguar, and Tanya."

"I feel like Dorothy in *The Wizard of Oz* with my own version of Tin Man, Scarecrow, and Lion."

"Do you have sparkly red shoes?"

"I'll find some," I promised. Every ounce of me was vibrating, awake, and full of life. That's why I trusted it. I was *alive*. I was ready to let it burn; it was time to fly into the unknown.

THE MEDITERRANEAN.

Exactly one week after getting my tattoos and almost five months after the day I had moved out of my house, the cool water tickled my toes while I breathed in fresh, salty air. The tiny pebbles adjusted under my feet with each wave, and seagulls lazily floated on the breeze, surveying the shoreline for their next meal.

For my part, I was rooted in a distant land but feeling connected at the core. Everything I would carry with me on this journey was packed in a Thule bag one hundred feet away in my seaside hotel room. Steph had said to pack clothes that represented Fuck Yes and No Less, so I kept it pretty simple: a pair of black jeans, blue jeans, white t-shirt, white tank top, black t-shirt, black tank top, duster sweater, crop sweater, intimates, curling iron (with adapter), light jacket, baseball hat, sunhat, swimming suit, three sundresses, two scarves, three necklaces, my four rings, black sunglasses, sneakers, flat strappy sandals and one pair of sexy black stilettos. I wasn't sure where I was going or how long I'd be there, but I felt prepared to mix and match my way through.

I may have packed with basics, but this was no backpacking trip—I was too old for that. I wasn't swimming in financial abundance, but I was thinking of this journey as an educational investment and freely using my savings, and, in an emergency, the personal loan I took out the day I was laid off. After that... there was no backup. I'd have to find work, doing whatever, wherever I was.

Two days before, I had been in New York City for Heather's engagement party and I booked my first destination to fill the seven blank pages in my passport. Sunshine and Expedia's last-minute bargain airfare landed me in Nice, France. I hadn't debated about where I wanted to go or why; I'd just booked it. I still felt a bit like Dorothy, minus the beautiful red shoes.

If my connecting flight from Lisbon to Nice was any indicator of how this trip would go, all I could say was men, men, *men*. I almost hadn't boarded the flight because I had been only one of five people who wasn't a man wearing a pressed and tailored suit. *Hello, Lisbon style,* I'd thought, looking at the crowd and subsequently down at my all black, casual commuting attire. Even the gate agent checked my boarding pass twice.

It turned out the men had been traveling together on a business trip for a car company, heading to the Mediterranean coast for a few days to test drive and launch their new fleet. I sat next to a youthful, handsome man who asked me questions in a thick accent for the whole two-hour jaunt. We'd flirted lightly, sharing stories in broken English over the European flight service. He thought I was brave for traveling alone, crazy for hiking around elk in the mountains, and cool for knowing about his watch—a Patek Philippe. He'd invited me to their automobile launch party in Cannes a few days later, and I'd said I'd think about it. I liked having no plan and intended to keep it that way, but it felt lovely to be invited. And it felt lovely to have someone curious about me.

The tune had changed in the Nice airport's car rental terminal. As I was traveling without an agenda or destination list, I thought having a car would allow the most flexibility. But the counter agent had nearly refused to give me the vehicle keys, as the mere thought that I could drive a manual seemed utterly preposterous. I grew up on a farm, thank you very much, and my dad made me do two things before I was allowed to get my license: change a tire and drive a manual. But the agent, clocking me as female and American, had assumed this was impossible. That made me mad: mad at society for having such judgments and unhelpful standards. Mad at my ex for not being here with me—he had always been the one to drive in foreign countries and on unknown roads. And mad at myself for being alone. I wouldn't have been dealing with that discrimination or delay if he had been there to accept the keys. True, I had been a little scared to drive, but I knew I was at least going to try. Approaching the car, I'd even gone to the passenger side door first—talk about habit. It just made my blood boil hotter.

Bone-tired and worried about the accuracy of the paper directions to my hotel, I had to keep going. So I drove through the afternoon rain, squinting to see the French road signs and pleading with other cars to stay out of my way in the roundabouts. But I'd made it. Harried and depleted, I'd arrived late and crumbled into my tiny bed in a tiny room with a big view. I'd opened the window to see an endless horizon over the Mediterranean waves—endless possibilities. With that mindset, the autumn breeze had drifted me to sleep.

The next morning, I'd started fresh. I'd fluffed my bedsheets and unfluffed the residual irritability of the day before. From my long-standing yoga practice, I knew that the tremendous power latent within an individual—lying coiled at the base chakra—is represented by the serpent. This was my time to wake the serpent inside—my kundalini—to embrace my personal power, face the dragon, and seize life, just as Kali would. I couldn't let a judgmental rental car agent keep me down.

Newfound conviction and the allure of coffee had rallied me out of my room, down the winding stairs adorned with historic black and white pictures of seashells, through the lobby with its double glass doors, and directly towards a café across the street, which boasted tables on the beach. Now, with my toes swirling in the sand, I slowly introduced myself to my new reality, the rhythm of the waves welcoming me to the dance with every crash. With a perfectly frothed cappuccino in hand, I felt present. Here. I had arrived, and it was day one on page one.

Today, I had no plan but to explore the coast, and I was brimming with optimism. I could do *anything* I wanted. Go anywhere, say hello to anyone I want. The south of France is dotted with historic beachside towns full of fresh seafood, local wine and cheese markets, bright umbrellas, and historic castles. To me, Nice was a bougie, sophisticated destination for European professionals taking a weekend holiday. That wasn't my trip's intentional vibe, but there I was, free to get lost.

It was liberating to be somewhere I wouldn't have chosen, almost as if it had chosen me. And for the first time, there was no partner to consult or joint budget to negotiate. No existential worry about whether I'd made the *right* choice, or if *they* would be happy—I was here solely for myself, guided only by choices that felt inherently right.

To invest further in my independence, I stayed off social media and didn't plan to communicate with anyone, not my friends or my family. I was going completely dark. Heather had protested, Jeannine had argued, and my mom had denied. But to go all in on this personal evolution and start from scratch, I had to fully detach. I had only caved on one detail: I would turn on my "Find My Friends" and sync with my dad. That way, even though I didn't know where I was going, he could see where I was—in case of emergency and all that. He'd been asking for this since I moved to Jeannine's in April, thinking that, since I was single, someone had to be looking out for me. *I'm thirty years old,* I kept saying. *I'm safe on my own.* But deep down, it felt nice that he wanted to protect me and stepped back into his former role without question.

The only person who was along for the ride was Tinder Tanya: she was my new gal pal, partner in crime, and voice of reason as I navigated this new world of dating. I wanted to meet strangers, go on crazy dates, and cross every comfort zone I had—a sexual education of sorts. I wasn't going to waste this time of exploration; I was going to seize it.

My only goal of the day was to stay near the water's vibrations, my medicine for recalibrating to a new flow. I'd heard of Nice's famous Colline du Château, a lovely spot with various hiking trails, statues, and historic ruins dotting its walkways, mosaic water fountains, and breathtaking views of both the city and the sea. It was only one and a half kilometers east of me. So, after savoring my first European cappuccino one sip at a time, I'd meander in that direction.

I was exhilarated and filling up with gratitude again. Dare I say I was childishly enthusiastic about the surprises to come? Although it was all uncharted territory, no chaperone was needed.

THE FIRST FEW days were a mix of warm welcome and challenge, but overall maintained a predictable pace. I was exercising my intuition left and right. It was odd that the randomness of it all made me feel more connected. I felt more in touch with the baker I passed on the street setting up his stall of fresh croissants, more compatible with the flowers that bloomed brightly whether someone was looking at them or not, and more aligned to the energy of the world as the passersby continued their individual rhythms and I mine. Separate but connected. I wasn't trying to direct or control anything, just engaging the flow.

Table for one, *oui*. Everything for one. I thought of not being alone as I sat down for lunch and wondered if anyone had matched with me after my late-night swiping. Ding, ding, ding. "Oh, hey, lady," I said to Tanya. "You have messages for me, I see."

This was a surprise. Three new matches. I had been in France for three days and stayed mostly off my phone. Being off social media certainly helped me embrace the day instead of fixating on how to document or share it. I was still clumsy on dating apps, but Tanya was proving to be an entertaining ally as I swiped through pictures and attempted conversations in the virtual world. *How do I say hello? Do I start with a joke? Or ask them how they are? Or simply ask to meet up? What would Jeannine do? Okay, I'll say hello and ask something about one of the pictures they shared. Like this guy, he's on a boat—maybe I'll ask about that.*

Wow, I could really get in my head about things. Too much internal debate and empathetic tendencies made me overthink a lot of the time; how could I learn to be more indifferent, less attached to external opinion, or just more confident that *anything* I chose to text would be okay? *I guess practice makes perfect, and you gotta start somewhere.*

"Hi! I just landed in France and will be in Nice for a few days."
Sent. Times three.

They could read that as desperate and forward, or maybe they'd find me demanding, like I had arrived and expected them to drop everything and take me out. Or they'd think, *Oh geez, another tourist, no thanks.* Oh well. My goal wasn't that complicated—I wasn't looking for much. I just wanted some fun, someone to surprise me. *Exhale,* my body remembered. *It's out there now, we'll just see if anyone replies.*

It was time to order lunch, so I put down the phone. Last time I was single, there were no apps, Facebook hadn't been invented yet, and I was still asking my parents for permission to be out late. This was a whole new world.

When the waiter came around, I ordered the catch of the day tossed in a light butter sauce with sparkling water and a lime wedge. Being on my own brought out my insecurities; I felt vulnerable sitting there by myself and could do with fewer speculative gazes. But the other diners probably didn't give two thoughts about it—it was all in my head. Having no one to talk to meant I had no distractions. When the mind is quiet, you're challenged to deal with things you've been hiding in the shadows. Fear crept in with thoughts like, *You're running away, this is irresponsible,* or *New York won't be waiting for you.*

I tried to reframe my attitude by focusing on what was right in front of me. I looked around the restaurant and noticed the beautiful chandeliers providing a romantic glow and the frosted windows. Estate-looking flatware and crystal glasses adorned the tables with a single rose at each. In spiritual alchemy, the single rose represents the mystic center of a person, our heart of hearts. It's a symbol of complete surrender and permanent transmutation.

Alright, I can calm my anxiety, I thought, remembering to be present. *All we have is right now.* It was liberating to live moment to moment, even if a bit alienating.

I needed to use the restroom. Looking around the quaint dining room, I noticed the familiar sign in a nearby corner. Was I comfortable leaving my purse marooned at the table, or should I bring all my belongings with me to be safe? Maybe the server would think I was done eating and clear the table too early, or worse, fear I'd dined and dashed. I guessed I'd just finish up and relieve myself on the way out. Basic things like this sent a twinge of sorrow through my heart: if I'd had a companion, it wouldn't be a worry.

After lunch, I walked out of the bistro and into the street. The fresh air hit me like a welcome wake-up call, and I deliberately added a spring to my step. That afternoon, I was heading towards Old Town: an intricate lattice of small streets, churches, and schools with laundry hanging out of windows, scooters tucked into doorways, and plants holding their spot in the sun.

A bright green awning caught my attention to the right, so I decided to go that way. I was learning that meandering through streets and getting lost in a city—when and where it was safe—was a great way to hone intuition while simultaneously choosing destiny. The truest gifts emerge from the delicate dance between action and surrender, revealing wisdom that cannot be forced, only received: they are the gifts from life you could have never known to ask for.

I WOKE UP easily in those first days. Early nights and avoiding alcohol—two things I learned are helpful to establish safety for a solo female traveler—had me sleeping better than ever. Rolling over in bed, still nestled under the covers in my tiny seaside room, I said, "I have a date," out loud to Fern, my phone's GPS, and Tanya.

I'd had a few interesting conversations going with potential matches, but after being honest with myself, I had honed in on who and *what* I wanted. Someone direct, no bullshit. Someone more experienced than me, and whom I found darkly sexy. Someone who would push my boundaries and take me on an erotic adventure. I wanted to experience the opposite of being in control and leading the way—I wanted to taste what it was like to submit.

The Guide had been up front about his intentions, and reading his messages made my tummy flip and nipples tingle. *Yes.* I'd raised my hand physically and figuratively when I read his date ideas, such as blindfolds or fantasy sharing, after we'd matched a few days ago. Tonight wasn't the start of forever; it wasn't for romance. Tonight was for tonight. We were going to meet at the location of my choosing, and at ten this evening, he'd bring a single rose and join me. I was to greet him wearing nothing but a robe or lingerie, and he would direct everything and anything from there. *Yeow.*

Be careful what you wish for, girl, I thought to myself as I rolled over, darting back under my covers as if they were Braveheart's shield. *Is this normal for app dates?* I wondered. *I've never put myself out there like this before. Vulnerable and exposed.* Something in my psyche was gravitating towards him, but would I be brave enough to go through with this? What if he laughed when he opened the door and saw me standing there, inexperienced and awkward... or what if he was a hateful, harmful asshole that manipulated women to fit his dominating desires? The fearful talk track was legit, but my innate intrigue was winning this war.

After I let my mind freak out on a few horrible tangents, I quieted my breathing and felt for an answer instead of thinking of one. My vibration was calm. I was relaxed. The nerves I was feeling were excitement. And when I tuned out the noise of the world and truly looked within, my soul simply smiled back. In a moment, I felt all of those tangents blow away like letting go of a balloon's string. I wanted this adventure; I'd matched with him and committed to him for a reason. I'd chosen this experience for tonight, and I would own it.

Confident again and coming out from under the covers for the final time, I smiled, tremendously turned on by the idea of what was to come. But there was much to do before meeting him. He was flying in from Paris, and I was transferring from my seaside hotel to a boutique castle in Cagnes-sur-Mer.

My plan was: yoga, pack up, check out, coffee, drive to Cannes to shop for something fresh to wear, explore Cagnes-sur-Mer, settle into my new room, have dinner so as not to faint later on, shower, and be ready by ten. Whew. It was more of an agenda in one day than I'd had on the whole trip. But I was ready.

But I wasn't ready. Even though I didn't need to pick out an outfit for the evening, I wanted to feel fancy and put together. My make-up game needed an upgrade. I've never been a girly girl. Growing up on a farm with an older brother, I was more of a tomboy. Since becoming an adult, I'd started wearing mascara, fallen in love with stilettos, and could pull off a dress, yes, but I'd never really been taught about makeup or clothes. *I'm in France*, I mused. *This is where modern femininity was basically invented. The French are undeniable fashion and style innovators.*

The ultimate no effort, no makeup, rolled-out-of-bed-like-this elegance seemed hereditary here. Sexy without saying so. Today, I decided as I approached the Cannes Sephora, I would ask for help. Today, I would embrace my softer side and learn how to appropriately color these cheeks and highlight these hips.

A very friendly woman in her late forties with bold black glasses took me under her wing and all around the store. It was an educational experience indeed: I had no idea the palettes that existed for eye shadows if you were looking for a smokey eye, or any of the various textures of lipsticks. I felt like we were in a scene in a movie as we added potions and paint to my basket for tonight's show. I was beaming, as if one of my newfound treasures, Diorskin Forever—an incredible pressed powder—would camouflage my impending nakedness. Besides that, I had *fun!*

Stepping back out onto the glitzy, shop-lined street, I smiled. Next on the prop list was an outfit. Did clothes even matter? I could just wear the robe in the hotel room. But what if there wasn't a robe? Or what if I needed an extra layer of separation between me and The Guide besides *just* the robe? Yes, I wanted a little more security and a little more mystery, so I headed to an intimates store recommended by my Sephora fairy.

"Bonjour," I attempted in an unpracticed accent.

"Hello," replied a polite voice from behind a clothing rack. "How may I help you today?" She, of course, spoke perfect English.

"I need an, um, elegant but sexy black matching set."

"Lovely. We have many options for you—props and toys as well." Oh? Really? I hadn't thought of that. "You are a 34C, small, oui?" I nodded as she correctly sized me up and disappeared into the back, leaving me to browse the intricate lace and satin pieces displayed out front. Stunning. They were like works of art: far more sophisticated than my Victoria's Secret go-tos. And expensive. I gulped a bit as I bit my lip, noticing a price tag for just a bralette (panties not included). Maybe a negligée would do, instead of a set?

"Please, relax. Here is a glass of champagne, and I've pre-selected an arrangement of styles for you to try on when you're ready in the dressing room." Now I felt like I was a customer back at Framebridge, being brought free libations to loosen the mood.

"Merci," I said, looking her in the eyes as she handed me the bubbling glass of joy. She had exquisite hazel eyes with flecks of gold, perfectly lined with charcoal accents and soft lashes. If I were the lingerie designer, her eyes would be the inspiration for a limited-edition garment. I perused for a moment and took a few sips before diving into the mystery pieces awaiting me in my dressing room.

Four outfits hung along the mirror. A gorgeous black and na-vy-blue corset paired with cheeky panties that would perfectly push up my breasts and tease out my bum. A complete black lace, hour-glass-shaped one-piece that had delicate flowers strategically placed to hide only the most intimate bits. A set made from strappy satin, which would make me feel like a present wrapped up and ready to be devoured, and finally, a barely-there, dark blue, low-rise thong and flirty bra.

How had she understood me so well, calculated me with a single glance?

Hungry for them all, I finished my champagne and tried them on. Each piece fueled my desire for the night or enhanced the idea of the version of me who would show up that evening. I was desperate to meet this sultry side of Whitney. I was ready to embrace her, and was starting to get a sense of what Coco Chanel meant when she said, "Beauty begins the moment you decide to be yourself." To-night was for me, even if that included a few cosmetics.

Later, I unpacked my bag and settled into my suite, trembling with anticipation, the hourglass of black lace gracing the bed, ready for action. The dark blue set I had been unable to resist was still wrapped in tissue paper. After reminding myself it was okay to loosen up my purse strings, I'd bought both. Although spending money on myself still felt taboo—like someone was going to slap my hand when I signed the receipt—I was proud of myself for do-ing it anyway.

The whole situation was liberating. It was so freeing not to wor-ry about *how* to show up. Or wonder whether he would kiss me at the end or worry about whether sex would be expected. I didn't even have to stress about saying the right things or asking the right ques-tions to sound interesting and charming. Nope. I knew where tonight was going and what it was about, no games.

I hung a few days' worth of clothes in the antique wooden ar-moire, and laid out my shoes underneath them. I placed my toiletries in the delicate and stunningly remodeled bathroom, complete with a pedestal sink, marble floor, open glass shower, and claw-foot tub, then noticed my reflection in the mirror. *Hi.* I quietly smiled to myself. *It's nice getting to know you.* And then I giggled. *You crazy bitch—I like you.*

Drawing a warm bath and sinking into the tub, I let my finger-tips trace the curve of my jawline as I relaxed into the moment. What I craved was to feel alive; to feel my body wake up. I longed to be touched with reckless abandon, free from judgment, expectation, or responsibility. *Soon,* I thought, as my fingers drifted to my col-larbone, lingering above the steady beat of my heart. Tonight would be my Zep Tepi, my first time in a place of simultaneous awaken-ing and forgetfulness. It was time to shed the constraints the mind imposed on the body and, for the first time, be free to transform the energy of unfiltered desire into hedonistic action.

AS I PEERED through the drapes towards the street beneath my balcony, I saw him quickly walking, his single rose silhouetted on the courtyard stone wall. He'd shown up. My breath caught in my throat and my palms warmed. I was so nervous. In about sixty seconds, I'd hear his footsteps coming up the staircase, and he would knock on my door. My eyes shot down to the new lingerie I was wearing, immediately insecure: *Who shows up to a first date wearing nothing but lingerie and a robe?* My mind panicked, questioning my sanity.

Knock, knock, knock.

Fuck. My heart raced. I opened the door, and there he was: he looked exactly like his profile picture. Better. He was a bit sweaty from the walk, and I could smell a touch of cologne floating off his body. His eyes were dark and curious as they took me in, his lips parting just slightly as his gaze dropped.

"Hi," I said, more with my eyes than with my voice. I stepped to the left, opening the solid wood door for him to enter.

"Salut," he softly replied with more confidence than my legs had in standing. He entered, unfazed by the romantic surroundings of the suite—the medieval chandelier, the velvet and gold fainting couch, and the sheer canopy roped off to either side of the decadent king bed. After he'd placed the rose down on the nightstand and draped his jacket over the chair next to it, I wondered if I should ask him how his day was or if he'd found the castle easily—the polite chatter one would expect from a proper girl. But I just watched him in silence, gripping the belt on my bathrobe like we were going through turbulence at the beginning of a long flight.

Removing silver links from the cuffs on his shirt, he walked back to me, standing still near the doorway, and stopped a few feet in front of me. He slowly reached out and laid his hands on the belt I was desperately clinging to. As he cocked his head to one side as if to ask permission, I moved my hands slightly out of the way so he could continue.

I couldn't believe we were still in silence, but I liked it. It was an electric flirtation, a staring contest of mounting sexual tension. Even if my inner child was squealing, ready to hide behind the curtain, I wanted this challenge. I stayed present and felt like I was staring down a lion.

His energy was dominant, but kind. He was already pushing me, and I could tell he wanted to push me quite a bit further, but he showed restraint. He was relishing in delayed satisfaction as he slowly undid my belt and let the sides of the robe open. He stayed in the staring match, not even glancing down as he let his fingers do the investigating. They started at my belly, right where the belt had been, and then wrapped around my waist and up my back to the clasp of my bra. Just touching, not undoing it, feeling the lace as he traced it to the front of my breasts and rested in between them before going in a straight line to my belly button and then the top of the connected panties. The tickle was almost killing me; my body longed for him to kiss me or pull me towards him. But he was experiencing me one layer at a time, and I had put on this lingerie to facilitate that very thing. Remembering that, I let out a breath I didn't realize I had been holding in. At this release, he stepped back, breaking off his physical touch and increasing my need for it. My legs wobbled and he finally looked me over from head to toe.

My long blond hair was loosely twisted at the nape of my neck. My makeup was light but impactful, highlighting widely bright eyes, and the only color adorning my body was the cherry red of my freshly painted toes. His chest rose and fell deeper, slower, and I realized he was taking this absurd amount of time as an intimate, proper introduction. He was inviting me to truly sink into the situation and appreciate the moment. *Don't mask it with frivolous commentary or rush it with hastened desire to get out of the beautiful awkwardness we're creating*, he seemed to be saying.

Well played. I liked it.

Then, like a switch had been flipped, he stood a bit taller, his smile curled up, and his eyes bore right through mine as he said, "On your knees."

What? I immediately thought. *How rude—that's not the way to treat a lady.* Then I remembered this wasn't the time for Midwest Whitney. This was the time for international, sexy Whitney. *Oh my god.* Did I want to do this?

"*If* this is what you want," he said, his words falling from his lips like silk, "you don't want to make me ask again." In that moment, I remembered I had signed up for this, I wanted it, and I chose to trust him. He'd given me an out, and I knew I would have one at any time should I need it. With that, I completely submitted to the situation and let my hair down, as well as the rest of my body.

THERE IS A meme floating around the internet that reads, "In my defense, the moon was full, and I was left unsupervised." It had been following me for months, and I'd finally lived it. The Guide and I sat on my balcony, sipping champagne, gazing up at a very full and naked moon. After we had tasted every bit of the physical, we chose to explore the mental. The conversation was open and honest, and he was charming with a blunt laugh and a French accent.

"So, tell me about yourself," he said.

"I lived in Vail for the past decade and plan to move to Manhattan after this trip. My life used to revolve around adrenaline sports, my ex-husband and work, but now I'm shifting my focus to things like tonight and getting lost around places like France."

"Sounds like a good change." He was clearly happy it had led me to tonight.

"What about you?"

"I'm in procurement for a major enterprise and a soccer coach."

"I could see you as a coach. Leading and teaching," I said with a twinkle in my eye that matched the stars in the night sky. "I used to coach, too—volleyball and ski racing. It was fun to break down something I knew so intimately and experience it through beginners' eyes."

"I just like to be in control and win. The attitude bodes well for work and play."

"You certainly don't seem to have a problem doing what's right for you."

"And why would I? Who else am I here to make happy?" he said as he rested his bare feet on the metal balcony siding.

"True, but you have society to appease, and I'm sure people you want to keep happy."

"Pffff, life is too short to focus on that. If you make yourself happy, they'll be happy."

Raising my eyebrows and pursing my lips, I decided this wasn't a moment for debate. I relaxed into my chair and went a little limp, exhausted from the past few hours. He gently touched my thigh with one finger and swayed his way north like a snake slithering in sand. "Relaxation yields sensitivity," he purred. "When you calm the body, you allow space to feel the delicate nerves in places you didn't even know existed. And sensitivity is necessary for even the best lovers to truly experience orgasm."

"I have no problem orgasming, as you well know," I said, closing my eyes to relax further.

"But there is such a variety of climax. I wonder if it's possible to have had them all."

"Are you suggesting we go back into the bedroom?"

"I certainly am, but this time with a wager."

I looked at him, and he continued, "I'll give you a new orgasm, one unlike the others."

Now I was intrigued. "And if you do, what do I need to give you in return?" I asked.

"Two nights from now, be my date." *Aww, that's so sweet,* I thought. He wanted to see me again. "There's a private sex club in Cannes, secret invite only, and I'd love to be your guide. Everyone must arrive in couples, and seeing you naively experience this world will be the ultimate prize."

I coughed, and let out a half laugh. "Excuse me?" This was not the type of date I was expecting.

No, no, no, no. Wait, what? Sex club? I'd heard about those parties but never thought of attending one. No, that was too much, too far—I wasn't comfortable. But if it scared me, should I do it? I didn't want to get bullied into action here, but I needed to investigate my immediate reaction. It was a unique opportunity sure, but could I trust him? I would have to if I said yes.

"Too much thinking," he interrupted. "Feel it. If you don't want to go, don't. But knowing what I do of you now, I can promise you, you won't be disappointed."

I paused, put my glass down on the small side table, and stood to go inside. Glancing down at him, I said, "You have to win the bet first," and strolled in with him only a few paces behind. Fuck comfort zones. I was here to cross them.

TWO EVENINGS LATER, I waited for The Guide to pick me up. He'd won the bet: the orgasm had been restrained like a long and teasing rollercoaster ride, before bursting like a firework. And the best part? It had all been just for me. He didn't even attempt a climax. My pleasure was his, and that's where he left our interaction for the evening—lingering.

It was fortuitous that I didn't have a set travel agenda to follow, or I wouldn't have been able to make spontaneous choices like attending the party. What was it about sex that intrigued me so much, anyway? Honestly, I wasn't entirely certain yet, but I felt a consistent pull toward embracing my inner vixen, adorning myself in whatever guise I desired, and reclaiming intimacy on my terms.

Yet as I stood alone on a dark, cool, cobbled street corner, doubt crept in. Our first date had been exhilarating—undeniably so—but stepping into a car with him, leaving behind all the familiar markers of safety, felt like crossing an invisible threshold. Perhaps I should text him and call it off. I didn't want to inconvenience him or hurt his feelings, but I also knew I couldn't proceed out of obligation. I didn't dare reach out to Jeannine or Steph for advice. This situation was far too bizarre to interrupt my commitment to silence. And Tanya, bless her, was helpful in introductions but offered no guidance beyond that point.

I want to go. A quiet voice was saying, *yes, please.* I was deeply curious, drawn to the forbidden worlds I had only glimpsed in films like *Eyes Wide Shut*, curious about relationships that operated outside what was considered normal from where I came from. I wanted to try it for myself, far from mountain trails and farmland roots. This was my chance.

I had no idea what to expect. I would have to trust my body completely, listen for the subtle cues of arousal or unease, and honor whatever boundaries might emerge from within.

And, well, my shoes deserved a night out. I'd gone shopping again and found my Dorothy slippers—a glowing gradient pair of limited-edition red stilettos that called to me from a small window and found their home on my feet. They were like the red balloon in a Banksy painting to the rest of my outfit: a sleek little black dress covering a plain black thong with only a thick gold chain draped down my bare back. I would normally say the shoes were out of my budget, but I wasn't here to be responsible. They were meant for me and for tonight. If I had been communicating with Jeannine, I'd have sent her a captionless picture, and she would have understood.

Pulling up in a new, silver Audi, The Guide got out to open my door, looking so exquisitely dapper in a sleek suit and polished shoes that my jaw nearly dropped. Slowly taking in the sight of me again, he looked me over from head to toe. His patience was such a tease. Finally, as he swept my hair aside and kissed my cheeks hello, he said, "I love your shoes, but you won't be wearing them for long." Blushing again, I got into the car and away we went.

GUIDE ME, HE did. We started on the dance floor, keeping mostly to ourselves amongst a variety of nearly bare bodies, adorned with fashion made from shadows and classy, jeweled ensembles. The women were like artwork: every one of them seemed to be made from glass but filled with confidence. I wondered if I looked like that from across the room, still clothed but inviting you in with every movement. The men felt more mysterious to me, more reserved as they kept their eyes low, their hands hidden.

I pulled away to head to the bar, and The Guide, not two steps behind, said, "Only one glass."

I raised my eyebrows.

"Liquid courage is exactly what I need."

"I will not have your choices swayed or your sensations numbed." He wanted everything to be deliberate, awake, and intense. I wasn't used to being told what to do, but conceded silently, thinking, *one point for the Frenchman.*

"Let's go on a tour," he whispered as I received my flute, then gently ushered me towards the back stairs, which were wide and smooth with velvet and gold railings, winding up. The walls were adorned with candle sconces, flickering stars of light, and small, compact-size mirrors hanging below them. Upstairs opened to a luxurious lounge area with plush sofas and draped walls. There was another bar decorated in crystals and stones of white, blue, and titanium, with no alcohol to be found. The Guide mentioned there was a hidden room to the right, designed with a closet front. As we entered, it was completely black, with tiny twinkling lights coming down from the ceiling like the night sky. I couldn't see a thing, not even my hand in front of my face. I could tell the room was round as we followed a curved seating area along the perimeter. And then we sat down, in silence... waiting. Waiting for what, I wondered? Did we intend to stay?

Then I felt a woman's hands go slowly across my knees and onto his, feeling us both up to the hips and back down. She said something in French to him, low and smooth. He replied, and then I heard his zipper being undone, and she started to pleasure him. He put his hand on my thigh to make sure I was okay, and I thought, *absolutely, go for it,* as I leaned back into the sofa. I could not care less if she pleasured him—but it didn't cross my mind that other people in the room might come over to us as well. Pretty soon, there were two more people at my side, a man and a woman I identified by their scents and the size of their hands. They seemed to be entertained by each other. *Okay,* I thought. *That's okay, I don't feel the desire to be included.*

But then their hands started to explore my body, and I began to feel claustrophobic—this was happening very fast, and I didn't even know what *this* was. I didn't feel comfortable. I didn't know who they were, or what they wanted, and I wasn't... *I was not just down for anything.* Thinking of The Guide in the middle of his pleasure, I hesitated; should I just leave? Or try to settle in, but politely brush their hands aside? Should I use our safety word? The Guide told me everyone here was very respectful; it was consensual play or no play. The hands on my body seemed to be getting more adventurous, and all I wanted to do was cross my arms and legs and curl up. I needed to leave—I grabbed his wrist fully like a handcuff, and immediately, with zero hesitation, he stood and we walked out the door while he zipped up his pants. Once in the light, he looked me straight in the eyes.

"Are you okay?" His sincerity and protection were clear.

"Yes, I'm sorry," I mumbled. "I mean, I wasn't comfortable, but I'm okay. Nothing horrible happened."

"Nothing horrible will happen. Not being comfortable is reason enough to leave. This is not fun for me if you feel forced or unsafe." My pulse slowed, and my trust in him grew.

"Thank you." The trust in myself grew, too: I shouldn't be afraid to speak my mind or ask for what I need. "Let's take a walk and see what else we find," I said, ready to abandon this situation for good and continue the discovery tour. He kissed me gently, grabbed my hand, and away we went.

We walked past rooms with swings, ropes, and stirrups, hallways with peeping windows in between erotic artwork and low lighting. There was a large room with a circular bed in the middle and an enormous crystal chandelier above it, surrounded by mirrors; gold and sparkling pillows were strewn everywhere, as if the cushions were waves in a sea. Bodies at rest and bodies in motion dotted the scene like an old Hollywood movie; everywhere I looked, I saw a world of raw desires within an air of elegance, fantasy, and respect.

"Do you want to join the room?" he purred.

"No. I don't think this public vibe is for me," I replied as I glanced towards the other couples looking in on the room alongside us.

"Maybe something more intimate then," he said, and we continued.

"Maybe a quick restroom visit, and a glass of water?" I asked.

"Lovely idea."

In the bathroom, I felt my nerves level out and start to match the rhythm of the atmosphere. *This is amazing*, I said to myself in the mirror. *I feel safe, this is all consensual adult play, and sexual adventure is at my feet. Deep breath… what do I want? I don't even know how to answer that, not even to myself.* Another deeper breath. *I'll know it when I see it, if I see it.* And with quiet composure, I smoothed down my dress, fixed my makeup and left to rejoin my Guide.

He spoke in smooth French, greeting others and exploring options, I assumed, and we wandered a bit more. I was eternally grateful I didn't understand. Glancing over my shoulder, a woman caught my eye from another room. A cozy room. She was lying on a white bed with her date, relaxed, and smiling in nothing but a forest green thong and pearl earrings. The Guide noticed my attention and immediately directed us her way.

She spoke in French, of course, and all I could do was notice her lustrous, long, chocolate hair and soft hazel eyes as The Guide responded. She crawled over the bed to me and onto her knees. Her full breasts and sharp hips perfectly framed a slender waist. Face to face, The Guide came up behind me, rested his hands on my pelvis, and whispered in my ear, "Kiss her." I wanted to follow that command. She seemed like an angel as I melted into her embrace; her date joined behind her as well.

"Turn your dress around," The Guide commanded. The dress' opening would reach the top of my panties, and its gold chains would be my only coverage in front. Every part of my body was aroused, and I did as I was told. The woman and I moved closer, nipples to nipples. Her hands slid into my dress and gripped my hips, her kisses trailed down my neck towards my shoulders, and she pulled on my chains, leading the rest of me down to the bed. It was exotic, liberating, and sensual. My heart swelled from feeling desired, and her soft embrace made me feel peaceful. The rest of the club slipped away as the four of us melted into our own world.

After leaving the private party, he invited me to see another side of Cannes nightlife, escorting me to the chic VIP sections of the Bâoli and Bookers night clubs. Even there, I sipped sparkling water as I didn't want to numb the electricity pulsing through every cell of my body, still on fire from our sexual adventures. My limbs bounced with anticipation and pleasure. It made me feel alive in a way no adrenaline sport ever had.

"Isn't it delicious?" He whispered in my ear as we silently cuddled on a bright pink couch under gold-dipped candles and swirling LED lights.

"You're going to have to narrow it down," I replied.

"Knowing. Knowing how in control you are. Knowing you're not afraid to go after what you want. Knowing that when you look around this club, no one here could imagine the experiences we just had. It's a temptress's secret that's in you now."

What he was saying was true: I liked feeling a little bit wild and slightly naughty. I liked all my senses firing in overdrive with pleasure and freedom. I liked embodying the sexy shadow in the corner rather than the light on display out front, and claiming what I wanted just because I wanted it. It was about time I woke up the rebel inside and fed my innate challenger archetype—the Enneagram type eight, which often questions the status quo and isn't afraid to take risks. I felt I was embarking on the black phase of transmutation—a death of my old self in preparation for a new beginning—and was on a treasure hunt through the chaos of my subconscious desires.

"Yes," I said, exhaling. "I like our tasty secrets."

After taking ample time to savor my realization, I looked up into his dark, mysterious eyes and sent him back all the energy that was coursing through me. Feeling like Kali herself, I licked my lips and kissed him purposefully. An internal flame was expanding: this vixen was playing with matches, and sparks were flying.

THE FOLLOWING MORNING, my phone erupted with notifications. *Ding, ding... ding, ding, ding.* "Quiet, Tanya," I murmured, my voice muffled by the pillow as I fumbled for the device. It was 6 a.m., a mere two hours after I had finally surrendered to sleep following one of the craziest nights of my life.

But it wasn't Tanya, it was Jeannine. She was in Switzerland, racing in the Swiss Epic, a grueling multi-stage mountain bike race that traversed the rugged expanse of the Alps. And in a single decision, a year of meticulous planning, rigorous cross-training, and unwavering dedication had ended in an unexpected way: she and her teammate were not going to finish the race.

Without knowing the details, I understood the enormity of that choice and empathized with how difficult it must have been to make. Her ask was straightforward: "Where are you, and can you get here?"

She had been my rock and foundation since April—much longer than that, actually—and nothing in the world would stop me from getting to her.

Mapping out the route from Cannes to Verbier, tracing the winding roads of the French countryside, I calculated that it would take roughly eight hours to traverse the distance. I allowed myself the luxury of an additional hour of rest before rousing and preparing for the road trip. By 8, I would be on the road and to Jeannine by late afternoon or early evening, factoring in necessary stops along the way.

Armed with printed directions once again, I hoped for the best and got on my way. Predictably, I got lost: I second-guessed lanes and directional signs and ended up backwards. I was so afraid of making the wrong turn that I worried myself out of the right one. I stopped at the next gas station and looked up my route again; because of a spotty connection, I realized the directions in Google

Maps stayed *active* once loaded, even if you disconnected from Wi-Fi. I hadn't paid for international roaming, so this was huge. I could preload my route, and if I kept the window open on my phone, follow it to my destination. No paper needed.

"Fern, you goddess," I said, thanking my GPS and tossing the paper directions into the back. "I trust you to lead the way."

I needed a soundtrack for this daytime adventure and remembered the French rap from The Guide's playlist on our drive home the night before. I flipped through local radio stations and finally found the perfect mix. I was captivated by the rhythmic flow, sultry voices, and sexy language that radiated from the radio—it made me want to melt into whatever, or whomever, was holding me. Although I didn't understand what was being said, *how* it was said captivated me. It may as well have been the language of the birds, something not meant for me to understand, and I relished in the freedom of it.

I drove hour after hour, singing and talking to myself, stopping at gas stations and thinking of nothing serious. My brain simply couldn't compute the emotions or events of the past week while running on such little sleep and lack of clarity. One thing made kilometer after kilometer of tired delirium unquestionably worth it: friendship.

Finally, I reached Le Châble, Switzerland, and started the long and winding road to Verbier, where Jeannine was waiting at the hotel. I was going a little cross-eyed and my bum felt numb from sitting all day, but the road switch backed up to the village and I couldn't help but be mesmerized by the beauty of the mountains. The sun was setting, and puffy horizontal clouds were turning shades of pink above the peaks, dotted with early autumn snow. It was an entirely different season from the sunshine of the Mediterranean. Driving from sea level to 5,000 feet elevation made me think of life in Colorado with its elevational diversity. Looking at the Alps, I could see efficient routes up and adventurous lines down. After so many years of backcountry hiking and skiing, my reflex to "see the line" had become automatic, almost like a video game.

Jeannine. I nearly collapsed from exhaustion and excitement when I hugged her. She seemed to fall into me with the same intensity. Although our reasons for being tired were quite different, we understood it was time for a good, long chat while we waited for my room to be ready. Cuddled up in the lavish hotel lobby bar with cold tequila, we started catching up.

My heart swelled with pride as she told me her story. I was in awe of her tenacity and physical courage leading up to this race, and even more in awe of her character and the awareness it had taken to quit. She and her partner completed three days of the scheduled five; they prepared together and rode together, but after mechanical problems, sickness, extreme fatigue, and weather, they made the impossible decision to stop. The team was rock solid, but the conditions were impossible.

When it was my turn, she was speechless as I told her all about my introduction to Tinder dates and The Guide.

"Of course, you would have stories like this. No, not normal beer dates or coffees. Whitney goes to posh sex clubs." We both laughed at the oddity of it.

"I feel so empowered," I said. The feeling was in stark contrast to the past year of restrained tension. "I mean, I was scared and nervous, but walking around the velvet rooms with dark corners, all my senses heightened, and I was so present, it was amazing. Everything else just faded away."

"It's certainly an exercise in risk tolerance."

"Look who's talking, Ms. Bruised and Bandaged, head-to-toe competitive mountain biker."

"Different type of risky business girl," she nodded for emphasis. "Are you going to go to another club?"

"No." We both laughed at the sureness of it.

"At least one of us is getting some. I fear that between my rollercoaster of a breakup and sore body, it will be a while before I even tempt the idea."

"Breakup? What happened? I thought the connection was charged."

"It was, but then things started to get confusing, and he pulled the plug right before we flew here."

"Has it been a blessing or a curse to be here without him on your mind?"

"That's the thing—he's still texting and checking in, which is frustrating. I'm tired enough, I don't need my heart being tossed around."

"No kidding. I'm sorry. But I'm still proud of you for giving a relationship a go."

"Well, you're making jumping back on Tinder more appealing!" she said.

"I suppose it was time for both of us to mix it up," I said, as the front desk agent walked over to tell me my room was ready.

"True. Do you have another date lined up?"

"No. Not sure where I go from here. I have to return my rental car near Paris, but that isn't for a few weeks," I said, gathering my purse and jacket to head to the elevators.

"Still rolling without a plan, I see?"

"Yes. Although now Switzerland is officially my second stamp. Two down, five to go."

"Does it count unless you stay and explore for a bit?" She did have a point. Fate had brought me here—maybe there was a reason.

We decided I'd stay with Jeannine and her small race crew for a few days to relax and enjoy filling page number two with raclette and a little watch shopping. Switzerland, after all, is the holy land for fine watchmaking, and neither of us could pass up the opportunity to witness the creatures in their native habitat. From Verbier, they were going to a lake house in Lucerne, and I'd join them.

Later, I contemplated Jeannine's remark about risk. Was I truly being reckless? It didn't feel that way. What was I risking with The Guide? My safety, my dignity, my heart? No, I didn't think so. The greater risk lay in the journey itself, delaying my job search, depleting my savings, all still without a home address. I wasn't gambling with fleeting uncertainties; I was wagering comfort and routine in exchange for transformation and blowing past my boundaries. But I didn't feel reckless. In fact, I rather enjoyed it.

SWITZERLAND WAS A storybook come to life. I fell in love with every small village tucked into mountain ravines and every bright green pasture with cows roaming free that we passed. Bells lazily swung from the cows' necks and rang out a soft chorus of presence into the air. I grew up with *The Sound of Music*, *Swiss Family Robinson*, and *Heidi*—although I was not singing and running through open fields, being in the country felt surreal, like I had crawled right off one of the water-colored pages. Waking up on Lake Lucerne, I felt tucked in by the blanket of fog, as protected as the sleepy fish swimming below the surface. The fresh, chilly air was a dramatic contrast to the warm, salty breezes of the Mediterranean.

The Alps continued to evoke the Rocky Mountains but didn't make me long for them. I didn't miss Vail—I liked being where I was, unexpectedly in Switzerland. I felt there was something special for me there, but maybe not right now, not today. Today was our last morning on the lake, and I was ready to press on.

The past week had unfolded in a rhythm of unhurried days, familiar conversations, and indulgent comforts like sleeping in late, lingering over meals, and savoring well-earned massages. The athletes had more than earned their rest. The race crew welcomed me with tired arms, and I was quietly grateful to become an unexpected addition to their recovery retreat. Quintessential Swiss delicacies like rich fondue and decadent chocolates were woven seamlessly into nearly every meal. There was a quiet elegance to the country: an elevated, refined energy rooted in honest labor and an appreciation for life's simple pleasures, executed with precision and pride. Even while bordered by a tapestry of neighboring cultures, Switzerland remained distinctly itself. That enduring sense of identity, unwavering in its subtlety, left me admiring the strength it takes to stay so true to one's essence.

"What's the goal for today, team?" I asked Jeannine over morning coffee.

"Watches and more cheese," she said, cracking the outside of her boiled egg.

"Want to take a walk on the wild side with me and embrace some sassy spontaneity?" I said, licking the honey from my finger. "I assume you have a better idea?"

"Come to Paris with me." Paris wasn't high on my destination list, but it was strategic as a rental car return point. The drop location was a direct train ride away from two large airports that could get me anywhere, even if I didn't plan to stay in the city. However, I had decided that I wanted a little more France and planned to explore Paris before moving on.

"I have the car to get us there, and the hotel is already booked. We could have some *real* fun, and if you fly home next Friday, you'll still make it back to work on time," I said.

She laughed and declined, but I knew she wished for more carefree travel.

"Why don't you stay here awhile and do some trekking? The weather looks amazing and there are so many trails to explore," she said.

"Another time, I would love that. But I'm still avoiding athletic adventures. I'm trying to embrace other facets of my personality, remember?" Plus, I didn't pack the right gear for that and didn't want to buy duplicates of what was boxed away in her loft.

"So, you're still committed, then? You don't want to come back with me?"

"No. I need to keep going," I said, although I was gutted at the idea of saying goodbye to her.

We enjoyed our last day in Lucerne, walking across the famous Chapel Bridge, which is the oldest covered wooden bridge in Europe. The bridge is lined with interior paintings dating back to the seventeenth century, boasts overflowing flower boxes through the windows, and has a prominent tower. The tower has evolved over the years from a prison, torture chamber, treasury, and now into a tourist gift shop—if those walls could talk, I wondered about the secrets they would share. We also visited the Lion Monument, a rock relief commemorating the Swiss Guards who died during the French Revolution, and walked through gorgeous cathedrals and into watch boutiques, appreciating the timepieces but not buying any. I may have been flexing my wallet, but I hadn't won the lottery yet. That reminded me—my lottery ticket was still in my wallet. I'd asked for "my career to surprise me" back in Vail right before I got laid off. I guess it truly did surprise me that day. Just entirely not in the way I wanted.

"Do you miss it?" Jeannine asked as we exited our last watch shop, Audemars Piguet.

"Yes and no." I looked away from her. I will always have admiration and fascination for the watchmaking craft—finished pieces from legacy companies are mechanical works of wearable art. But the memory of being laid off still left the taste of metal in my mouth. "I can't imagine being in that world right now. And it's probably healthier for me not to." I felt the anger rumble in my belly, snarky comments quickly bouncing around my mind. She was quiet.

"Why don't you go to Geneva before Paris? You could set up factory and showroom visits, meet the craftsmen, and maybe reignite your curiosity?"

"The horological museum would be cool," I agreed, turning off the bitter, internal dialog. "But no. I mean, I'm still curious about gemstones. But not in the commerce kind of way—I feel we only comprehend a tiny amount of what they're capable of, frequency and healing-wise. I don't think they exist on Earth just for beauty. Things that form over millions of years have more power than that... maybe I need to investigate their scientific and energetic potential."

"Like quartz? That's widely used in technology, and diamonds are abundant in medical devices," Jeannine explained. "Think semiconductors and water purification."

"There you go. Maybe my career will take me in that direction," I added. "I'm beginning to loathe the idea of working in luxury goods again."

"Jewelry as well? Or just watches?"

"Everything. Like them or hate them, Framebridge is at the top of the global industry, and how could I top the position I created with them?"

"Yeah, I see your point."

"But besides that, I got into the industry for a love of stones. And right now, I don't feel connected to it anymore." I thought of my rings and the small rose quartz angel I had with me. "I hope there's something different waiting for me in the professional world, because I feel this door is shut."

"You can always open a closed door if you change your mind," she reassured me. "Your experience and expertise aren't going anywhere."

When it finally came time for Jeannine to leave, she was ready to head back to Vail, unpack her racing gear, and get back to the routine that would carry her into the winter season. I, on the other hand, was faced with a fresh slap of loneliness after having this unexpected connection with home, friendship, and a job I used to love. I felt like Swiss cheese, missing all of those pieces of me. It even made me miss my ex—not so much him, but the part of me that *was* him. I was desperate to feel whole, and the reality of being alone again sent me into a mini tailspin. I still had five blank pages to go.

After I drove her to the airport and made sure she was able to check in with her copious amount of bike luggage, I beelined to a parking lot and sobbed. Shaking and confused, all the fury I'd been pushing down came roaring up. I couldn't imagine starting my six-and-a-half-hour drive to Paris with waterfalls blurring my vision, so I sat there and rode out the storm, letting the waves of doubt and abandonment ring through me.

Alone again. I looked around my rental car at the vacant seats. Was this what I wanted?

AFTER THE POST drop-off, parking lot waterworks stopped, I remembered that I was in no rush—I was on my own timeline. I meandered through countryside towns, stopping at flower shops and cafés along the way, and took in the ease of my lack of schedule. I fell in love with the autumn grape vines that seemed to hug every farmhouse. I picked up a handmade white and blue striped sweater, and ate a long lunch while being serenaded by jazz on an old radio. By early afternoon, I decided I wanted to free myself of the car and headed straight for the drop-off site via the autobahn. Thinking I had mastered getting directions on Wi-Fi, I loaded up Fern before departing the last market. Still seeing the countryside but zipping at a faster pace now, I crisscrossed big roads but never seemed to take them. I thought it odd, but kept going until I came across an internet hotspot and checked again. When I reloaded the directions, I realized that my maps were still avoiding toll roads. This whole time, I had been playing a giant game of Mario Kart, zooming around the gardens of France without ever getting to take the drawbridge to the castle. When I finally made it to the drop location, I had only minutes to spare before they closed. I hustled to the train station, knowing I was cutting it close to the next departure for Paris. Moving quickly proved to be a daunting task with a rolling suitcase. Fortunately, a group of five uniformed police officers noticed my distress and offered to help.

They asked, first in French and then in broken English, where I was heading. The look on my face as I held up my ticket said enough, and one of them carried my case down the stairs, under the tracks, back up the stairs, and to an open position on the platform, while the others walked along. *Decent escort*, I thought, smiling and trying to keep pace.

Graciously thanking them, I waved as they went back to their evening. Eventually, I made it to my hotel in Saint-Germain and checked into my new home. Cozy and safe, this location was central for walking routes and the train. After dropping my luggage, I was famished and walked the windy, dimly lit streets of the popular neighborhood until I found a bistro with available outdoor seating. Exhausted but happy, I feasted on red wine, escargot, bone marrow, quail, and asparagus. My first Parisian dinner: to die for.

Now, standing in the shadow of the Eiffel Tower, I replayed my journey from Switzerland and could do nothing but laugh. But I had made it. This morning, I'd walked the few blocks to the Seine from my hotel, then walked west to the Eiffel Tower, passing Notre Dame, the Louvre, the Palace, countless vendors along the riverbanks, and corner cafés framing the streets. The sun was warm and the wind tickled as it danced with my hair and swirled around my feet. Most of the flowers had shed their petals, but the grass was still green. Taking in the Eiffel Tower's magnificence with its proud but elegant steel trellises and unique architecture, I wondered if this had once been someone's dream. Friends, lovers, and tourists sprawled out on blankets with white wine, cheese, and baguettes to enjoy the afternoon. As I took in the scene, I wished Jeannine were there, or that I had a date to join me.

I didn't purchase the tickets to "avoid the line" and found myself looking at a mini-Disneyworld level wait to reach the top. I'm allergic to lines and highly impatient; it may make me miss key sights at popular destinations, but I've never been one to wait. So I decided to take in the view from the park. Lying on the grass with nothing but my jacket to recline on and sparkling water from my bag to drink, I got lost imagining the city skyline from above, visualizing the city as a bird would see it.

Switzerland had been a welcome reprieve from the world of sex parties and late-night dates. Jeannine's non-judgmental and inquisitive support was also extremely calming—I might have been diving into the deep end, crossing comfort zones, and doing what I wanted, but I was grateful for a voice from home assuring me I wasn't entirely crazy, and that they still loved me.

The Guide lived in Paris, and I was half interested in setting up another date. But right now, my focus was on quality me time and embracing other experiences I had been missing, like exploring museums, attending the theater, and, if I was lucky, finding a perfect new dress or bottle of perfume. I always think of the last spritz of your favorite perfume as the final page in a good book, the empty bottle containing all the experiences from every time you wore it. You might get another bottle of the same scent, but the story will never be the same. On my first night in Paris, I finished the bottle I had brought with me.

THE NEXT WEEK passed quickly. Like an Energizer bunny on steroids, I had the best time bouncing around Paris. I'd watched the famous *Moulin Rouge* from a box seat, took a river cruise down the Seine, and shopped for hours around the Champs-Élysées. I had only accumulated a few small bags out of respect for my budget and the limited space in my suitcase, but I loved slowly meandering through the shops and trying on statement pieces. A bright red scarf found its way into my heart and around my neck.

I got purposefully lost in the Louvre only to find the Mona Lisa a few displays over from where I ended up. On my way out of the museum, I stood at the top of the stairs, marveling at The Winged Woman. An incredible example of Greek sculpture, the Goddess Nike was depicted returning victoriously from a flight. Centuries of war and movement have left the piece incomplete; she is missing her feet, arms, head, and the front of her foundation, the bow of a boat. Yet, her mere presence still inspires respect. Perfect in its imperfection. Strength in its vulnerability.

Besides the city staples, I often found myself off the beaten path: I loved to stroll through quaint neighborhoods, marveling at the creamy limestone architecture with its wrought iron balconies, tall windows, and ornate cornices. The buildings stood strong and, I imagined, their welcoming courtyards had housed generations of families.

Traveling between the arrondissements, I would jump on and off trains without an agenda. Doing this, I stumbled upon one of my favorite destinations yet: Père Lachaise Cemetery. The sacred energy called to me even in the subway, and I'm grateful I noticed a sign mentioning Jim Morrison. With fallen leaves and dried flowers gracing the narrow cobblestone rows, low tree branches protected the headstones and monuments. I was nearly alone walking around the holy site, and quickly found the unmarked grave of the famous singer from The Doors. *He wasn't here for a long time*, I thought, *but he seemed to have a good time.* Famous for his unique voice and poetic lyrics, his impact on music reached generations after him. What a powerful legacy cemented in such a short amount of time. Jim Morrison, of course, died at twenty-seven like so many greats: Robert Johnson, Kurt Cobain, Janis Joplin, Jimi Hendrix, each with legendary status. I wondered, what would my legacy be? Although, Jim started out resisting his frontman position, singing with his back to the audience in early performances. I guess we all find a unique way to center stage in our lives.

Distracted by my grumbling tummy, I left to find lunch. After fifteen minutes of walking, I grabbed a side table under a bright red awning and sat happily waiting for the server. In Paris, it was impossible not to feel like you were in a movie. Being a single, American female, I loved it; my romantic imagination was in overdrive. Even if my recent encounters were far from headlining a rom-com, I felt love here. Part of that was a love of silence—without checking in with Tanya or any other social media, I was simply tuning into myself. What *did* I want to do? Eat? See? Taking a sabbatical from overthinking, my guard was coming down and my mind was quieting.

Americans have often said that Parisians are rude, but that couldn't be further from the truth. They simply can't be bothered to overinvest themselves. The polite and chatty girl in me found it a refreshing break from small talk. Before, I had been scared to travel in countries where I didn't know the language and, surprisingly, I found it glorious. Without understanding the conversations going on around me, I was finally able to tune out the noise.

We subconsciously process everything the mind understands, from chatter at the table next to us, to advertisements on the radio, to seeing a text pop up on our phones. All that static keeps the mind working overtime. But the sound around me was now in French, and since I didn't understand it, my mind wasn't processing it; it was more like music. The introvert in me relished the reprieve. Fear wasn't creeping up anymore either, and I was discovering a strange confidence in the void, a beauty in silence and solitude. I was learning to tune into my intuition again for more than just street directions. I was remembering how to create space for divine inspiration and to be in touch with my internal world.

One of my favorite Alan Watts quotes came to mind: "It is only when there is no goal and no rush that the human senses are fully open to receive the world." My senses were rising from a deep slumber and starting to flex again. If we can avoid all the static, who knows what information we are capable of receiving?

ON MY SEVENTH morning in Paris, I was worn out from constant activities and decisions. Option anxiety had settled in: too many rights or lefts, in or out, ride or walk micro choices had piled up, and I just wanted to lie there and sleep. My body, my mind, and my spirit were all exhausted from relentless stimulation. But how could I justify staying in bed and wasting this special time? *Suck it up, buttercup, and get out there*, I told myself. I reminded myself that this is what I wanted—solo spontaneity and diversified exploration.

I chose to visit the Galeries Lafayette, infamous for their store window displays. They mirrored the impact of Bergdorf's windows in New York, which I used to use as inspiration for creating such displays at Framebridge. I caught a whiff of nostalgia and sought them out.

Of course, as I'd come to expect, my initial destination unveiled the inspiration for my next step: the Palais Garnier Opera House was right around the corner, and I meandered over to take in the grounds. The interior was as regal as I'd been told, with gold details, overlapping grand staircases, and hand-painted mosaics covering every inch of the ceiling. As fate would have it, there was a performance that evening, and it turned out it was easy to get a last minute seat as a single person. I didn't have time to return to my hotel, and I wasn't as dressed up as I would have preferred—this would have been a classy excuse to wear a formal gown—but my body would feel the music all the same.

The opening immediately captivated me with a striking set and lighting design. By the second scene, the dramatic duet between the heroine and villain pulled me into the story, and a heartfelt aria transported me out of body. By the end, I was unaware of linear time or space and sat, suspended in another plane of existence, in complete surrender to the character's emotional journey. Sound is such a powerful vehicle for transportation.

As the curtains closed, my hands tingled with musical electricity. The fact that I didn't understand what was being said or sung made little impact on what I felt; instead, I found that it was that very lack of definition that brought me truth. In the void of processing, the break between thoughts created a space for energetic and emotional comprehension.

With tears streaming down my cheeks, I closed my eyes and bowed my head in gratitude before rising to join the standing ovation. Witnessing the artistry of the team it took to orchestrate this performance was inspiring: from costume creators, prop architects, and musicians to the stage performers and writers themselves, it was a community affair. I respected their passion as I saw them all take a final bow. In Colorado, live music had been a regular part of life, but country and classic rock concerts were a far cry from the magic I'd found at the opera.

Filled with internal romance, I walked out into the crisp evening air. Weaving and swinging around streetlights and trees, as if they were my dance partners, I made my way back to my temporary home in the Saint-Germain. I've always been enamored by cities at night, and Paris was quickly becoming my favorite. The city of light certainly did sparkle.

Growing up, I had loved *Phantom of the Opera* and *Rigoletto*, even singing "The Melody Within" at a solo ensemble competition one year. Humming the song as I walked, I remembered the lyrics clearly: "It's not easy, you must listen, with your heart for what lies hidden…"

Thankful that I'd rallied to get out of bed that morning, I realized getting lost during the day had repeatedly helped me find myself at night. So, I promised, tomorrow, I would show up again. And again. And again.

I HAD REVITALIZED Tanya but was yet to make another intriguing match. I was getting a little restless, so the next night I joined The Guide again. In a stark contrast to the bright lights of the stage, we went underground—literally, down what seemed like a three-floor staircase—towards cozy corners and sleek shadows. In my imagination, we were using runes and roses to navigate a labyrinth of passageways surrounding the catacombs. Archways were laced with esoteric messages, and passing below each one was an opportunity to enter various chambers carved out to host secret meetings, exotic encounters, and elaborate escapes. In reality, we were a few floors below the private residences and luxury shops we'd passed on the street to get there.

With each step downwards, my red heels steadied my buzzing body with confidence and my muscles relaxed. I could feel the Black Jaguar from the oracle cards walking next to me, seeing clearly in the darkness and walking confidently into the unknown.

Entering the parlor, I was hit with dizzying lights, crystal reflections, masks, mirrored floors, and platinum ceilings draped with glamor and intrigue. Guests paid no attention to our entrance, fixated on their own worlds. The Guide's strong hand slid to the lower left of my back and, with a twitch of his little finger, directed me.

Round three: a castle suite, a private party in Cannes, and now an exclusive club in the heart of Paris. As we eased into our opulent surroundings, I found myself wondering, *is this who I am now?* Dating not for romance, but for erotic exploration? I adorned myself in lace and smoky eyes, not with the intention to impress, but to embody a persona I had no plans to keep. Could this even be called dating? Likely not. I accept that intimacy came in many forms, and relationship dynamics were as varied as the people who shaped them. Still, for me, this was an arrangement—nothing more. Each encounter with him became a bold drop in the narrow chalice of my sexual experience; I was awakening something once dormant, indulging in the thrill of the forbidden, and allowing my inner rebel to stretch her limbs. And yet, none of these evenings had left me feeling *whole*. Then again, not every experience is meant to be complete. Some are meant to stir, not settle.

Swaying on the dance floor, we mixed and mingled with various couples, eventually finding a few ladies from Italy with bracelets stacked to their elbows, hair to their breasts, smooth thongs, and high heels, their partners watching from nearby booths. Blending with the DJ's rhythm, I found harmony; my frequency settled in and blended with the crowd. Accustomed now to new bodies, scents, and touches swirling around my personal space, I was comfortable with my boundaries, welcoming what I wanted and gracefully passing off what I didn't. It was a space of physical intimacy but emotional emptiness. There was pleasure to be had, no doubt, but my heart didn't desire to go into the backrooms that night. Anything more than dancing felt like an intrusion. So, we danced, we danced, and we danced. It was hot and poetic and free.

The whole night left lingering sensations but also a feeling of closure. Sealed with concentric circles of grace and gratitude, I knew this would be my last date with The Guide.

"Merci," I said, my sweaty body shivering in the outside air a few hours later.

"My pleasure," he said, as he draped his jacket over my shoulders.

We walked a few blocks and, unbeknownst to me, towards another destination.

"I love balance," he said, breaking the silence as he led me up a new staircase. The shadows opened as he turned me around to face a glowing, soft sunrise over the silhouettes of Montmartre. The view over the sleepy city was breathtaking: rays of light wove around trees and buildings, extending their golden carpet.

"Light to our dark?" I said, watching the day rise around us.

"Night to day."

"Our rendezvous have been quite the introduction to Tinder dates," I mused, making him laugh.

"Don't expect to find another like me."

"I believe not. You will forever be my Guide."

Stopping to look me in the eyes, he said, "You're very bold, Whitney. I won't forget you."

"You better not," I said, wrapping my arms around his waist and hanging on to the idea of being important to someone.

"Thank you for trusting me."

I smiled, we kissed, he ushered me towards my Uber, and I waved goodbye.

Driving back to my hotel, there it was again: smooth rap coming through the car speakers. I'd crossed comfort zones I didn't know existed, and was being escorted back home by a beautiful, melodic lullaby. But this wasn't the new me—tasting was one thing, becoming was another. I didn't know what the dating world held for me, but my heart told me I wouldn't find it in the sexy, dark, velvet rooms of those clubs. And maybe not in France, either. Maybe it was time to move on.

I WAS READY to figure out passport page number three. Traveling alone had been both exhilarating and demanding, a delicate balance of empowerment and vulnerability. With each passing day, the act of showing up solely for myself became more natural. Staying anchored in a single hotel room for almost two weeks was stabilizing as well. It allowed me to immerse myself in the full spectrum of emotions and experiences that arose when I wasn't fixated on foundational logistics.

I had discovered that, while I adored Sancerre, I preferred the crisp minerality of Chablis when paired with fresh Normandy oysters. I'd learned that a warm, buttery chocolate croissant in the morning had near-medicinal properties. And I'd realized the body is meant to be explored like a personal treasure map, each touch an invitation to deeper understanding.

Paris had nurtured brilliance—Hemingway's prose, Coco Chanel's revolution, Monet's impressionist visions, and the daring reinvention of Nouvelle Cuisine. It was a city that inspired courage, innovation, and romance. But as intoxicating as it had been, I knew it was time to move on.

Sitting up in bed, I plucked my laptop off the small nightstand and placed it next to me on the pillow. I closed my eyes and imagined the feeling of happiness. When I feel happy, what else is in the vision? Slowing my breathing, I tuned into my body, asking what it needed in this moment to feel joy.

Water. I envisioned crystalline waves shimmering under the sun, a mirage of whitewashed buildings framing the horizon, a warm breeze brushing my skin, and the soft, shifting sand beneath my feet. An island. I sensed being surrounded by this water.

I ran through possibilities: Malta, Ibiza, Mallorca. And then I noticed Sicily—I'd never been. Sunshine was in the forecast, and it was only a fifty-six euro direct flight from Orly. After a quick three-hour plane ride, I'd arrive in the third country to stamp my passport. France, Switzerland, then Italy. All had been spontaneously decided and embraced without an agenda.

I booked a hotel near the Catania airport for my first night, rented a car for two weeks, and sketched out a loose itinerary, tracing a counterclockwise route around the island. The finer details could wait; I'd figure them out once I arrived. For now, my focus was on a proper farewell to this enchanting city.

I decided to end my time in Paris as I had begun, on the Eiffel Tower's lawn. But this time, I would curate the moment with intention: a bouquet of flowers (for myself), a bottle of rosé (also for myself), and a spread of cheese and a freshly baked baguette—a farewell picnic for lunch. The romantic in me couldn't envision a more fitting goodbye.

And speaking of romance—I wasn't ready for love, but the idea of sharing a meal and a conversation called to me. I hadn't dined with anyone since Switzerland, and something about a Parisian prince—one who would open doors, pull out my chair, and make me feel like a lady rather than a vixen—felt undeniably alluring. My heart called out with fairytale main character energy.

Hello, Tanya, I thought. *We have a new mission and precisely twenty-four hours to bring it to life.*

I retrieved my phone from the tangled sheets and opened Tanya's app, more out of curiosity than expectation. I had browsed profiles in recent nights before drifting to sleep, yet none had piqued my interest enough to meet in person. My inbox overflowed with private messages and an unsettling number of unsolicited photo requests. Was this standard Tinder etiquette? Perhaps. I wished I had Jeannine's take on the matter.

A sudden pang of loneliness tugged at me—a longing for the ease of friendship and familiar voices. Maybe my struggle to find a match wasn't about the app or the men, but about me. Maybe I was still uncertain of what I was truly seeking. With fresh resolve and a spark of optimism, I continued swiping.

No, no, no, I thought, swiping left. Then: *Wait.* This one stood out. Handsome with an easy, genuine smile. Something was captivating about his presence, which seemed both refined and adventurous. In the second photo, he exuded a boyish charm, dressed in hunting attire, a beret, tall boots, and a vintage rifle slung effortlessly over his shoulder. Yet in the next image, he was polished and composed, wearing a suit. Not the kind reserved for weddings, but one that suggested a professional occupation. Intriguing.

Then came the snapshots of his travels: trekking through Africa, riding a motorcycle in Nepal, crafting homemade gin. Yes. I wanted to meet this elixir of a man.

I sent him a message right away. Quick to connect, his response was swift, thoughtful, and—most importantly—engaging. He asked questions, showed genuine curiosity, and, to my immense relief, demonstrated fluency in English with not a single inappropriate request or mention of private clubs. Triple yes.

He asked me to meet the following weekend, but I mentioned I was only in town for that night, then probably gone forever. To my surprise, he said, "I guess we're meeting tonight." He proposed a little bar near his place and asked if it was convenient for me.

You're kidding, I laughed out loud after entering the destination into Google Maps. I had unknowingly walked right past it on my very first day here, stopping for lunch just a few doors down.

Serendipity was in motion. This was meant to be.

Feeling energized by my decisiveness that morning, I leapt out of bed to get ready for my picnic. I slipped into a black linen dress, paired it with little white sneakers, a black scarf threaded with gold accents, a light jacket, and black sunglasses. I left with my hair down and a smile on my lips. I was going to end my French adventure with two incredible dates. One with myself, and one with… The Duke.

GETTING OUT OF the Uber just a block away from Le Recruit-ment, where I was to meet The Duke, I was nervous. I wasn't feeling the usual anxious, pre-date nervousness—the pressure of wondering, *Will this go somewhere? Does he like me? Do I like him?*—since we both knew I was leaving tomorrow, and when permanence isn't the priority, people tend to drop their guard. Vying for acceptance to get another date was off the table, leaving only the here and now. But at the same time, I still cared—it was still nerve-wracking to put myself out there and exciting to see what was going to happen. This was my first proper first date. Ever.

As I approached, I saw him through the glass, ready with a table by the window. True to his word, he had come straight from work and was still in his suit and tie. It wasn't until that moment that I realized I had never been on a date with a man in a suit. He looked effortlessly elegant, exuding a quiet confidence that made me feel, suddenly, very much like an adult. All of this was hitting me as we locked eyes through the glass. He immediately stood, pulling out my chair with an old-world grace as I walked through the door. It all sent a delightful thrill through me. As I leaned in to greet him with the traditional French kisses, I batted my lashes playfully, murmur-ing, "Merci, how kind of you."

This was going to be fun.

"What an unexpected pleasure," he said.

"There's no time like the present," I said. "So, how did the fi-nancial markets treat you today?" He was an investment portfolio manager.

"Typical, but not important. Tell me more about your trip so far. A solo odyssey has been a dream of mine for some time—it's fascinating to meet someone in the middle of theirs." With that, we launched into hours of discussing travel—where we'd been, where we wanted to go, the importance and impact of volunteering, the pace of easy country life, and the need for relaxing. Casual drinks turned into a long, divine dinner, and we chatted until the place was empty, losing nothing in translation.

"I'm French, I love doing nothing," he said, leaning back into his chair, full, entertained, and charming.

"Society here has certainly made relaxing an art," I agreed. "I would love to venture into wine country and get a taste for that."

"Life is meant to be enjoyed," he said, waving his hands for emphasis.

"I agree with that," I said, more with a smile than my whispered words.

"What do you think about imagination versus reality?"

I leaned back, considering the question. The Guide came to mind: how much of that encounter had been shaped by reality, and how much by the story I told myself about it? Although reality was inviting, leaving some things to my imagination was ideal.

"We need both, I suppose."

"That's an easy answer." He smirked, inviting me to go deeper.

"Imagination inspires... reality grounds?" I added, testing the balance.

"I think people can get stuck in their imagination and use it as an excuse not to participate in the real world."

"On the flip side," I countered, "some people become prisoners of a limiting reality because they've lost touch with their imagination. What makes you think information from the imagination isn't real, anyway?"

"Because fairytales and dreams aren't tangible, they're not real."

"Like Santa Claus? You may not be able to touch him, but his presence is certainly real to a child who believes."

"He's not real. The child believes in magic, and Santa is just a symbol for that."

"So, you believe in magic, then?" I arched a brow, my curiosity piqued. "I happen to have a budding relationship with things unseen."

He exhaled, amused. "I think we could go round and round with this conversation." It made me want to kiss him even more.

"Good," I said with authority, "I like a conversation with no finish line."

"Then it's decided. You will visit me at my country house so we can relax and drink wine like the French, and debate—"

"Like Americans." I interrupted. "I'd love to join you. But as you know, my flight leaves in the morning."

"You will come back. For tonight, the least I can do is offer you a private tasting of some of my favorite homemade gin."

"Oui, Monsieur. That sounds like a perfect dessert."

He gracefully paid the bill, not even acknowledging my attempt to reach for my purse. As we stepped outside, his arm looped through mine, the cool night air wrapped around us. Just beyond the awning and away from prying eyes, he paused, tilting his head slightly in invitation. Our first kiss was unhurried, light, and sweet, a natural extension of the evening's easy rhythm.

Finally, I allowed myself the indulgence of running my fingers through his thick, curled hair—blonde with a hint of auburn—in the glow of the streetlights. He traced a gentle line along my cheek, his touch lingering before subtly guiding me into a graceful, almost cinematic dip.

His townhouse was only a block away. A multi-level home with a private courtyard, it was precisely the kind I had been wistfully imagining behind the grand, ornate gates scattered throughout Paris.

Gin and olives led to cozying up on the couch, which led to venturing upstairs to find our bodies as in sync as our conversation. He undressed me with reverence and ease, striking a dance between tenderness and control. It was beautifully simple to focus on him and only him. I opened under the weight of his body and traced the flex of his muscles as they moved around me. He focused on my neck and trailed down to my belly until I grabbed his mouth to meet mine again. All of me was excited to give and receive, and our physical flow was a welcome show to which we both subscribed.

Afterwards, my head lay peacefully on his fresh pillow as the breeze floated past the linen curtains. I could see ivy wrapping around the window frame and the original stone wall radiated warmth in the filtered light. The atmosphere was beautiful and the sex connective;

it was tempting to stay. But I had an early flight to Italy in the morning, so, after a silent snuggle, I got up and got dressed. He wasn't surprised and, always the gentleman, got dressed so he could see me to my car.

"We'll always have Paris," I said as I turned to face him one last time, quoting *Casablanca*, my grandmama's favorite movie.

"Paris will call you back," he said with quiet certainty. So French. His confidence felt like a promise—one I wanted to believe. I ran my fingers through his hair and traced his slightly scruffy beard as we melted into one last, sincere kiss. The Duke had been the quintessential Parisian date, leaving me with more than just a memory. He left me inspired. Inspired by the effortless way we can connect with kindred spirits across the world. Inspired by the reassurance that men of depth, charm, and integrity do exist. And most of all, he reminded me that I was worthy of sitting across the table from them just as I was, with my relationship history, financial insecurity, unclear future, imperfections, and all.

COMING OFF A lovely evening, I was surprised to wake up feeling frustrated and cranky. At the airport, I sat in a vacant waiting area as I stewed about the morning. Packing my suitcase was a chore for the first time, and I nearly missed my ride. I had arrived early only to find that none of the cafés past security would open before my flight departed. No caffeine, no comfort. But beneath the surface of these inconveniences was a deeper ache, an overwhelming, hurt feeling I just couldn't shake.

Still, I guessed that my plane ride leaving France wouldn't be like the one entering it. I thought back to the 737 filled with suited men and wondered how their car launch had gone.

Taking a deep breath, I tried to reframe: I was on time. I was en route to the third page in my passport and really had no reason to complain. Taking another breath and focusing on something mundane for a moment, I looked at my boarding pass; group three, row three, seat F. Departure time: 8:36 a.m.. Departure date: *Shit*. That was it—the date. That day, my ex-husband would be handed a manila envelope containing his copy of our signed and notarized divorce decree. Obviously it wouldn't be a surprise for him, and our divorce wasn't final until the mandatory waiting period was over, but I knew seeing the official paperwork for the first time would sting, nonetheless.

That's what I had been feeling. I felt *him*: his reaction, his pain. A reverberation through the ether. I had absorbed it, and it fueled my irritation, filled my chest with unease, and brought hot, uninvited tears to my eyes.

There was something else in that envelope, something far more personal: his wedding ring. The same ring he'd left by the sink when we moved out. When preparing the documents, I chose to return it—it had never been mine to hold on to. But the symbolism must have felt like a slap in the face. I imagined him opening that envelope and being hit not once, but twice. Once by the law, then by the life we'd lost.

I glanced down at the yellow sapphire engagement ring I now wore on my right hand and twirled it absentmindedly. Our connection, though severed in name, remained energetically intact. When we felt things—*really* felt them—it was as if the emotional current traveled directly from one of us to the other. The invisible thread still hummed. My tears rolled quietly, one after another, falling down my cheeks.

He hadn't been on my mind at all, but I felt him as intensely that day as I had on the days he came home from snowboarding, lucky to be alive. My heart didn't seem to recognize any distance between us. He was physically absent—I was half a world away and alone in a nearly empty airport—and yet it felt as though he were right in front of me, his eyes meeting mine with confusion, resentment, and the echo of broken promises. We were both moving on, I knew that. But it still hurt. My heart still ached over the version of us that once was, but mostly it longed for the missing parts of me. The hollowness was haunting. Would I ever be able to fully move on?

By that evening, I was exhausted—utterly and physically spent. The day had gone from bad to worse. Some asshole at the airport called me "la pute" as I accidentally tried to board the flight before him. Then I arrived to find more rental car resistance; at the counter, I'd learned my reservation had been canceled due to insufficient contact information and flagged as a suspicious, last-minute booking. They thought I was a scam. After explaining the situation, they had finally agreed to rent me a car, but at a higher daily rate with mandatory, non-refundable insurance. Neither my confidence nor my budget had appreciated the situation.

And after all that, for the first time traveling alone, I felt unsafe. The hotel I booked was *not* what was advertised—it had bars on the windows, narrow dirty hallways, and a parking lot buzzing with what felt like drug dealers and purse-snatchers.

As I walked up, a man had hollered at me from across the street, first in Italian and then in English, saying that ladies drink for free at all bars around the corner. "Come and dance on stage, we are all friends... very nice." When I hadn't responded, he'd started walking towards me, waving his hands, and I had almost run to the dingy hotel entrance, fumbling with my belongings along the way.

Then, after arriving in my room, I sat up like a statue on my horrid bed and thought, *no. Absolutely not; I'm not safe, and I'm not staying here.* My phone still wasn't working in Italy yet, so I drove all around trying to find Wi-Fi to look for an alternative, safe hotel, but hit no vacancy at every turn. Desperate, I thought I would go to a Starwood property and try to play the employee or preferred member card. My ex had worked for a Westin in Colorado for years, and he was never one to be on top of paperwork, so maybe I was still listed under his employee account for discounts and rooms.

I found a Sheraton and pleaded my case with the women working the front desk. I was alone, I'd booked the wrong hotel, didn't speak the language, it was getting late, and I was scared. After conversing amongst themselves for a few minutes, they told me if I waited in the lobby until 7 p.m. and no one came to rent the room they had to hold until that time, I could have it. Done—worst case, I could stay somewhere safe for a few hours, and fingers crossed the room would remain vacant.

Sitting there waiting, I thought about men. Being afraid of them was certainly a departure from my recent ambitions. But the thought of being assaulted was real. I was emanating sexual energy into the universe, but was I attracting *this*? "Asking for it," as some say? If something awful did happen, would people say I "deserved it"? Fuck me, what a tragic thing to think. I sat up straighter in the lobby chair, annoyed; fuck the societal talk track that even put that idea in my head. I should have free will to explore my sexuality and still have *complete* agency over when and how I do so.

I thought I could do this alone, but maybe I couldn't. Should I go home? My hands were starting to sweat as I fidgeted with my purse, looking for nothing. My legs crossed and uncrossed, toes nervously tapping the ground. Why couldn't I rebound from the day's crippling energy? I needed cold water on my face and space to shake the anxiety and doubt from my limbs.

In the lobby restroom, tired makeup and dried-out spaghetti hair greeted me in the mirror. Before today, things weren't exactly easy; there were bumps and twists in this lonely journey, but I was still feeling a flow, following signs to keep going. But maybe it was all a lie. Maybe it was just my mind seeing what I needed to justify this selfish escapade. Maybe I was indeed running away instead of facing reality, like some family and friends had suggested—what made me think that I was capable of anything more? What an idiot. I should accept failure and go back to the US. Maybe I didn't have the courage to fill all seven pages; it was time to go home. Why did I have to go halfway around the world to hear myself think, anyway? Why couldn't I figure out my identity back there?

The cool water wasn't cleansing away any doubt. Instead, it only temporarily cleared the debris from my cheeks to make way for new tears. A fresh surge of emotion took over as my heart ached for my parents. I missed them; I wanted to cuddle up in my childhood bedroom and have them tell me everything was going to be alright. I grabbed a rough paper towel from the aged dispenser and ugly cried as I blew angry snot bubbles from my nose. Crumbling into a faded, cushioned vanity chair in the far corner, I broke down, head on the counter, hands above it, praying for escape.

I was so frustrated with not feeling like myself. Go or don't go—what the fuck did it matter? Is our life laid out for us? Destiny or fate? Is free will just an illusion, and are all these big choices simple jokes from the grid? I showed up, life. I took the red pill and abandoned reason, but I did not feel free yet. I did not feel powerful. I was trying to trust in myself, but it was miserably confusing—maybe I was done. Maybe I was broken, and it was time to acknowledge that. Maybe it was time to throw my passport and all its stamps in the trash. What if I drove my rental car straight into the Mediterranean and *drowned*? It would take days for anyone to even alert my family that I was missing or dead. No one would know because I'd shut them all out.

As time went on, my thoughts went from questioning to desperate, and confusion and doubt took root. When anger started sprouting, I finally took action, unwilling to let it consume me. I stood up, bounced my legs, and shook my arms to free all the negativity. Looking like a frantic ragdoll on a vibrating dance floor, I let my body go wild. Weird, contorted movements ricocheted off each other and around the bathroom I went, totally unhinged and flailing, as if I were full of lightning. Finally, as I noticed a tingling sensation overtake my fascia, I slowed my movements, and subsequently my breath. The tears were gone. The electric surges were done. Empty; there was still a slow pulse of self-loathing and sorrow, but I was empty.

It was like all communication channels had shut off. My mind, intuition, my heart: all quiet. The tiny room became a dark and eerie void. Just... *there*. What do you do without thought or emotion? How do you embrace this space or get out of it? More internal silence. No inspiration, no ideas, no help. But then I heard someone enter the gentleman's bathroom next door and was jolted back to the fact that I was at a Sheraton and must walk back into public to face my fate.

I pressed my cheeks and gave myself an internal pep talk in the mirror. After regaining some form of composure, I left the restroom and walked back to my lobby chair on autopilot. The front desk manager waved me over with some papers. "Please fill these out about your car, we have the room for you." I felt immediate relief; at least one hurdle was being lowered.

"Thank you for your patience. Due to company policy, we must reserve this room every day until this time in case a diplomat arrives."

"A diplomat?" I echoed. Did I hear her right? What employee information did I give her? Thinking they would find out I was a fraud and kick me out moments later, panic quickly returned.

"Yes, you'll be staying tonight in our diplomatic suite. It has a closed-off bedroom, separate kitchen area, two bathrooms, a living room, and a boardroom with a private deck boasting views to the sea on three sides." I couldn't speak. "With your employee discount, the room will be eighty-nine euros for the night." Now I might faint.

"But I'm not a diplomat," I squeaked out.

"Yes, that's okay. We simply must hold it until seven in the evening in case one arrives. Afterwards, anyone may use it."

She continued with breakfast and parking details, but it felt like I was watching a silent film as the quiet in my head from before returned. I could stay, I would be safe, and I was going to be in a suite for under a hundred euros. Oh, my. Thank the universe for kindness and rescue. Thank this wonderful woman's empathy and creativity that helped me in my time of need. And thank the bathroom for holding me safe for the past hour. All I had to do was get on the elevator, and I would be finished with this day.

I ENTERED THE diplomatic suite, depleted and solemn, stumbling over myself through the doorway. I was oddly enamored with the soundproofed walls around me; I hoped I wouldn't need them, but it was comforting to know I had a decent buffer. After finishing room service, I prepared for bed. Wrapped in a hotel bathrobe, I curled up on the balcony as the sun dipped beneath the horizon, my thoughts returning once again to my ex. It wasn't lost on me that I owed this refuge, in part, to him, and a tangle of conflicting emotions stirred at the thought. His habitual negligence with paperwork had worked in my favor. How ironic when shards of glass from a broken past come back around to help put you back together.

The sea lay still below, its surface stirred gently by the breeze, dancing to a rhythm entirely indifferent to my unraveling. Nature bears no burden of heartbreak; it simply endures. And yet, beyond reason, I sense that it knows. It listens. It responds in silence to all that stirs within and around us. Below, the city hummed, cars moved from offices to restaurants and homes, doors opened and closed, and voices sang with anticipation as people eased into their evening.

I withdrew from the world below, nestled between potted palms, and sank into the plush embrace of a lounge chair, the final farewells with my ex looping quietly through my mind. Goodbyes that sealed a decade-long chapter of life and love. First, the goodbye to our community, when I had attended his going-away party last July. Then, our private parting days later at the airport. And finally, the last time I'd heard his voice, just before boarding my flight to Nice nearly a month ago.

Attending his party had been one of the hardest nights of my life. My breath caught as the panic returned, and I gripped my bathrobe tighter—talk about putting on a brave face in a state of utter despair, feeling on display with rumors flying all around you. *But if I hadn't gone*, I still justified to myself, *people would have been talking about that instead of celebrating his move to Hawaii.* We'd decided I should be there to show unified support and suppress gossip. But truth be told, the only thing being suppressed had been my emotion.

Most of our friends remained individually supportive—sad, but supportive. Still, many were shocked; my mountain family had only known me as his wife, so not serving that role anymore left a confused space around some relationships.

At the end of the evening, we'd realized that our flights—his to Hawaii, mine to New York—departed on the same day, just forty-five minutes apart. We chose to go to the airport together, and Jeannine had graciously dropped us off. After checking in, we'd shared a tearful breakfast, gently reminiscing over random memories and kindly asking about pending plans, before walking to our respective gates. (Which, as fate would have it, were only three apart in the vast expanse of the Denver airport—you couldn't script it.) We'd hugged softly, the embrace still charged with emotional connection, and looked at each other with fear-filled tears, silently wondering, *will I ever know a love like this again?* And then he had boarded his Swiss Air flight.

I'd watched him, dressed in jeans, a blue plaid button-up, his skateboard strapped to his hiking backpack, as he walked away from me down the jet bridge. I'd paralleled his plane, hollow and heartbroken, walking in the terminal as it taxied away until it reached the runway, then took off. Not a minute later, the bell had rung to start boarding my flight. Stunned as I was by the enormity of the moment, I'd recognized I might have just watched him fly out of my life forever. Tears had streamed down my cheeks, and I'd closed my eyes to pray for the strength to move. Eventually, I'd turned and walked in the opposite direction, my internal struggle shoved down as I boarded my own flight.

And then there was our final farewell. At the very moment of my departure on this so-called grand journey, who had I called? Him. His voice had been the last one I heard. All I had wanted was for him to say he was proud of me, but he hadn't. The lack of validation had stirred my insecurity, and three Basil Haydens later, I'd landed in Nice with a pounding headache and no comfort to show for it.

Back in Sicily, the sunset had vanished, but all I could see was red. Rage boiled hotter than before—I was getting mad. *Really* mad. My bathrobe was becoming claustrophobic, and the chirping birds sounded like nails on a chalkboard, anxious disharmony rising all around me. I closed my eyes and vividly saw him again, disappearing down that jet bridge, heading toward a new life, toward rediscovering himself. But this time, I wanted to scream: *Why? Why didn't you deposit that stupid check? Why did you stop having authority over your life and look to me to control everything? To fix everything? Why didn't nearly dying cause you to step back? Why did you stop listening to your intuition, to your body—you ignored the signs. How could you choose joints over presence? I am so mad at you for breaking my heart, for not fighting. I am furious you let us get divorced. And I hate myself for still needing you!*

My gut twisted; it ripped my heart out to feel all of this, to admit all of this. The intensity of it shattered something in me, and I couldn't control it anymore—the emotions I had buried deep within my soul erupted, and it was time to simply be pissed. I couldn't *hold* any more. It was time to have the composed girl take a seat and let the wounded warrior scream.

I remembered the soundproof walls, sprinted to the master bedroom, launched myself onto the king-sized bed, and wailed into the firm pillows. With the firehose of fury finally unleashed, I cried, screamed, and cursed every resentment into existence. Not limiting my rage to romantic scars, I vented about Framebridge for laying me off and yelled at the universe for not protecting me. I was angry with everyone but myself—for once, I didn't want to be strong. I wanted to break.

I was done hiding. Done holding it all together. Done putting on a brave face. No one checks on the people who always seem strong, but we're the ones who often need it most, because we don't know how to ask for help, let alone receive it. And there, in that diplomatic suite, I finally admitted it: I needed help.

This is too much, I said out loud, through haggard breaths as the anger started to subside. *This is too much*, I repeated, begging the unseen for comfort. Everything solo was too much. Emotions to process, life to figure out, travel to plan—I didn't want to do it anymore.

Wiping my face and releasing my death grip on the covers, I exhaled. I needed help, but how? How could I help myself, and did I even understand the mess I was in? Confident the diplomatic suite had never entertained such brazen incivility, I got up and returned to the balcony for some fresh air. The tide must have come in; the waves were much louder now. The sky stretched out like a pure black canvas, and the stars shone like tiny police interrogation lights, all pointing at me, expecting answers. Stunned into submission, I sank back into the lounge chair and decided: in the morning, I would check my bank account. Numbers didn't lie—if it was low, I'd investigate return flight options. Maybe it was time to call it quits and be practical. Practical, I could do. Maybe quitting this crazy journey was how I could help myself. But return where? Where was home anymore?

Enough, I thought. *Get over yourself; whatever you choose to do is a luxury because you have a choice at all. So keep your whiny ass here until you remember something you're grateful for, then go to sleep.*

I reminded myself, *I have pain because I had love. Polarity creates contrast, and I must endure the pendulum shifts.* Still, frustration and sadness were at the forefront, and it took a while to settle. But as the bathrobe gently wrapped around my tired limbs, I thought of the moss from the farm: cool, soft, and resilient. I was grateful for moss. Simple, yes, but true. Once again, authentic gratitude had the power to bring me back—back into the light.

That day had been a moody thunderstorm, but as my head finally hit the pillow, the world pitch-black and calm all around, I accepted it. It was over. I fell into a deep, dreamless sleep.

WAKING UP, I felt lighter, cleansed, as if the emotional fire that had consumed me yesterday had burned away an unseen weight I'd been carrying. My energy felt clearer, my vibration less tethered to the remnants of heartbreak. It was a new day, and I was nearly halfway through filling up my passport pages. I had a rental car for a few weeks and had pinned a seaside villa near Cefalù to book—if I stayed.

Logging into my bank account, I hesitated, bracing for the worst. Yet, to my surprise, the balance remained in the black. I still had half of my savings left and hadn't touched the personal loan or credit cards. A flicker of possibility sparked: maybe I should continue. Did I have the will?

Full-on spontaneous, solo travel was draining me. I needed more balance. Structure, without suffocation. Company, without obligation. What if I joined a tour or tried to meet up with another friend? No, I didn't want to reach out to anyone I knew—overlapping with Jeannine was an accident, not the plan. Instead of immediately researching flights home, I googled "last-minute group trips." If I eliminated some of my headaches, like logistical planning and decision fatigue, maybe I could keep going.

Why Not India? My mind inquired.

Uh, because I don't want to go to India, I replied.

I wasn't entirely sure why I resisted the idea so much—I knew the country had delicious cuisine, a rich cultural heritage, and diverse landscapes. Maybe it felt a little religious for me. Was I on a pilgrimage?

Regardless, the sign from Jeannine's apartment kept flashing in my psyche. *Why Not India?* It asked again. Maybe a dramatic change in environment would be good for me. But if I were to seek out a quieter destination for spiritual reflection and introspective meditation, I would head to Japan: that was top of my list. The Zen practices, elegant structure, and respect for the order of life appealed to me—I would choose manicured stone gardens and bonsai trees over the dusty, busy streets of India.

To appease my curiosity, I decided to look at flights and group tours with Intrepid Travel for both destinations. I'd gone on a safari with Intrepid in Tanzania and had a credit from a separate canceled trip. Oh, Africa—another destination that *always* called to me, as if I'd lived there in another lifetime.

But immediately, Africa was out. South Africa, Mozambique, Madagascar, Botswana, Congo. It was high tourist season, and everywhere was top price or sold out, including flights.

Japan was possible, though. There were interesting tours with last-minute spaces available, specifically in the central region around Kyoto, the cultural capital, which would be a priority for me. Autumn would be an incredible time to visit, with vibrant fall foliage draping the temples and mountains, temperate weather, and hot ramen bowls to cuddle up with at the end of the day.

But I also needed to investigate India. I'd spent about a month in Nepal, volunteering and trekking the Annapurna Circuit, so I didn't fancy focusing on northern India. I knew that I would want to see Jaipur—it was home to The Palace of the Wind, which resonated with me. While on a camelback trek with Heather in Morocco the fall before, our guide had named me Azu Tenabaunt, which meant First Daughter of the Wind. I came to understand it was because when I introduced myself as Whitney, they thought I said Windy. Oh, well—it stuck.

Jaipur is also called The Pink City, and as a girl who had never embraced pink, I thought I needed to. After all, I was trying to awaken my femininity. India's Golden Triangle tour seemed to cover this and more.

Time to look at flights and dates. I *could* make Japan happen, and I liked the idea of it. But India was undeniably more in flow. Half as expensive, half the distance on the map, and seamless with timing. I would need to be in Delhi in two weeks for the group's departure, which meant I'd need to return my rental car only one day early. Plus, there were ten spots available in India, which meant I would be joining a partial group. As much as I wanted to choose Japan, my intuition sang India.

I signed up.

Yes. I wouldn't be alone. I wouldn't be in charge. I could sit back and just experience it. All of this research made me realize how much environment affects your energy—from expectations to reality, even the idea of a place can change your vibration.

Page number four was now planned. I continued to search Asian destinations for logistical reasons, and read about Thailand, Cambodia, and the Philippines. I speculated about things I'd *never* done: I'd never spent any consecutive days or nights on a boat, and I wondered what it felt like to be suspended between land masses, floating while you slept. There was a catamaran sailing tour around the islands near Phuket that caught my interest, which departed three weeks after my tour in India concluded.

Interesting gap, I thought.

It felt full of possibility, but not daunting. If I signed up for the sailing adventure, I'd have book-end tours planned and still have space for solo spontaneity. I liked that. It felt like an honest balance.

Done—Dusty India and Watery Thailand were both booked. Pages four and six were planned, with five and seven still open. Plus, my credit paid for *both* tours. Hallelujah.

I never even checked flights home; that idea had been a desperate distraction. Although a dramatic return to safety might be enticing, I needed to keep going. And there was one place in the world I'd been wanting to visit more than anywhere—it was usually considered too far and too expensive, but it never hurts to look, right? I wondered… if I flew from Delhi to New Zealand, landing somewhere in the South Island, drove north to Auckland, and then flew to Thailand from there, could that work? Not exactly an efficient flight pattern, but I wondered if it was possible.

I was nearly squealing at the top of my lungs, bouncing around the diplomatic suite as the Expedia page loaded with flight prices and availability. *No way.* It was hard to believe, but *fuck* yes and no less. I would go to *New Zealand.* I could rent a car there for three weeks without a tour or agenda, which was perfect. India on a tour, New Zealand on my own, Thailand sailing with a group. I couldn't have planned this better if I had been working with a travel agent years in advance—page number six was sorted. I was falling in love with quick decisions, big or small. I was learning that all you can do is make choices with the information you have in the moment; if the situation changes in the future, you have the free will to make a new choice. But right here, still in my bathrobe and sitting at the board table as if I were a diplomat myself, these were my choices. I was rising from the ashes, and the resurrected vibe felt like confidence. What about page number seven? Without hesitation, I banished the thought. Best to leave that one open to fate.

I wandered around the suite with my coffee before packing up my belongings and departing for Cefalù. Moving my laptop to the head position of the boardroom table, I imagined myself leading a meeting, surrounded by influential government leaders and business executives. If all eyes were on me and I had their attention to pitch anything I wanted, what would I be sharing with them? *What vision would you share if you were given a room filled with everyone and everything you needed to bring it to life?*

Food for thought for my drive. I was off.

THE NEXT MORNING, I settled into the modest kitchen of my rented beach bungalow, the scent of salt and sun lingering in the air. With a flick of the remote, I tuned the TV to VH1 Italia. As the familiar pulse of nineties beats filled the room, I found myself dancing barefoot across the cool tile floor, a carefree rhythm guiding me as I prepared breakfast in my pajamas. This was my first lodging since I'd left the US that had a kitchen, and I hadn't realized how much I missed cooking. The day before, I'd stopped at a charming farmers' market perched along the cliffside coast, filling my basket with vibrant ingredients: farm-fresh eggs, rustic rosemary and thyme bread, crisp greens, handmade pasta, pesto, salamis, cheeses, and a kaleidoscope of sun-ripened fruits and vegetables. And, of course, a few bottles of local wine.

That day, I decided to do *nothing*. The villa was rented for a week, and I didn't want to go further than the beach. No sightseeing or city exploring. No long restaurant meals or seeing where a random direction would lead. Just nourishing food, reviving my yoga routine, and maybe a nap.

For weeks, I had been in constant motion, driven by an unspoken urgency to keep moving, always chasing the next experience as if stillness meant stagnation. But then I'd hit a wall—*hard*. I had begun to understand that long-term travel required a different rhythm, one that allowed for intentional pauses and days set aside for recalibration. I could navigate a wide range of social interactions, but solitude was my true recharge.

I was learning that sometimes doing nothing was the most productive thing I could do, provided it was a choice, not a default. That day, I drew a line in the sand: I would not leave.

My 5-Year Plan workbook was on the table, a parting gift from my dad which I hadn't cracked open yet. I had no desire to plan my future, but maybe it was time to start thinking of it again. *What type of life do I want to build? What are my priorities?* I was sure the workbook could pique my curiosity.

Before I dove in, though, it was finally time to check my email and WhatsApp messages from home. With this rollercoaster still bucking me around by the hour, I couldn't even begin to answer the simple question, "How are you doing?"—still, it would be nice to see life updates from others.

I'd received an email from Jeannine. She was still reeling from our unexpected rendezvous in Switzerland—she looked at the pictures and thought of me often. Framebridge was rolling right along, she reported, and business was starting to pick up for the winter. Snow was flying, lots of it. The loft missed me, but had been full of friends spending the night as they passed through town. She missed me, too, but hoped more than anything that I was happy.

I miss you, too, girl.

An email from Heather followed, full of wedding updates. The exact ceremony site and date had been decided: June 2017, in Arezzo, Italy, a two-hour train ride from Rome. There were accommodations onsite, and she'd set aside a room for me. She also sent links for bridesmaid dresses and, as MOH, would like me to select my favorite first.

Oh! More shopping.

Finally, an email from my parents. They'd made a daily habit of checking "Find my Friends" to see where I was, and had been treating it as a video game: where in the World is Whitney? Everyone at home was doing well and had been asking about me. Mom was busy with fall clients, and the horses were healthy. Dad had been flying a lot lately and had recently gone to Canada for a fishing trip. They looked forward to seeing me for the holidays and waited every day for a phone call. I missed the farm. I missed my parents. I desperately wanted a hug. But no, not yet.

Life, I thought. *It changes, but it goes on. Other people's lives go on as normal, even though mine feels suspended, floating in a moment that's neither past nor future. I'm starting not to resent that anymore, though.* In fact, I liked it. For now, silence was sacred.

Stepping away from the noise, social media, outside opinions, and the expectations of others wasn't isolation, it was preservation. This moment was about deepening my relationship with the one person I was just beginning to truly know—myself.

With that, I closed my laptop, silently sent them all love, tucked my workbook under my arm with a blanket and coffee, and sauntered down my private cypress tree-lined driveway to the beach. Swaying with the Italian pop tunes in my head, I needed expansive views before transitioning into future focus.

One day of doing nothing became two, then three. I hadn't realized just how much I'd needed a break from being in public. I felt safe on this secluded property and went between my garden and the beach, dipping into the sea and walking along its shore. It was heavenly to sleep late, ignore my makeup bag, and enjoy a few extra glasses of wine sitting by my outdoor fire pit.

Due to its powerful, mesmerizing effects, fire is the ultimate meditation partner—simply watching the flames induces relaxation. We're wired to find the pattern in things, but because fire is impossible to predict, our brain gives up trying and simply relaxes. Feeling Kali by my side, I held a burning ceremony for things I was ready to release. Watching words such as *codependent* and *fear* curl and burn on small pieces of paper was remarkably healing.

I also texted with my dates so far. The Guide encouraged me to seek out his community here, assuring me there were plenty of willing partners to escort me to a party. I was flattered, but no—I was happy to scale back and continue learning about myself one-on-one. Speaking to The Duke was like a continued conversation with an old friend. We had solid rapport and support for each other; he understood my need to *go* and respected it. My heart was still raw, and I needed to have tender gloves on. My walls were up, and that was okay.

WITH TWO DAYS left to experience Cefalù before driving west to Trapani, I ventured back into society. Cefalù is a picturesque beachside town with a walking-only historic center and a famous twin-towered cathedral. Locally owned restaurants and shops, colorful craft markets, and white buildings all nestle between the turquoise sea and the gently rolling hillside.

I was out and about for a few reasons: I felt rejuvenated and eager to explore, I'd run out of food, and, finally, I had a date. Settling into a quiet seaside restaurant, I found a private spot beneath blue-and-white striped awnings with yellow flowers painted on the weathered wood tabletop. As I waited, I watched seagulls glide effortlessly above the shore while small children danced with the waves, their laughter rising and falling like the tide. I felt content, grateful that I had taken the time to rest and realign. I was looking forward to introducing myself to someone new. *Who was Whitney today?*

My afternoon fling was with The Sailor, an American Navy Officer stationed in Italy. He happened to be from Minnesota, and I was looking forward to spending time with someone who understood what the Midwest felt like in the fall and how to make a real Bloody Mary. I wasn't nervous about going to a club or wondering about a language barrier; I was just a girl, sitting by the sea, waiting for a boy.

The Sailor introduced me to Negronis. I'll never forget the first sip of the delicious, bitter cocktail. I'll also never forget following his lead and drinking three of them without lunch. Feeling a little too comfortable with my man from America, I relaxed into sarcastic banter and extra rounds. It was wonderful; his international gossip could have fueled a live mic night at any comedy house, but his broad chest housed a beautifully romantic heart. He was taller and more muscular than any of my dates, with buzzed hair and a paler complexion. A very handsome Navy man indeed.

"So, besides the little you shared on your Tinder profile, tell me about yourself, Whitney," he said.

I shared my story, and he said, "Big changes for such a young gal."

"I'm getting pretty comfortable with change, that's for sure."

"I've been in the Navy since I was eighteen and haven't questioned it once, so I can't say I know where you're at. But it sounds like you're finding your way. Maybe you'll even see the light and realize it's way more fun to be a Viking fan than a follower of those dingy Packers?"

"Oh. Those are fighting words, mister. Don't get me started on the Hall of Famers, championship records, and the fact that we're one of the only professional sports teams in the world owned by the fans and not some billionaire wannabe player."

"The stock options are dope, but Green Bay? Call y'all crazy for being outside in that cold, game after game. Obviously I'm no stranger to bitter winter weather, but we have a *dome*."

"How's the season going? I haven't watched a single game."

After that, we got lost chatting football, Thanksgiving traditions, nieces and nephews, and speculating about the next time we might both be stateside. I relaxed in his presence, melting into the familiarity of our conversation. They say laughter is good for the soul, but its true power isn't understood until you've endured its absence. Letting go in a fit of real, belly-deep laughter felt like medicine—simple, honest, and long overdue.

After lunch, we strolled the cobblestone streets of the medieval city and found ourselves at the foot of a famous cathedral. The doors were open and a children's choir was rehearsing, the soft melody of innocence floating through the air. Linking arms, we ascended the sweeping stone staircase, our steps slow. Inside the aged wooden doors, we found seats among the pews. There were a few tourists inside taking pictures, mostly parents and locals near the front, coaxing their offspring to stay in place.

I tilted my head back, letting my gaze drift over the intricate mosaic ceiling as my imagination ran wild. What must it have been like to live in that era, to walk the earth at the time as Christ? Perhaps Christ, in some form, was present even now—after all, who's to say where history ends, and myth begins? Or that legend isn't certainty? I suppose it's a matter of perspective and perception.

Diving into religion and spirituality seems to be a terrain of paradox. Faith asks us to believe in the unseen, yet scholars demand proof. Spirituality encourages freedom and personal truth, while religion can sometimes feel like a list of rules.

And then there are universal spiritual laws, which are not confined to any one religion, but reflected in many. These laws are considered fundamental truths about the nature of existence, consciousness, and energy, transcending specific doctrines or belief systems. Perhaps it's not clarity we're meant to find, but wonder; not answers, but the courage to keep asking.

Fascinating. We have a mind to question things, intuition that whispers beyond logic, bodies to taste and feel, and hearts that pulse in harmony with the universe. Faith, dreams, and the quiet knowing within us all interact in ways we can only begin to grasp—and that's just what we can identify. Beyond our labels, beyond our understanding, an infinite realm of possibility exists, one that hints at something far greater than we yet perceive.

Slightly tapping my left leg, The Sailor brought me out of my head and my focus back to the present moment. Sitting in the pew, right by his side, in this majestic church. Motioning towards a side door, we made a silent exit as the song continued to ring through the tall and arched holy chamber. After we were clear of the exterior walls, he stopped on a stair below me and grabbed my waist, smoothly pulling me in for a playful kiss. As if in on the game, the warm air danced my hair around us and flipped The Sailor's hat right off his head. He quickly bent down to retrieve it and I looked up toward the sky. Above us, a beautiful elderly woman perched on her tiny balcony, observing the world around her. She noticed us, but paid as much attention as she would to the pigeons—I wondered how many scenes she'd watched from that exact spot. Closing my eyes, I visualized her point of view, and saw a straight line to the sea: endless waves and sky. No wonder the happenings of strangers below seemed unimpressive.

My date with The Sailor and my Negroni haze ended a few hours later. He told me a local legend in which a man, possibly now a ghost, ventured out every evening to the farthest rock on the point, where only the truly committed fishermen spent their days. The man called out to the water for his long-lost love to join him—a siren call to a mermaid, one might say—until the sun set, every single night. With honesty in his eyes, this Midwest Navy man proclaimed he would have a love like that someday. And I trusted he would.

For now, he was the siren call that I'd needed. A voice that connected me to a little piece of the Midwest, to a little piece of home.

A FEW DAYS later, on a calm and beautiful day with light clouds overhead, I drove inward, passing heritage vineyards and hillsides dotted with farmhouses and endless stone fences, away from the crystal-clear shoreline. I was en route to a rented apartment in Trapani, which seemed like a lovely town on the west coast. It was also a port for boats going to the Favignana islands. Back in Paris, when I Googled images of Sicily before booking my plane ticket, these exact islands were featured in the pictures that drew me here; the desire to see them for myself directed me to my next destination.

Being in no rush to get there, I decided to veer off course to the south and visit Di Giovanna Estate Vineyards for lunch, then walk around the Greek ruins at Tempio di Segesta on my way.

"Ciao, signorina," a charming *maître d'* greeted me as I walked through the metal gates.

"Ciao," I returned.

"What brings you to Di Giovanna today? May I interest you in some wine tasting or lunch?" He was clean and well-dressed, a little taller than I, and boasted a warm smile.

"Yes to both. I read about your 'Picnic in the Vineyards' option and am interested in learning more about that." The sun was out and the smell of fresh harvest hung in the air. The grapes were gone, marinating in chambers to ferment into wine, but the vines still held the allure of flavor.

After a quick conversation, I was packed and ready to go on my picnic, instructed to walk until a spot under an olive or fruit tree called me to stay. I was armed with a wicker basket filled with Sicilian gourmet products, including breads, olives, cheese, prosciutto, fresh fruit, and of course, my choice of a bottle of Vurria wine. I selected the Syrah, thinking the bold tannins would fit this autumn afternoon.

What a lucky girl to be here. Settled under an olive tree on the hillside with a view into the valley below, I stretched out on my blanket and unpacked my treasures. Leaving Colorado, I wanted to experience the opposite of married life—the opposite of monogamy and consistency—and get a tourist pass for a thirty-year-old dating virgin. *Check.*

There was an invigorating energy in meeting someone new—the anticipation, the unpredictability. I never quite knew what I would say. Conversations were surprising and held a certain spontaneity that simply didn't exist with someone who had known me for years, who knew all my secrets.

Kissing felt like a thrill ride, a heady rush of sensation and discovery. I had almost forgotten that no two kisses were ever the same. But sleeping beside someone? That was a different matter entirely. It still felt too intimate. Both my body and subconscious resisted it, as though dreamtime required solitude—a sacred space where I could retreat and protect my peace.

Tanya and technology were instrumental in allowing me to connect with a variety of people. Choosing who to see in person was a workout for my intuition, though, as a profile doesn't give you a lot to go on. Each date became an exercise in self-acceptance, an opportunity to relinquish the habit of molding myself into what I thought someone else might want. Instead of striving to impress or please, I had embraced curiosity and asked more questions about *them.* When I stopped trying to prove something, I noticed they had the freedom to show up more authentically, too. Dating was proving to be an interesting, multilayered experience, one that was reshaping me in ways I hadn't anticipated.

With a happy wine glow and full belly, I drove the hour or so to Tempio di Segesta. Once I arrived, I appreciated the long walk up the staircase to the ruins. I was also pleasantly surprised to find only a small group of students and a teacher exploring the grounds besides myself.

I sensed a magic in the columns, dating back to the fifth century B.C.—the wind whispered secrets as it slithered around them. They have a complex history: some say displaced Trojan citizens built them, and some believe they were constructed by an indigenous Sicilian tribe.

After walking around the ruins and marveling at their prominence and design, I wondered how much life they'd witnessed, how many conversations had been held in this courtyard, surrounded by strong archways. Traditionally, arches symbolize strength and support, but in mythology, they also represent elevating the spirit and mind towards higher ideals. Finding a welcoming bench, I sat down to ponder such theories.

I wished I understood the hermetic alchemy lessons from teachers like Thoth or Hermes better. I wasn't destined to be a scholar, but Dr. Grundland's comment about having a philosopher's soul stuck with me. What did that mean for me?

"Mi scusi?"

"Yes, hello," I replied, looking up to find the teacher from the group. She seemed to be in her late forties or early fifties, with short, tidy hair and a flowing outfit of off-whites accented with a bright pink scarf. Not a school uniform.

"May I sit?" she asked in proper English.

"Please do. Is that your class over there?" I gestured to the loose, exploring children.

"For the day. I'm a historian who chaperones the local students here once a year as part of their history studies. This bench, tucked away over here, is always my rescue as they have their lunch and are free to roam."

"Oh, I'm sorry, I can leave. Would you like your privacy?"

"No, no. Not necessary at all. In fact, I'm pleased to see a visitor here. Usually, the tourists go to the larger ruins on the south of the island."

"Yes, I researched those as well. But this just happens to be on my drive today, so it's a bit fortuitous."

"Ah, the unexpected stops. Don't you just love those?" She smiled.

"I'm traveling right now by hopping from one to another," I laughed.

"Success?"

"Hits and misses. More hits, though. I almost turned around and went home, but then a piece of home found me here and I see it as a clear sign to keep going," I said.

"What home are you talking about, and how did it find you here, in Sicily?"

"Home is where I was born, in Wisconsin. It found me here on a date—I met a man from Minnesota, and spending time with him made me *feel* at home without being there."

"Fantastico. Ask and receive, right? Almost like you manifested him out of thin air. I believe home is on the inside. See, I am from Egypt, but history has taken me all around the world, so I've had to accept home is wherever I am."

"I'm beginning to agree, I think. It's unbelievable how connected you can feel to something, even if you're physically far apart." I looked out at the ruins. "Egypt—now that's a place I would love to visit."

"It'll welcome you when you do," she smiled again and elegantly rose from the bench, pressing down her skirt.

"Have a wonderful afternoon. And thank you for the chat," I said, rising to thank her.

Leaning in with the customary two kisses to say farewell, she said, "Meant to be. You may have just provided the sign I needed as well."

"Best of luck."

She walked back to her students.

I had no idea what sign I'd provided, but I supposed that information wasn't meant for me. Feeling energized from our brief conversation, I decided to finish up my rounds at the ruins. Walking always inspired my thoughts, and something she'd said still bounced around in my mind: that I'd *manifested* The Sailor. Surely not. Someone like me couldn't have such a profound influence on my reality. But what if she was right? Ask and receive. I was asking for home—begging for it, actually—and the universe sent a piece of it back to me. Certainly not in a way I would have expected, but undeniably, nevertheless.

What about the other dates? When I first landed, I had been craving bold, sexual experiences. The Guide had provided a few check marks there. Then, my heart had called out for a chivalrous prince, and I'd found The Duke. And now, when I needed a piece of familiarity, The Sailor. Check marks, all three. *Damn. Thank you, universe. How powerful is that? How incredible?* I was trying to connect the dots, thinking back to all the books I'd read on energy and spiritual laws... could it all be real?

Instinctively, I grabbed my left ribcage where my tattoo lived. Part of the acronym I had tattooed was *MM*, standing for "manifest magic." When I'd gotten the tattoo, I had known it was relevant to me and believed our thoughts matter, but maybe the phrase meant more than that. Maybe it was a reminder of what I could *do*—and that I needed to live the message again to truly believe it! I looked back and forth at the countryside. What else was possible? And what other secrets did my tattoo hold?

I wondered if my next date was part of this beautiful puzzle. Yes, I had a date lined up for Trapani. I didn't have an intention with this one, but I was just excited to continue meeting new people. He was a true local, so Tanya and I called him The Mayor; as someone born and raised in the area, I was sure he knew a secret or two about the town and its inhabitants. Similar to all my other dates, the texting conversation was minimal, but enough that my gut told me to show up—something was there. Tanya agreed. She'd proved to be a steadfast ally. I had been skeptical at first, but she helped me clarify my desires and wade through the muck of self-doubt and overthinking. Whatever the experience or lesson from The Mayor was, I was ready.

MY APARTMENT IN Trapani was a treasure chest of old-world charm. Every corner of it breathed history: wrought iron railings curled like vines, filigreed picture frames adorned the walls, and handwoven oriental rugs softened the wood floors. Sunlight spilled generously through the dining and living room windows, bathing the space in a golden hue. I was falling deeply for this island day by day, drawn to the intoxicating mix of romance and rebellion that came with its disconnection from the mainland. Life here felt tucked away from time itself; in the quiet simplicity of daily rituals, shopping for produce, and folding laundry, I was finding magic in the mundane again.

The Mayor had promised to bring everything we'd need for dinner and casually asked if I ate fish. I perched on the windowsill, watching the horizon burn with the sun's descent, waiting. When he arrived, my pulse quickened as I crossed the fifteen steps to the door. Dressed in a flowing sundress with only a touch of makeup, black stilettos, and of course, my rings, I opened it, heart steady, lips curled into a smile. Thinking back to The Guide and his lessons around anticipation, I remained quiet for a beat, taking in the sight of him.

"Buonasera," he said. "May I come in?"

"Please do." I opened the door, sashaying to the side, and he stepped in, linen grocery tote in hand, and leaned in for the two-kiss reception. He lingered a bit on the first cheek, and I stayed close enough to absorb his scent of cedar wood and spice, until he landed the second kiss with a little more intention. His soft hazel eyes gave me a look that made it clear he was *interested*. He wore a crisp, collared blue shirt, fitted jeans, clean shoes, and a light leather jacket. His hair was a bit longer than his picture, with a beach wave that framed his face. My cool girl attitude fluttered away, and my energy swirled. Everything in me was intrigued. Aroused, too.

His body language was confident but not rushed, and his style was youthful but chic. We chatted while he cooked dinner. It was flirtatious, although a bit bumpy. At one point, he put his hand up, saying, "Let's just be for a moment, Americans talk too much." This made us both laugh. He was fluent enough in English, but since it was his third language, I needed to speak plainly. I loved the slower pace and simplicity it demanded.

By the time dinner was over, words mattered little. As a true chef (though not by trade), he insisted on tidying up the kitchen. I returned to my seat in the window, though the sea was dark and the sky dotted with stars. He came up behind me and laced his hands around my waist, kissing the curve of the left side of my neck, just behind my ear. It was sensual and even tickled. I loved it. Closing my eyes slightly and leaning backwards into him, I consented. When I turned around to face him, he knew we were on the same page. His nimble fingers began undoing the buttons at the bust of my dress, one by one, until his hand found my bare hips. Hoisting me up onto the windowsill and into the night air, my legs wrapped around him, our lips never separating. Not taking the time to fully undress, yet thoroughly exploring each other, our bodies entwined like twister players as he moved me up against the interior wall en route to the front bedroom.

It didn't feel like the first time our bodies had met. It was as if we were long-lost lovers reuniting after being continents, or lifetimes, apart. It was as if our auras were doing the communicating, removing the individual protective shields and enhancing the flow of passion. And that kiss.... There is an art to kissing, a rhythm between give and take, lead and follow, and he was adept at it all.

Afterwards, we sat mostly dressed in the window again, finishing our wine from dinner. The conversation was captivating, rolling from generational expectations—family and purpose were very important to him—to resumes and career reinvention. He said something that particularly resonated: "You don't have to be a professional at something, educated and experienced, to succeed. You simply need to *know* you can do it. And so you shall."

This, I responded, was always how I'd felt; I'd never limited myself because I didn't have the right pedigree to go for it, and I believed mental conviction played a big role in success. After an hour of verbal stimulation, we fell into kissing again and heard a group of teenagers laughing below in the shadows around the beach. Although unrelated to us, their laughter grabbed our attention. Looking down at the waves, I noticed the stars reflecting on the water.

"As above, so below," I said.

"Shall we test that theory?" he asked.

"What do you mean?" I asked, thinking philosophically, not literally.

"Sex was great up here, looking down. Why don't we go in the water and try it looking up?"

I nearly leapt out of the window in a giddy dive, but I let my eyes do the talking. We simultaneously went for our shoes and down to the beach. There were other people around, but it was very private; we found an easy place among the rocks to leave our clothes, and into the water we went.

The cool currents danced around our bodies, and in the midnight light, we blended like the sand below our feet. The intimacy was gentle, feminine, almost morphing with the tide. We both appreciated the rawness of it—being outside, embracing the wild of the darkness. The moonlight blanketed the bit of skin above water, and I saw my apartment windows twinkling in the distance, repeating out loud, "As above, so below."

AFTER OUR FIRST date, The Mayor and I continued seeing each other. The next evening, he picked me up and we dined at a small waterfront restaurant. We barely made it through the meal before making more plans. A local band was playing two nights later, and he invited me to go dancing with his friends. I couldn't possibly say no. We decided I shouldn't continue traveling south as planned, and for the first time on my journey, I stayed—I stayed for him. I stayed to keep experiencing us.

When my apartment rental ended, I moved into his family's unoccupied beach house just south of the city. Everywhere we went, he ran into someone he knew, living up to his mayoral nickname. His friends welcomed me with youthful stories, explanations of local delicacies, and enthusiasm for friendship, which reminded me of the impact of community. In Vail, I had a wonderful, deep, and treasured circle like that. I knew I needed to be on my own, but I still longed for that feeling of belonging.

Unlike my previous dates, I hadn't consciously manifested The Mayor, but it must have been what my heart called for: to *feel* again. A faint scent of love, of belonging. Something in me opened and settled because, without hesitation, I slept next to him—all night, peacefully. I loved waking up to his presence, seeing his bare chest rise with each restful breath. Our mornings quickly morphed into a routine: with minimal talking, but paying sweet attention to the other, we would have sex, make coffee, and get ready for the day—he for work and I for exploring.

One day, I finally set off for Favignana, the island that had brought me here. There was something extraordinary about following through on an idea, watching a dream take shape in the tangible world. As humans, we're wired to imagine, to project, to paint places in our minds before we ever set foot in them. But I'd learned the trick: use the vision to get you there, but once you arrive, surrender. Let the place introduce itself, instead of dimming its true personality with the burden of expectations.

Favignana was proof of this fact. I expected to find a beautiful cove of turquoise water and relax in the sunshine—instead, the wind greeted me with wild arms, and every cell in my body itched to move. I was too alive to sit still. I found myself weaving along hidden trails, leaping from one rocky path to the next, threading through the island's secluded inlets and stone pillars. The energy of the past few days had begun to unshackle something in me, and my limbs, my mind, my spirit, all stretched into movement.

Eventually, I found a bench to rest on and unwrapped the sandwich I'd packed that morning. I'd always been a diversified diner. In my career, I would hire chefs to cater events and even did a few covert critique missions. But I loved everything from classic diners to Michelin-starred restaurants, from food trucks to avant-garde tasting menus. Thinking back to the proverbial "food on my plate" discussion with my volunteer kids, I realized that when you're rediscovering or rebuilding a life, it's best to be mindful: go slow, be deliberate, and keep it simple.

That day, I chose simplicity—bread, butter, prosciutto, cheese, and a pickle on the side. I'd also begun to nourish myself with things that couldn't be wrapped in paper: a sense of self-worth, curiosity, resilience, salty tears, sun-drenched smiles, and yes, a metaphorical magic wand, always within reach.

Finishing my sandwich and worn out from the impromptu exercise, I noticed an ache growing in my stomach. Not of exhaustion, but of approaching farewell. My flight to India was in two days, and I needed to spend the final night near the airport in Catania, on the opposite side of the island. The thought of leaving clawed at my chest. I didn't want to. But I must have been *meant* to; if I were still rolling without a plan, maybe I would have chosen to stay. But because I had prebooked the tour, I didn't have that option. My journey was pointing me onward, and I knew I needed to trust that. Our love affair was destined to expire, but we had one more night.

After returning from my journey, the sunset looked as if it had been painted by Aphrodite herself. Layers of vivid pink, orange, and yellow overlapped in the distance and swirled with soft clouds. Back near his house, we sat curled up on the beach, nestled against a dune for shelter from the wind, watching tall grasses wave goodnight to the sun. The Mayor wrapped his legs around me, and I leaned into the warmth of his arms and chest. Gently, he traced his finger in slow circles around my navel.

"What are you doing?" I whispered.

"This. Your manipura. It's on fire. You're full of courage and glowing yellow."

Tears welled in my eyes, but I kept them fixed on the ocean. His words pierced something inside me, dissolving my doubt and replacing it with clarity. I felt seen—not as a role or an idea, but as myself. Just a woman, embracing her power. Whispers of "Windy" Whit had started to sway in the tree branches, and the message came again: *Keep going.*

ONCE AGAIN, MY Thule bag was packed and I was ready to roll. I returned the rental car unscathed—another satisfying victory. From the labyrinthine backroads in France to the swift precision of the autobahn, and now the winding curves of the Sicilian coast, I had handled it all, manual transmissions included. I was starting to believe there was, quite honestly, nothing I couldn't navigate.

So much had transpired in such a condensed sliver of time. I'd never subscribed to time as a rigid construct—though we created it for order and communication, in reality, it's fluid. Age, for instance, is a measurement of time, but not of character; maturity doesn't adhere to a clock. In just six weeks since leaving New York—and mere days since I had nearly surrendered to doubt—I had expanded in ways that felt like lifetimes folded into one. And here I stood, confident and exhilarated. Ready to fly to India.

With three pages filled and four to go, my passport wasn't just accumulating stamps, it was collecting stories, written with unexpected encounters and unforgettable characters. Europe had given me what it could, but it was time to embrace a new land. It was time for a new view. And it was time to suspend Tanya's wise counsel. My heart and body were a little overwhelmed and it felt right to grant her some well-deserved PTO. Exploring my sexual freedom had been exhilarating; being with different men allowed me to see different sides of me. I felt neither anxiety nor guilt over my choices, but I was ready for a reprieve.

At the airport, I watched the planes ascend and descend in rhythmic procession. Watching them transported me to childhood: still in diapers, standing on the weathered picnic table on our farm with my eyes to the sky, watching Dad's plane pass overhead. That simple memory stirred an ache in my chest. I missed my parents.

On impulse, I checked my email and smiled at three new messages from them, filled with affectionate questions and lovingly mundane updates. Their words read like gentle nudges: a quiet plea for a reply—any reply. They didn't want much, just something more than tracking a red dot across a digital map as proof of my existence. Little did they know where they would see my next ping radiating from. I wish I had a portal to see the look on their faces when my dad announced, "She's in India. INDIA!" I pictured them pulling out the old steel globe, fingers tracing across continents, spinning toward a place that felt impossibly far.

I also yearned to text my girlfriends for their reactions to my recent dating escapades. I longed for their insight, their laughter, and their grounding perspectives. Beneath the surface, I sensed that these encounters weren't merely about romance; meeting men had become the medium through which the universe was communicating, delivering signs, and quietly urging me to recognize patterns. What if we really were co-creators of our reality? Was I manifesting these connections, these echoes of desire, through the frequencies I was projecting?

Still, despite the pull toward my family and friends, I knew I had to hold the line. The space between me and everyone else felt uncomfortable, even painful at times. But it was necessary. This particular path was one I had to walk alone, undefined as it was. Whatever this was—healing, awakening, reinvention—demanded solitude. I made a quiet promise to myself: *Protect your peace.*

So I walked down another jet bridge, unreachable by design, and boarded another flight.

DELHI FELT LIKE a fascinating new planet. At first it was busy, loud, and full of chaos: thick, overlapping electrical cords hung between the buildings, nearly blocking the sky. Scooters and rickshaws whizzed in every direction, and there was barely an inch of storefront without advertisements on it. But when I stopped trying to navigate the endlessly crowded streets and started going with the flow of the crowd, a calm wonderment settled in. I started noticing the details: vibrant colors from the mosaic lanterns and hand-woven rugs held their place amongst the dust, and I saw that the walls of the temples were carved with beautiful mandalas, lotus flowers, Bengal tigers, elephants, and *Om*. There were symbols everywhere.

It's fascinating how many esoteric messages exist in architecture, and how seemingly simple symbols can hold so much. Throughout history, symbols have been used to encode complex spiritual truths, carrying messages from the divine into the material world. They are found across all cultures, often sharing similar themes and meanings. Take the circle, for example—it could represent the Sun, Earth, one mind, first matter, complete connection, infinity, or a hula-hoop. Here, it seemed the carvings acted as guardians for the city's inhabitants, offering messages of peace and faith.

I certainly felt like a foreigner, but I was carrying a lightness with me and felt immediately connected to the rhythm of spirituality I sensed here. With daily bindis and street shrines, religion was more than a day of the week—it was a way of life. Dynasties and traditional customs were still influential, but there was a modern fever that seemed to have settled into the youth. I didn't fully understand why India yet, why Jeannine's sign had beckoned me to go, but I was grateful to be there.

I had a few days to myself before joining the group tour, which I spent meandering through the city by day and retreating to the quiet comfort of my hotel room each evening. The jet lag lingered, and the prospect of dining or dancing alone held little appeal. Cuddling up with my thoughts was company enough for now, and I protected a few evenings of solitude before stepping back into the energy of shared experiences and group dynamics.

"Let's go around the table and briefly introduce ourselves," our guide suggested on our first evening together. We were sitting at a few tables pushed together in the corner of our hotel's ornate rooftop lounge.

It was an eclectic group, and I specifically connected with Blake, a lady in her seventies from New Zealand and the only other solo traveler, and Alec and Anne, a newlywed couple from the UK, honeymooning their way to New Zealand, where they'd celebrate a second wedding. Blake was a film producer and had travelled the world for inspiration and culture immersion her entire life. Her parents had ignited this fire by, in her words, throwing her baby-self in a backpack and trekking everywhere. Alec was a very successful software engineer, and Anne was a language expert, moving from political interpretation to teaching. Completing the group were two friends from Canada in their fifties, and two couples: one from France, one from Vermont. I loved the mix and appreciated the group's intimacy—we were only at half capacity, so there'd be plenty of room everywhere we went, from seats on the bus to extra rooms at night. After introductions concluded and our guide explained our daily itinerary, we broke off into separate conversations.

"Your journey sounds very exciting," Blake began.

"A rollercoaster for sure. Seems like you're familiar with the idea."

"Are you keen to share more details? I'm always intrigued by a hero's journey." We covered the reasons why I left, and the destinations, dates, and highs and lows so far. She shared with me a few pivotal moments from her travels, home life in New Zealand, and her goal for this tour: to connect with Ganesha, the remover of obstacles.

Our banter had been supportive until she bluntly interjected, "It sounds like you simply replaced one form of adrenaline with another." I was taken aback.

"I did not. I'm on this trip to discover *new* things," I retorted. I was getting away from the adrenaline focused lifestyle. She continued, "So far it sounds very cinematic, yes, but certainly not a character film. Are you going to delve into internal transformation? Everything you've described has been external." I stared at her. I was diving into both—I was trying to focus on my feelings and listen to my heart. "I'm sorry, I don't agree with you. My goal has been to embrace a spherical approach to life and broaden my horizons, and I think I've been doing a pretty good job so far," I said as the heat flamed in my cheeks, full of conviction. She clearly didn't get it.

"Sure, but you're still existing on the same dimensional plane: physical, external. Being more spherical, as you put it, should include inward attention and the diversity of your mental and emotional self as well."

"I have been. I've been doing things that scare me, and I've been separating myself from external validation. And I guess that's why trips like this are solo," I said to calm my nerves. "I'm just trying to figure it out one day at a time."

"Sure—" I could tell she was only winding up.

"Well, so much to chat about, but I'm afraid the pillow calls my name."

She exhaled, "Good idea."

We took our cue; it was time for sleep, and the whole group followed suit.

Unsolicited opinions were one reason I wasn't staying in touch with anyone back home—I certainly didn't need a stranger being so judgmental about my choices. I also felt frustrated that I'd fallen right back into the pattern of justifying myself. I shouldn't care what she thought. And I didn't need her advice. My hot head hit the pillow hard. Thank goodness I was bone tired—tired enough to drown out my inner ranting and sleep.

ALL I HAD to do was set an alarm and be ready. Ganesha was already removing my obstacles; I had no other decisions to make. After enjoying a coffee and a small breakfast, all I had to do was get on the bus. Thank God, all the gods, I could finally sit back and relax. We explored an urban food tour through the markets of Delhi, where spices and tastes I'd never encountered before teased my senses. We also visited Jama Masjid, Delhi's oldest mosque, learned about the history of the Sikh religion at the Gurudwara Sis Ganj Sahib, and toured Humayun's Tomb. The first days were full of sensory overload and incredible discoveries; I loved learning about the history and unique characters that had carved India's chapters. I was taking in so much new information that I barely had space to focus on myself or my own life much at all. Blake and I exchanged small talk but refrained from intimate inquisition. I usually sat close to Alec and Anne on the bus and found our fascination with India to be very in sync.

We were in Jaipur now, and the day had been filled with various jewelry, textiles, and art bazaars. We'd visited a shop where we tried on and designed custom saris, stopped by the Hawa Mahal—the Palace of the Wind, which I had been especially excited about—before heading over to the Royal City Palace to meander through its extravagant rooms, secret passageways, and manicured gardens.

That evening, we added a special stop before dinner at my request: sapphire shopping. The group had readily agreed to the excursion, looking forward to browsing local gems and fine jewelry themselves. I wouldn't have the opportunity to visit a mine on this trip or go deeper into the adventure of the stone, but the chance to sit down with a local dealer—who our guide assured me had an honorable reputation—was perfect.

Maybe it was time to embrace new magic, I thought, looking down at my rings. I wasn't one for buying many souvenirs; I felt that true souvenirs, and what my money usually went toward, were experiences. But a sapphire from India because I was in India? That superseded normal travel purchases. I was on the hunt for a small, bright red ruby. Sapphires come in every color; a ruby is a sapphire in a specific shade of red.

Sitting down with the men at the store was intimidating at first. They guided me up three flights of stairs to the buying table and took their time bringing out the first tray of pouches. In my experience, loose stones are usually stored in parchment paper with their ID number and specifics—like carat weight, color, clarity, cut, etc.— noted in the corner. Prices are never divulged until you ask, and even then, they're usually not final.

But looking at the first round of options, I nearly laughed. I had explained what I was looking for, and they clearly didn't take me seriously. All stones have beauty; I wasn't trying to be rude. But the stones they brought out were cloudy, poorly cut, and maroon-ish—not what I had been looking for at all. The second tray they brought was the same, albeit with slightly larger stones. The third tray started to clear up, and the fourth finally had a few that caught my eye, though nothing particularly striking. The fifth tray had a stone included by mistake; I opened the pouch and saw not a ruby but a bright padparadscha, more pink than orange. Its sparkle was radiant; it danced with femininity and sass, matching the vibration I'd been emanating on this journey. Padparadscha means "lotus blooms," and blooming was I. After a little negotiating, I was sold. I purchased the unexpected treasure that represented *me* just as the store was closing.

I thanked my group for waiting as we departed. Still buzzing from the encounter, I felt both wise and respected; it was deeply gratifying to draw on a piece of my past and stand as an expert amid a roomful of underestimating glances. A fragment of my former self, the boss, was stirring back to life.

Though gemology no longer felt like my path forward, I had chased my thrills in the industry, and while it would always remain a part of me, something new was calling. I slipped the stone into my purse, savoring the quiet pull toward a new chapter.

By the fourth day, I finally relaxed into someone else planning the agenda: I stopped peppering our guide with questions over breakfast and started a habit of daily yoga and a little journaling. Sometimes I would practice in my room, and sometimes I would take a bath towel and find a private place on our hotel grounds to be outside. It was nice to quiet the mind and listen to my body, stretching or holding where needed. I was certainly not an instructor, but I had practiced enough to link my routines. Our group had taken notice, and now nearly half of them had started joining in on my practices, drawn to the rhythm I unknowingly set. I welcomed the company, and it boosted my ego to be in a low-stakes form of leadership again, guiding us from position to position.

That night, we practiced yoga atop a private palace as the sun dipped below the horizon. Our silhouettes, framed by the spikes, dots, and curves of the ornate railing, stood against a sky ablaze with deep orange hues, like a scene from a postcard. Below us, the city's energy simmered while a luminous moon began its ascent. Afterwards, I sat in a meditative perch, watching the changing of the celestial guards on my own.

My hands tingled, and the energy seemed to expand all around me. I just sat there bearing witness to the world and thought of nothing. For the first time in a long time, I was inspired to pray. I didn't feel the urge to bring my hands together, connecting them in front of my chest like I had when I was a child, or to have a premeditated prayer lined up, like gracing dinner or reciting the lord's prayer. It felt more like I picked up the phone to have a conversation; I was present with an open channel.

Dear Lord and Mother Earth, I began. *Hi. I feel you. I sense you in and around me. I'm grateful for that. I'm grateful for much, but I also know more change is coming. I pray to you for the courage and grace to let go of my professional past and face a new financial future. I pray you light a path for me, so that I may walk into a new world as a new me. Give me the conditions for reinvention and I promise I'll step into them; I want to trust this knowing inside me. Please help me.*

I sat in silence for a spell, as gentle tears filled my eyes. *Thank you,* I closed.

I couldn't explain it, but it felt like my words were welcomed. I bowed my head and stood to return to my room feeling light, liberated, and supported. If not in reality, in faith.

THE NEXT DAY would begin with an optional hot air balloon ride over the city, followed by an exploration of the Amer Fort, where elephants escorted tourists up the winding pathways and through the two-story entrance gates.

The elephants were magnificent: their gray skin was adorned with intricate paintings, their faces crowned with jeweled headpieces, and their backs draped with bright colored silks. I hoped with every part of me that they were treated with kindness and honored as equals. Elephants had always carried a profound symbolic presence in my life, embodying humility, wisdom, spirituality, and deep compassion. As a group, we chose to walk to the fort rather than ride these majestic beings in a silent gesture of respect for their dignity.

The fort is especially famous for its Sheesh Mahal, or Hall of Mirrors. Walking through the countless chambers of ornate design and intricate art took my breath away; staying close enough to one wall as we walked, I let my fingers trace the masterpiece. There was so much energy held in every piece—centuries of mystery, life, and secrets. Catching my reflection was inevitable in such a place, and almost frustrating; I wanted to appreciate the beauty around me, not be distracted by my unkempt hair and tired eyes. I finally wrapped a scarf around my head and concluded that time in front of a mirror was certainly not on the agenda.

After, we walked the streets in a crafty part of town. It's always inspiring to see art in the process of being made, and I was excited to wear my treasures to dinner that night. My new bracelets were made from wood, semi-precious gemstones, and lacquer.

We were staying at a heritage property and planned to dine with the descendant who would have been the regional king. The palace was incredible: peacocks roamed freely, and the high halls were covered with paintings, tapestries, ornate gold candle sconces, and mirrors. There were mirrors all throughout the palace—not like the mosaics in the hall, but full walls of custom-cut reflections. Stone pedestals supported artifacts, and full-sized stuffed animals lined the walkway. The local taxidermist must have been busy; there were hunting prizes, stuffed and positioned, everywhere.

After a friendly meet and greet, we all sat at a decadently set table in the courtyard. There was a mirror under each place setting, mirrored vases holding tall white flowers, and yes, a mirrored menu card. What was it with mirrors? I certainly saw the beauty in the light they sent around the room, prisms abound, but I was beginning to feel claustrophobic from my reflections.

"Have you been to the United States?" I asked the king. He sat prominently at the head of the table, wearing loafers and a jodhpuri suit. His dark hair matched dark features and framed a boisterous smile.

"I have. Two of my sons are at Penn State," he answered proudly, "I visit a few times a year. Americans, what do you think about the presidential election?"

Others quickly dove in with opinions. I hadn't thought about it at all, but from magazine covers to radio mentions, it proved difficult to get away from US politics anywhere in the world. As they debated the candidates, I wondered what it would be like to be a king here in India. Instead, I asked, "Taking it back a step, how do you all define being a leader?"

How's that for deeper focus? I thought, glancing at Blake.

As we discussed what the world needed from those with influence, I asked myself more questions: what did being a leader mean to me? What were the essential characteristics of leadership, and what did respect, power, or influence represent in my life? I knew I liked the collective feeling of importance, especially having experienced the lack of it recently. But did I deserve to be a leader of anyone anymore? Looking down at my plate only to be confronted with my face again, I angrily turned over the menu card and closed my eyes to get away from myself. Taking a deep breath, I thought, *Fine, then I will ask myself. Why does my own reflection send me running for the hills right now?* No understandable answers came to mind. I just felt an unexpected urge to cry.

Maybe Blake was right. Maybe I had more to internalize and learn about myself. Maybe there was something missing I needed to see before skipping ahead to the next phase of life.

I shoved down the volatile emotions and looming questions and looked up. Bright-eyed and fully focused on my companions, I enjoyed a long and delicious meal of local delicacies and got lost in the king's stories. Everyone chimed in with questions and bursts of laughter. It was a family meal made up of diverse backgrounds, varying future goals, and conflicting global outlooks. I smiled looking between my fellow diners and was grateful to be at the table.

THE SUN WAS shining as we walked the Old Quarter of the local village and stopped at a traditional rural temple. What the temple lacked in grandiosity, it more than made up for with intimate charm and humble beauty. With a few hours to wander on our own, I found my way into a small meditation chamber. Seeking solitude and space to think, I was called to it because I had to duck beneath a simple carved banister to walk inside. It had wooden cutout partitions with the flower of life depicted all around the room; clear glass windows representing various symbols of sacred geometry were at the top of each wall, and there were no crystals, gold, or mirrors in sight. Instead, it had a humble altar near the north wall with stairs before it and a few dark satin cushions on the ground. Sitting in the corner was an elderly man who looked to be well past eighty. I smiled at him, and he at me. I didn't feel called to approach the altar, but instead sat on a bench near him in the back. There was an intrinsic sense of balance in this small room, and my energy blended with the patterns that surrounded me.

I could hear other tourists walking by, chatting and snapping pictures. They passed the small door, not bothering to investigate the unassuming room; their voices echoed like little bird chirps bouncing off the glass. Light danced in through the windows as if fairies were putting on a play, and I peeked through the wooden cutouts, noticing only bits and pieces of the view outside. The perspective made me realize that sometimes you need a clear view to take in the big picture, and sometimes there's a lesson in seeing only one small piece of it. Maybe I needed mental wooden cutouts so I could refocus on specifics instead of fixating on the overwhelming scope of my life.

I needed to see the small screws on the blaring neon road sign— the screws that held it together. I settled my gaze on a large mandala engraved on a floor tile in front of the altar, trying to let my mind go blank. If my life was that neon sign, what did my screws say? What did they represent that I needed to focus on? What were the pieces that held me together, and were they the *right* ones?

I expected to feel calm and see visions of my family and various successes. But I quickly became antsy, as a montage of images from backcountry skiing to boarding airplane after airplane, to sexual encounters and lavish purchases laced my consciousness. My heart raced as every image flashed quickly—all I felt was adrenaline. Thrill after thrill... *Oh shit*, I thought. Maybe Blake was right? Even though I was seeking something different, I had still replaced adrenaline with adrenaline. I'd swapped athletic challenges for sexual extremes, and subbed in materialistic things for professional validation. All these activities had just flooded my nervous system with endorphins; the pendulum had shifted without moving beyond the same 3D identity. Everything I had been focusing on was external; I hadn't spent any time figuring out the answers to harder questions. If being a wife, a homeowner, and a professional didn't define me anymore, what did?

Silence. My mind went blank.

Even more alarming was the fact that I didn't even know what questions to ask to figure it out. I thought of my new aversion to the mirror. What was I afraid of seeing? What wasn't I ready to admit about myself?

I opened my eyes and recalibrated to my present surroundings, my head still spinning and fingers a little numb from sitting there for who knows how long. One thing I was sure of was that I was reluctant to focus on the details. I had been avoiding something, even if I didn't know what it was. But I finally understood Blake's point of view: it was time to go deeper. I needed to understand why things had happened—why I was here, traveling through India, caught between lives. I needed to understand *who* I was, not just what I was.

I shook out my legs and arms as I stood up from the bench. Taking a deep breath of gratitude for this tiny room, I found a smile and prepared to leave. I respectfully tilted my head to the gentleman in the corner, and, to my surprise, found him grinning ear to ear.

He stood and walked towards me, so short he would have been just above eye level if I had still been sitting. He handed me a single red rose that fit in the palm of my hand. Then he placed a small red bindi in between my eyes, and said only one word: "Light." Then he said it again—"light"—motioning with his hands expanded around his face like rays of the sun, repeating, this time, "Be light."

WE WERE SIX hours into our ten-hour drive to Agra. It was a day filled with riding around the countryside listening to eighties rock and Indian pop playing through the bus speakers. The stretches between stops were unbearably long with absolutely no restrooms in sight. More than anything, I wanted to relieve my bladder; dust, small villages, and the occasional wandering donkey lined the road, but there was not a single place to stop. My desperation escalated from fantasizing about peeing in a bush to actively calculating how to aim into the small opening of my water bottle right there in my seat.

Dear lord, please let us stop soon so I can find a bathroom. Exploring far-off places wasn't all roses, all the time.

To distract myself, I pulled out my 5-Year Plan workbook to search the pages for questions that might illuminate my internal journey. In Sicily, I had only glanced over the exercises about lining out one's professional purpose with tangible goals and actionable steps. But I was hopeful there were chapters on self-reflection as well.

Here we go:

Chapter 7: Questions to Uncover Your True Self
Understanding who we truly are underneath all the social conditioning helps us build more authentic connections and pursue a more intentional life. These thought-provoking questions will help you peel back the layers so you can connect with the *real* you.

- What is your mindset towards change?
- How do you behave when there's nobody else around to see it?
- What are the masks that you wear in everyday life?
- What emotional situations tend to trigger you in your everyday life?

- What is one challenge that keeps showing up in your life over and over again?
- When was the last time you felt truly strong and capable?
- What is a small way you can leave the world a better place than how you found it?

Just a single page into the reading, I leaned back into my bus seat, eyes drifting to the passing landscape. My naivety made me wince. I had yet to uncover so much of myself—there were so many layers I hadn't known to peel back. But I arched my brow with a hint of self-forgiveness; at least I was aware now. I thought of the spot where the bindi had graced my forehead the day before.

All my eyes were open.

Thankfully, my bladder held out until our next stop, though I only narrowly avoided sitting in a puddle on the bus. A few hours later, we were checked into our rooms, refreshed and changed for dinner, and walking alongside one of the Seven Wonders of the World: the Taj Mahal. Palm trees lined the street and shone like football stadium lights in the moonlight. The scene transported me to Friday nights in Wisconsin, wrapped in a letterman jacket, face painted, ribbons in my hair, ready to cheer on my high school team.

I sought out Blake right away and was finally eager to talk.

"You're right," I admitted softly.

She only looked at me in return, her grey eyes hidden behind black-rimmed glasses.

"You're right," I repeated, more firmly this time. "I was replacing one form of adrenaline with another. And I was only seeking external experiences instead of taking the time to look within."

"What have you concluded?" she asked, tilting her head slightly and nesting deeper into the folds of her linen scarf.

"That this is the tip of the iceberg. Awareness is one thing, but peeling back the layers will take time, intention, and likely, guidance."

"Metacognition takes time."

"What's that?"

"Awareness and understanding of one's thought processes," she replied. "Just one element of the inner journey. The path toward self-actualization, uncovering your true potential and intrinsic abilities, as you said, will take time. And a few good mentors. Also," she paused, "I have to thank you."

"Thank me?" I said, looking at her sideways.

"Yes—advice we give to others usually applies to ourselves. And in this case, it certainly did. The obstacles I needed to remove—why am I here to connect with Genesha? All internal."

I just smiled at her.

"I've been down this road a time or two, but still have layers to go." After a few comfortable steps in silence, she continued, "You know, most people think we are here to find individual purpose and to control our destinies."

True, I thought, *most people would like to think their existence matters and that we have free will.*

"I believe it's much simpler than that," she continued. "We are here to be human. That's it. For example, people sometimes come to India to embrace their spirituality—as if spirituality is separate from us, or something to be attained. But the truth is, we're not humans trying to experience spirituality. We are spirits, choosing to experience being human."

What a concept.

"Whitney, part of the human experience is external and part is internal, but everything—all experiences—are part of *be-ing* human."

A light bulb came on; everything I thought I knew or felt evaporated.

"Well, if we're just here to *experience*, who's to say what is good or bad? Or happy or sad? It would all just be… part of being human," I said. If I adopted this thinking, how would it reframe my choices, emotions, or judgments?

"Exactly."

Back in my room, two thoughts permeated my mind: spirit and sex. The topics fascinated me and guided me around the world—there is power and intimacy in both, yet you would think they'd be on opposing philosophical ends. What Blake had said about spirit resonated with me: inside of us, or part of us, is a spirit that wants to understand what it's like to have a physical body, feel powerful emotions, and experience impermanence.

Understandable, I thought. There are limitless ways to wake up the body and feel human things. For example, being present with not only the taste of food, but also being aware of the tiny taste buds allowing you to experience it. The first time you had a truly sour candy—even the *thought* of it makes your mouth water. Feeling wind on your face and seeing goosebumps rise on your arms. If you really take the time to notice tiny adaptations to different people or atmospheres, our bodies and sensory capabilities are exquisite. What a gift physical experience is. No wonder spirits want to give it a whirl.

THE NEXT MORNING, we got up before the sun to take in the breathtaking white marble mausoleum with minimal crowds. I was fascinated by the story: the Taj Mahal was built in remembrance of the emperor's third wife. Today, divorce is somewhat taboo, but historically, having many marriages and partners wasn't only accepted, it was expected—especially for prominent and royal families. If society's rules change with the century and by the class, why did we hold ourselves so damn accountable to them? *Maybe I should step back and recreate my* own *moral compass,* I thought, *populated with spokes I completely embody. For example, ones that don't make you out to be a horrible, unworthy person if you've gone through a divorce.*

Thinking of my own failed marriage, I wondered about that word: failure. Was it a failure just because it ended? Or were individual parts of the marriage considered failures while others were deemed successful? Maybe marriage was like a test in school when you were granted an all or nothing grade. All I knew was that my ex wasn't going to erect a mausoleum in my name, and that had to be okay with me.

The idea of him was quite strong again, his presence nearly palpable as I walked around taking pictures. Was there a jarring planetary alignment going on or something? Was today an astrological day for me to live in the past? Noticing the date on my phone as I framed a shot, I realized our divorce was official and final. That day. The Colorado mandatory ninety-day waiting period was over, and legally, we were one hundred percent disconnected. I could change my name back anytime, and our assets were no longer mutual. It was done. My eyes instantly welled with tears, and my heart sank. How could I still be physically feeling so much from something so over?

I looked at my hands and spun my engagement ring. Did the energy of the love it represented keep us bound? I had been wearing the ultimate reminder of broken promises. My rings were a part of me; symbols from my career and purposefully designed, they made me feel deserving, and they made me feel *special*. But my spirit sang another tune—it said they were in disharmony with the version of me striving to grow into the future. It was time to say goodbye on every level. It was time to give the rings a death—a burial of sorts. Thinking of Kali, I remembered that death is not to be feared. Though many believe death to be scary, I have never and will never subscribe to that idea. I'm not afraid of death—not at all. Why would I be? It is the only thing in life that is guaranteed. And although many speculate about what happens after we leave these bodies, we do not know for sure. But *how* we view death while we're alive is a choice—a choice that affects us our entire lives, either calling in fear and resistance or calling in love and faith. I choose faith.

Yes, I needed to permanently say goodbye to my rings, symbolizing the death of a double love—marriage and my career in gemology. Those chapters in my story were entwined, and I had to find the courage to walk away.

It was no mistake I was there on the exact day my divorce was finalized. The Taj Mahal became a beacon for me; a symbol of individual strength and power not in death, but rebirth.

That evening, it was our final night together as a group. Since we'd become fast friends, everyone traded details about where life would lead and how to stay in touch. I mentioned New Zealand as my next destination, and Alec and Anne invited me to their second wedding in the middle of January. I thanked them for the invite but knew I'd be back in the states by the holidays.

We shared a rickshaw back to the hotel. Anne and I exchanged a few of the bracelets we'd purchased in the markets, but she seemed quite excited about something else entirely.

"I'm pregnant," she said.

I nearly squealed myself out of the rickshaw and hugged them both. They had just found out a few hours earlier and wanted to tell someone; otherwise, they'd keep it a secret until their celebration in

January. What an incredible surprise for their family and friends. And what a highlight for their honeymoon memories. Babies—the ultimate embodiment of innocence and new light.

"Do you want children?" Alec asked.

"Yes," I answered without hesitation. "Absolutely. I'm meant to be a mother. You know, for years, people asked me when my ex and I were having kids, and my answer was always the same: *I have so much to learn about life before I'm ready to teach someone about it. But someday!*" As a newly single woman, I certainly hadn't thought about children in a while—but my heart still knew this longing for kids to be true. The beat of motherhood had been strong for as long as I could remember and wasn't going anywhere. No situation or season in life lasts forever, and I trusted that someday I'd be in a relationship again—one in which I was grounded and wise enough to step into parenthood.

I instantly felt the urge to give Alec and Anne the rose quartz pink angel I'd been carrying in my purse since my last visit to Wisconsin, the one that paired with my goddaughter's and niece's to keep us connected. Rose quartz represents love—self-love, specifically—and helps protect mothers and children. I thought Alec and Anne's baby should have mine to accompany them on the rest of their journey.

Yes, give freely, I thought. *Love does not mean possession, and the energy will find me again. Right now, their child calls it, and I'm in a new pattern of becoming lighter, literally and figuratively. Give the angel, give up my rings.* It was as if Ganesha was helping remove obstacles I didn't even know were there. He was helping me remove the blinders from my third eye and the locks around my heart. *Thank you, my friend*, I thought. *I don't believe I'm seeing the whole picture, but I'm confident I'm starting to regain focus, with a full spectrum of color. I want to dive into that color, breathe into it, and send millions of brightly colored, sparkling lights into my cells to heal what is needed.*

SKIPPING THROUGH THE Delhi airport, I hummed to myself, listening to music through my headphones. I was back in the airport and back in my happy bubble. My bag was checked, I had made it through security, and I was looking for a window seat to kill a few hours before departure. I was ready to simply watch the planes again. There were signs for Diwali everywhere—the festival of lights celebrating the inner light that protects us from spiritual darkness. How incredibly in sync with my journey; of course I ended up in India around this time. Part of me was disappointed to be leaving before the actual festivities, but all of me was grateful to be in the middle of the anticipatory energy of it all. It was infectious and blooming in me like spring. How timely: the Southern Hemisphere, where I was heading, was entering spring, too.

Page number four was complete. India: what a surprise. Sometimes the things we resist —the destination and unsolicited advice—are just what we need. My focus had started to turn inward and I was feeling more like myself, leading yoga flows and waving goodbye to the old while ushering in the new. I was starting to feel energetically empowered to imagine *different,* and confident in the fact that different was waiting for me professionally. It felt inconceivable for my vibration to return to its previous state.

What did this mean for what came next? How did I feel about New York? I hadn't thought about moving in weeks, and I didn't want to. How could I look for jobs if I didn't know what I wanted to be? Was New York the right place to figure it out? Maybe I should just keep traveling, budget permitting—I loved meeting people from all over the world and hearing their stories of life, love, and even politics. I had received both scrutiny and support for my choices, yet I was starting to care less about either. Heather and Steph would be proud.

I ruminated on Blake's theory: being a spirit with the foundational purpose of simply experiencing being human. That perspective made every experience valuable, both internal and external. That idea would also encourage a drop in both harsh judgments and attachments to outcomes. There was an echo of freedom in this ideology I'd never envisioned before—I felt charged with an internal light that was starting to radiate in all directions. *Radiate light... That's it!* It was the second half of the acronym tattoo I had gotten before I left: in its entirety, MMRL stood for "Manifest Magic Radiate Light." The signs and messages about light were everywhere... *Wow,* I thought. I felt light coming from within. I was there around Diwali, and even the elderly gentleman from the prayer chamber repeated "light" like a prayer when we parted. *Be light.* Maybe his wisdom was connected to insights from my higher self.

My excitement circled back to "Manifest Magic," something I thought I had figured out. But maybe I needed to understand *how* I processed emotions to respect and potentially direct them. Maybe it hadn't been about what I was asking for all along, but about the emotion I had been radiating—the frequency I had unknowingly sent out into the universe, which it understood even when I couldn't articulate it. Not *ask and receive,* but *feel and receive.* Something about this realization resonated in my soul, as if my spirit was leaping to its feet in a standing ovation. I laughed at the visual.

Like the Cheshire cat, I was grinning ear to ear; I was ablaze with an internal fire of new understanding. I had lived one of my favorite quotes from Oliver Wendell Holmes: "A mind stretched by new experiences can never go back to its old dimensions." I looked around the strangers' faces in the waiting area as if someone else might be in on this massive discovery. No one was paying attention to me. Not caring that I was alone in the glory, I almost sang the discovery out loud: "Manifest Magic, my emotions co-create my world, Radiate Light, emanate a frequency of pure spirit." I finally understood why the intuitive download from my dream so many months before felt right—the words and letters that demanded to be tattooed on my ribcage were already part of me. But now I was living their meaning again; I was granted the chance to experience the power of inception again. Now their meaning was rooted in story. It was deeply, authentically mine.

The only tattoo left to internalize was the Pleiades on my left arm. *Time will tell,* I thought. *My future is still completely unknown, but my vision of possibility is getting brighter.*

I WAS BACK behind the wheel, settling into my rental outside the Christchurch airport. Christchurch was my first and only planned destination in New Zealand. I had a beachside bach rented, and it was a quick twenty-minute drive away. My Thule bag rested contentedly in the back, my purse claimed the co-pilot seat, and my extra travel layers lay discarded in a heap. It had been an exhausting thirty-eight-hour commute, and the local time was approaching 6 p.m., an hour before sunset.

As the driver, I sat on the right side of the car, a considerable departure from everything I was used to. Still, I could manage this. I had also, perhaps ambitiously, rented a manual. I hadn't realized the gear shift would be on the left. A curveball, but not insurmountable. The pedals and clutch were in familiar places—small mercies. I took a deep breath. I could figure this out.

Then I turned on the navigation system and froze.

Japanese.

The menu, the instructions, everything—in Japanese. Navigating without directions? In a language I couldn't even attempt to decode? Flashbacks of getting hopelessly lost in France bubbled up instantly, and this time, I didn't have Fern connected to help.

I stared at the console, willing it to translate itself. My mind was blank. *You're tired, not helpless*, I told myself, fingers tightening around the steering wheel. I had to be able to sort this out. I looked for symbols: "settings" was usually represented by a gray gear, and language options often came with flags. There it was: the British flag. *English.*

Relief washed over me.

Maybe this hiccup with the GPS was a sign I needed to visit Japan next. Or maybe it was something subtler, an invitation to gauge my immediate reaction to the situation and recognize my own capability sooner. I wish I hadn't reacted with anxiety. *Oh well*, I sighed. At that moment, the sky began to blush with color, and I concluded that the sunset was calling. Drama had been averted, and I was on my way.

The bach was utterly charming—peacefully set below tall trees, tastefully decorated with beach colors, and thoughtfully furnished with matching arrangements. A welcome note awaited me alongside fresh fruit, a bottle of wine, and a plate of cookies. As tired as my limbs were, I knew the beach was a mere hundred feet away, and I couldn't deny the call from the ocean a moment longer. The path to Woodland Beach was lined with magnificent pine trees, their trunks rising like skyscrapers and needles forming a soft, fragrant carpet beneath my feet. The forest gradually gave way to white sand, and as I neared the shoreline, tall grasses swayed in the breeze. I pressed my bare feet into the earth, letting the tension and fatigue from my journey drain away. As I stepped onto the beach, the view left me speechless: nothing but the ocean. It was humbling and profoundly calming.

To the far right, mountains loomed in the distance, framed by forest and grassland. To the left, more of the same: a mirror of untamed beauty. There was a light breeze, the sky was turning a deeper pink, and only a few other people dotted the shore. In that moment, the vitality of humans' connection to nature struck me with clarity. We are not separate from it—we *are* it. Living, breathing organisms, we are composed of the same matter and energy as the trees, the sea, and every creature around us. We are meant to be woven into this fabric, not detached from it.

Sitting down with a plastic glass and my wine, I started softly crying. *Arrived*, my spirit sang. I felt settled, like I was finally at an ultimate destination. Maybe it was the exhaustion, maybe it was the ocean or the mountains in the distance, or the lovely reception at my first rental. Whatever it was, my heart felt at peace, like something switched back into place inside me, as if a watch gear or disc in my spine had been off kilter and was now slotted back into position.

I had officially reached page five of my journey. Traveling from Europe to India had turned out to be the greatest gift I never knew to ask for. *Why not India?* The universe had known long before I was ready to listen. But listen, I did. Had the sequence of events unfolded differently, I might never have met Blake, nor begun to shift my perspective in such vital ways.

Now, in New Zealand, I felt the need to continue walking this path of awakening, to keep redefining what balance meant, and to release the outdated pieces of myself that no longer served me. In their place, I was making space for something new. It seemed wise to keep Tanya on extended PTO for the time being—I wasn't convinced that dating was what I needed, since it might only serve as a distraction. Perhaps I should find a yoga studio or two instead.

I sat by the waves, breathing in with their rise and fall. I often found myself gazing at the sky in broad daylight, imagining the constellations hidden beyond the blue: a quiet reminder of our place in the vastness of the universe. Why not? The stars were always present, even when unseen.

Watching the transition from day to night grounded me in that truth. Just because something wasn't visible didn't mean it had ceased to exist. In that stillness, I finally calmed. The darkness arrived gently, and night quietly guided me back to bed.

EVEN THOUGH I was a tourist on holiday, life went on: I realized when I got ready the next morning that my hair needed a trim and a color. And I still had to pee all the time. So that day, I decided I'd live life doing the normal, mundane things: check up on email, stock up on groceries, do my laundry, get my hair done, and find a walk-in clinic.

"How much are we cutting today, dear?" asked the salon owner with a last-minute vacancy.

"Just a trim so we're healthy. Keep it long, please."

"And for the color? You have beautiful natural highlights; I don't want to overdo it."

"Thank you. I agree, a natural look is best, but the dirty blonde around my face isn't doing me any favors, and I'd love to brighten it up. Maybe lighter up top and a bit darker underneath for some depth."

"Easy as—let me go mix up some color." She was in her late forties, blonde, and fit. The salon had three other stylists working on clients, a sleeping dog in the entrance, easy music playing, and a beverage and lounge area in the back.

"What have you done so far in New Zealand?"

I raised my eyebrows. "Went to the clinic down the road, actually," I said. She hesitated until I continued, "I just landed here after a few weeks in India, and knew something was off with my bladder. Turns out I have a UTI."

"Ah, I see. Not fun, but an easy fix," she said, then added, "The restroom is over there."

I laughed. It was my first UTI, so I hadn't recognized the symptoms. Truth be told, I was worried it was something worse. The sympathetic doctor said it could have been caused by holding in urine for too long or a lot of sexual activity, and I was guilty of both.

"Your healthcare system is incredible. I was seen right away, and it was only $86 for the doctor visit and prescription. I couldn't imagine it would have been as smooth in the US, even with insurance."

"We try to take care of people around here. No sense to make it too complicated."

"I also appreciate the free Wi-Fi everywhere, and clean public restrooms."

"Well, there's more to New Zealand than restrooms, dear," she said with a kind smirk. "Where else will your trek lead you?"

"I'm open. I'd like to drive as far south as Queenstown and I have a flight out of Auckland in a few weeks, but that's all I have planned. I'd love some recommendations if you have any."

With that, she lit up. She rattled off hiking routes, vineyards, hotels, Māori heritage sites, and even told me about a gemstone beach. All of them seemed worth visiting, and I could barely take notes as quickly as she chatted.

"Wait a minute!" I interrupted her. "You have to go into more detail about the gemstone beach. And what do you mean there are no snakes here?"

"The gemstone beach is at the far south of the island on Te Waewae Bay. It's rugged and remote with excellent surfing. You can find jasper, garnet, and quartz amongst the rocks. And we don't have any snakes. The only predators to humans on land are other humans."

"Alright. It's settled. I want to move here." The entire salon laughed. "No, really, I was reading that GMOs are nearly banned. So you can trust everything from the grocery store to restaurants. Is that true?"

"Yes, we certainly prioritize what we put in and on our bodies, and thrive on embracing an active, family-centric life. Now, the exchange rate and economy are a different story. Many Kiwis leave in their twenties to live abroad and make money before coming back to settle down."

"Interesting. If I were to stay, I'd be doing the opposite," I added. "Even though I'm not exactly in my twenties anymore." I thought of my identity crisis as I entered my thirties, which was also a reminder to check my bank account. The need to reenter the workforce was speeding toward me.

My time at the salon reminded me how easy it was to be back in a country that spoke English. I had thoroughly enjoyed not understanding the language up until then, and had learned a lot from the void of processing. I was not uncomfortable traveling alone anymore, eating alone, or driving alone. But it was time to see if I could consciously separate myself from the chatter around me and remain deliberate with my engagement.

After the salon—with fresh hair, a fresh prescription, and energized to dive into page number five as an upgraded version of Whitney—I was back at my bach, sprawled out on a blanket under the trees, mapping out my route and priorities. I was in New Zealand, for goodness' sake; it was the only destination on my journey that had been on my bucket list. And so far, it had superseded any idea I'd had of it—which, yes, was partially because I had never daydreamed of going to a clinic for a UTI. But I was learning that life could physically slow you down if you weren't listening, especially to your body. It could, and would, happen anywhere in the world.

Now for the fun part: what to do next. I had my rental car—which I named Little Bull—three weeks until I flew to Thailand, and a laundry list of activities and destinations from the salon ladies. The adventure seeker within me was beginning to stir, restless and eager for the rush that made her feel most alive. Queenstown, renowned as the adventure capital, offered every thrill imaginable: dart boating, kayaking, bungee jumping, mountain biking, helicopters, ziplines, you name it. Though I was committed to my inner growth, I also craved the visceral reminders that I was alive. It was time to plug that back in.

Nelson, the sunniest part of the country and known for its stunning landscapes and golden beaches, had been highly recommended today and seemed like an excellent target after mountain activities down south. I could use some more sunny beach days and coastal hiking, so I researched and found a place called Abel Tasman National Park, located on the northeast tip of the South Island. It was also en route to the ferry I needed to take to get to Wellington on the

North Island. From there, I would drive to Rotorua and then up to Auckland to explore Waiheke, Takapuna, and, if I had time, the Bay of Islands and Cape Reinga.

Whew. First, a budget check.

I averted my gaze as my account details loaded, then winced. The balance was far lower than anticipated—alarmingly so. My savings had all but evaporated. *Damn.* I hadn't noticed some pending charges before, which had since been processed. But I couldn't just throw in the towel. Everything I had been researching—helicopter tours and immersive day trips—came with a steep price tag. In hindsight, perhaps my planning should have leaned more toward trekking routes and self-powered experiences; Thailand was already paid for, and if I could stretch my funds until then, I could make it home afterward.

But had I come this far just to ease up on the throttle now? To return home penniless, but full of memories? That felt misaligned. Somewhere inside, my rebellious inner voice rose defiantly: *Screw it—transfer the loan. It's just sitting there, waiting for you to admit you need it. You'll regret it forever if you don't. This is your life's education—your one shot to live without limitation. Abundance will return. You can't evolve with a scarcity mindset. You'll earn it back. You always do.*

I transferred it. The loan would carry me through the next month, buying me time to decide what might come after Thailand. Decision made. My credit cards were still untouched, the inner rebel noted with satisfaction. Emboldened, I allowed myself to wonder what it would take to live here. Would it hurt to research more than just tourist itineraries? After all, if I could manifest men, why not relocation requirements?

AFTER ONLY A few days in Queenstown, I found myself declaring, without hesitation, that New Zealand was utterly addictive. The food alone was enough to win anyone over; Fergburger, the legendary local burger joint with queues snaking around the block at all hours, lived up to the hype. The people exuded a warmth free of pretense, the kind of friendliness unaccompanied by hidden agendas, and the night sky gleamed with a clarity made possible by the pure, unpolluted air.

As I strolled past mountaineering and outdoor shops, I thought of my gear packed away in storage boxes. Back in Vail, the first snow would have arrived by now, and the ski season was on the verge of starting. I hadn't missed an opening day in a decade. Yet, standing there, I felt no ache, no pull in my heart to return. Even the thought of familiar faces and shared mountain rituals didn't stir a longing in me; those connections, for all their history, felt slightly out of sync with who I was becoming. Not forever, I hoped, but certainly for now.

Next came the camping displays, and with them, flickers of summer memories: hiking through wildflower meadows, tubing down rivers, dancing under the stars at music festivals. I examined my heart again for desire, and still found it absent: there was no wistfulness for Colorado. Strangely, that felt freeing.

And then, as if to affirm that I was exactly where I was meant to be, I saw it in a crystal shop window: the very same rose quartz angel I had gifted Anne and Alec for their growing baby. A symbol so specific it couldn't be a coincidence—another one had found me.

It had felt so good to give without expectation of a return. But it was also reassuring to see it come full circle; I still loved the idea of completing the triple bond with my nieces, so I popped into the store and tucked a new angel into the pocket of my purse. Welcome to the ride, my friend.

By letting go of one small piece at a time, I was giving what was meant to come back to me the opportunity to do so. And if it didn't come back, I was giving it the freedom it needed to live another life. Maybe I was starting to break—or at least bypass—a few patterns of my own.

And possibly starting a few new ones. A few hours later, I had signed up for round two. This wasn't a date. It wasn't jewelry or internal debates. I was about to go *skydiving* again. It had been advertised all over Queenstown, and the temptation to embrace the freefall was too hot to ignore.

"Are you ready?" my tandem partner said.

"Yes," I shouted above the engine. I was ready for everything. I was the only one jumping today, so, lucky for me, I got to go first and last.

The ride to elevation had been relaxed; light banter and gear checking passed the time. But when it came time to open the airplane door, I felt my belly flip as I was whipped by the rushing air, and it fogged my googles. High above the mountain peaks, lakes, and clouds, I was abruptly transported back to Moab, seeing nothing but desert and feeling only my ex's presence behind me.

As if playing a trick on me, my consciousness jumped back to the current moment as we stepped out on the wing. Shaking my head, I tried to clear the mirage from my vision to see New Zealand again, but it didn't work. I squeezed my eyes shut hoping for clarity, but when I opened them, I wasn't on the wing—I was still *in* the plane, watching *myself* fall towards the ground. It was as if I was seeing through my ex's eyes: I was existing in his memory, seeing what he saw, feeling what he felt. A sword sliced through my heart, and I felt his pain as he watched me dive away from him, speeding irreversibly away from the life we'd built, our paths forever diverged. It wasn't anger; it was an innocent, tormented realization of loss.

I'd never focused on *his* feelings during that time. But the vision was piercing; I felt connected to him in the void between heaven and earth. As if embracing the same vibration again, the intensity of the pending fall had put me right back there. Something was unfinished, connecting us through time and space. It was intense and jarring, and made me question my motives for being there. Was I trying to retrace our steps? Or subconsciously calling to him? No, I squeezed my hands into fists. No, I was not. I was here for me today. I was jumping for only me.

"Ready? We jump in 5, 4, 3, 2..."

We jumped, and I closed my eyes. Memories from our marriage morphed from one to another: the moment we met, laughing on chairlifts, saying our vows, crying after losing friends. Their intensity pulled me into a black hole, and I was about to combust. I was lost. And then my instructor yanked the cord; the jerk slapped me out of my mental spiral, and we floated. The unexpected twenty-five-second freefall of history was over. I was confused, but my mind was empty. The air was pure with silence, and the only thing that seemed real was the feeling of our bodies following gravity toward the ground. It felt like the vacuous silence after a battle, the nothingness that symbolized both ending and beginning with the dawning realization that no one really won the war. *Maybe this is my float after our battle.*

"Do you want to take control and give us a few spins?" he asked, holding out the hand grips that direct the canopy.

"Yes," I said. I wanted to take back control. "What do I do?"

He gave instructions on how to turn, glide, and direct the flight that was taking us home. I loved it. I could make us waltz with the wind. I felt free as the breeze, and I could hear the song of the sky.

All too quickly, we landed smoothly in the soft grass. He detached my harness and asked how I was. "Incredible. You have no idea what just happened. Thank you." It was as if the jump had taken me to the far-reaching sides of the pendulum I'd been riding before landing me squarely in the middle, free to choose my new path. I felt electric. It was still intimidating as all hell to jump from 10,000 feet, but I was in love. I'd told Jeannine before I left that I didn't want to live in the gray—I wanted to experience extremes of color. Adrenaline was back in my life and demanded its place in the sun;

feeling it flow through my veins had unlocked things that needed to be released.

I found the color that transmuted fear to courage in France, the emotional color of heart expansion in Sicily, swirls of spiritual color in India, and now fireworks in New Zealand.

I was sparkling, and back with a bang.

THE FORECAST FOR the next day was spotty with showers of spring rain, so I signed up for a last-minute wine tasting tour. After that, during my final two days in Queenstown, I planned to take a three-stop helicopter ride with beach and glacier landings and a thirty-minute stopover in the infamous Milford Sound, then go on a dartboard and kayaking adventure through the valley where many scenes from *The Lord of the Rings* had been filmed. I decided my wine tour would also be a research and "planning real life" day.

Sitting at the bar on our last stop for the day, Trevor Valley Winery, I sipped on a cool white wine and perused LinkedIn for jobs in New York, read emails from Heather with apartment leads, and searched for a bach in Nelson.

"Ready to try the rosé?" asked the sommelier.

"Yes, please. The chardonnay was light and crisp—just delicious," I said.

"This rosé will be light as well. It's quenching, fruit-forward, and finishes dry. It pairs extremely well with our fresh salmon or onion, blue cheese, and walnut salad. Shall I bring you a menu?"

"Sounds wonderful, thank you."

"I'll be back."

After booking my bach in Nelson and remaining uninspired by leads in Manhattan, I saw another open tab on my desktop. I had been researching New Zealand visas for foreigners. The idea of moving here was random, of course, but not horrible; I could qualify for an essential skills visa with my gemology background.

It didn't take long to find a jewelry store similar to Framebridge. All I had to do was look up official retailers for specific watches, and I found the kind of store I was looking for. In New Zealand, it turned out there was only one company that carried lines like Patek Philippe and Rolex: Eberly.

The world of gemology and horology is quite small; there is one language and one education that is transferable all around the world. I didn't see open positions listed on their website or Indeed, but decided to send a random email to the "Contact Us" page. I introduced myself and explained that I was traveling through and was compelled to inquire about working with them. I included my resume to be efficient and ended with a request to meet while I was in Auckland; I clarified that I'd love to visit them even if they weren't hiring, as I was always interested in meeting like-minded professionals.

Clicking through their website, I was familiar with almost all the lines they carried—they were even family-owned and did custom work. The idea of working behind a counter in sales again was hard to swallow. It was a long shot, anyway, but I would never know what was possible unless I tried, and gemology was the only thing that qualified me for the visa.

Eventually, another vineyard employee brought over a menu.

"Here you are, miss. May I make a suggestion?"

"Please do."

"Order the tasting menu. It may take a few hours, but it features everything local and fresh our country has to offer this season, and, paired with our wines, offers an experience not to be missed."

"Wonderful idea. However, I'm part of the tour over there," I said, gesturing to the small crowd tasting and shopping in the gallery room.

"Yes, I see. Your guide is a good friend of mine, and he mentioned that," he continued. This man was cute. It seemed like he had a plan—and a sly smile.

"Researching me? Should I be concerned?" I laughed.

"No, no. Please. I'll leave you for a moment with the menu. But today's special includes a ride home from me, if you happen to stay past your tour's departure."

He did have a plan. He also left before I could reply—oh, my. I hadn't turned Tanya on yet in this country and hadn't even thought about men since Sicily. But it seemed they were finding me. It felt incredible to meet a human in the real world instead of on an app. I didn't even know his name. He was charming, and I was intrigued. I checked in with myself and didn't feel nervous—he didn't give me a creepy vibe.

Would spending time with him alter the internal odyssey I'd vowed to begin in India? No. Surely I could mix in a little external stimulation—personal evolution shouldn't be all or nothing. Was I going to stay?

Yes, yes, I was.

He was bold, and that was sexy—I wanted to play with that. I could be bold, too.

"Tasting menu with a side of a ride home later," I said before he could ask.

"You won't regret your choice, Miss. I'll ensure it," he said before immediately walking away.

The sommelier came back to my table. "I see your order has been put in with the kitchen. The GM will take care of the rest—it's been a pleasure."

The General Manager? Smooth. We'll call him The GM, then.

Through unbelievably delicious bites and wine that I would have bought in bulk, The GM and I chatted and laughed. He certainly threw a few extras onto our dinner, and I wasn't complaining.

"So, tell me a little about yourself."

"My background is in luxury and extreme sports. Events, specifically. Although I'm traveling right now, I sense a permanent move is closing in."

"Perfect. We need a specialist for weddings and whatnot—you're hired."

"Well, thank you kindly for the offer," I said, thinking that weddings were the absolute last thing I wanted to plan. "That's very generous of you. But after a bit more time vagabonding, New York is calling my name."

"Seriously, though, why not move here?"

"I did some research, but Queenstown is a little too similar to Vail—resort town, mountain lifestyle, and all. I need a little city to balance me out."

"Auckland, then. There are over a million people there. I'm sure you can find an opportunity."

"I'm excited to check it out," I said, thinking of the email I just sent. Not having seen a reply, I didn't dare mention it. "At least it's on the water and has a major airport."

"So, it's settled. Auckland it is. I go up there all the time—I'll come visit."

I smiled, "I love it when major life decisions are so simple."

"They're still yes or no choices," he said.

"I see your point, oh, wise one. And remind me, how old are you? Just curious."

"A ripe and ready twenty-three."

I nearly spit out my wine.

"You must be an ambitious twenty-three to be the General Manager."

"I've been working here since I was fourteen. I've done every job we have."

"Not many people understand their business that well. I'm sure your staff and products thrive because of it."

After a few more rounds of tantalizing bites and sips, it was time to head back to my hotel.

"Thank you, Whitney, for surprising me on a Tuesday with the best customer conversation I've ever had."

"Thank you for the bold invitation—I appreciate your hospitality."

"I would love to show you more of Queenstown if you have time before you drive north?"

"Dinner tomorrow?"

"I'll meet you here at 8. We can walk."

"See you then," I said, reaching for the door handle.

"Wait—" he jumped out of the car and walked around to open the door for me.

"Charming," I smiled.

In one smooth motion, his arm was around me and his lips on mine. Holy hot, he was a fun kisser. Enthusiastic. As he released me a few moments later, I felt a bit dizzy from the wine and kiss both.

"Thank you," he said, ushering me towards the door, "I look forward to seeing you tomorrow."

"Likewise. Goodnight."

A FEW DAYS later, I drove the West Coast from Queenstown to Abel Tasman National Park. The 4 Non Blondes were crooning through the stereo, keeping me company: "And I say, hey-ey-ey / Hey-ey-ey / I said 'Hey, a-what's going on?'" Hearing them brought tears to my eyes—"What's Up" is the song I share with my mom and grandmama; we've been singing it together since I was little. Just like their love, the song will find me anywhere in the world—time or distance, life or death, will never change that.

The roads were windy and narrow, covered in a dense canopy of lush, green trees. My time in Queenstown had been electric, and I was riding high on all cylinders. Besides skydiving and wine tasting, I'd gone on a dart boat ride—an activity unique to New Zealand in which you fly across a few inches of water up the river. After, we'd kayaked back down the river, exploring caves with clear turquoise water and stopping for lunch on the riverbank.

Once again, my muscles had jumped at the opportunity to stretch, and my lungs had quickly expanded with invigorating mountain air. My body had cheered with enthusiasm for exercise; I had been back in my element. Wise words from Enzo Ferrari had come to mind: "You can't describe passion; you can only live it." I hadn't forgotten about my internal journey, although it wasn't top of mind. It just felt so comfortable to focus on physical activities, and I welcomed the return of passion.

Continuing to ignore my responsible side, I'd also gone on the helicopter adventure. It had been my first time riding in one, and it was now officially my favorite form of transportation, hands down. Landing on a glacier had been out of this world—we'd gotten out to walk around the snow, and even found time to climb the slopes a bit. I'd loved being surrounded by nothing but peaks again, and it had been the first time since leaving Colorado that I'd missed the mountains. I missed the feeling of being on a summit with expansive views in every direction.

My time with The GM had been fun. I'd easily adapted to his youthful energy and had quickly let go of the strings tied to my heavy balloons—the ones that carried my big questions, flaunting flashing signs that said *New York, Money, Apartment.*

We'd gone to dinner and he had showed me the local spots around town. We'd stayed out late, playing pool, frisbee, swings—whatever we'd come across. I felt twenty-one again; his age was balanced with a confident maturity, and his enthusiasm for potential propelled me to believe moving here was a viable option. Why not? I'd appreciated the distraction, and although our time together had been sweet, I wouldn't encourage him to visit me in Auckland.

Since then, my drive had paralleled and crisscrossed the river almost the entire way. I barely came across another vehicle, so I began to recite "apex, turn; apex, turn," as my race training came back to me. I've always taken a GPS's estimated time of arrival as a challenge, and even if I didn't beat it, at least I had more fun driving. Even though I didn't know these roads, I felt connected to them. Driving a manual certainly helped with that, feeling the vibrations through the steering wheel when the gears shift and punching the clutch at just the right moment to go faster. The rhythm induced a light flow state. But all of a sudden, there were flashing lights behind me. Where had that police officer come from? Shit. I pulled over at the first safe spot.

"Excuse me, Miss, did you notice that the speed limit goes down to 25 kph back there?"

"No, officer, I apologize, I didn't. I'm in for a long commute today up to Nelson, and the car just got away from me."

"Tourists like you are what make the roads so dangerous. Slow down—if not for yourself, for others that might be on the road." I was ashamed; I should have been more responsible. I felt like a schoolgirl being sent to the principal's office.

He wasn't letting me out of this one, and hastily handed me a ticket that needed to be paid within forty-eight hours. Otherwise, my foreign license would be revoked. My impulsive driving delivered me a swift fine of $150 NZD.

Only a few minutes later, continuing at a slower pace, I popped out of the forest to find nothing but ocean straight ahead. I had finally reached the edge—the border between land and water. It was time to veer north, following the dramatic coastline on a narrow road carved into the towering, jagged cliffs. One sudden gust from the Tasman Sea nearly lifted the car from the pavement and served as a reminder of nature's absolute command of this place. I noticed the trees on the hillside weren't growing vertically, but diagonally, permanently shaped by the relentless wind. Survival here meant adaptation. The landscape had an almost surreal quality to it, like something pulled from the pages of a Dr. Seuss book.

The ocean crashed on the rocks below; powerful, forceful landings that sent plumes of sea spray forty feet high and waves out as far as the eye could see.

This place is charged, I thought. *Charged with raw, untamed energy. I love it—I need to soak some of this up.*

I stopped at a viewpoint and sat on the hood of the Little Bull with my eyes closed, doing some long, slow, intentional square breathing. This was the moment: time to attune myself to the elemental power of this place. And release the weight of that speeding ticket. Yes, I had been driving too fast—but I couldn't deny it had been fun.

I have a job interview, I suddenly remembered. The day after I emailed Eberly, they'd responded warmly with interest. They'd invited me to visit the store while I was in Auckland and had mentioned they were in the midst of an expansion, which meant a potential opening. What serendipitous timing!

Still, I hesitated as I drafted my reply. The prospect of working again—of reentering structure and responsibility—stirred a quiet panic beneath the surface. Had I grown too accustomed to this freedom? To waking up at leisure and following my instincts instead of a schedule? A part of me recoiled at the idea, as though employment signaled the end of something sacred, this inner and outer exploration that was just starting to redefine me.

Work didn't have to stop me, I supposed. And I had been so genuinely excited for the opportunity that I'd accepted their invite and the date was set. Besides, this could be more than a job—it could be a way to stay in New Zealand.

Sitting on the hood, I felt a resounding *yes*—one that rippled through my bones. I needed to get my head in the game and make it happen. If I wanted New Zealand, which I was really starting to, it was time to work for it; either that or start taking real action toward New York.

The nostalgia on the radio earlier had also made me decide it was finally time to call my parents. At least I could do so with happy, concrete news: I had made personal progress, there was a sort of job interview lined up, and I was on the verge of making a solid plan. That would mean something to them. I should also call Jeannine; she could do some background research on Eberly and give me the industry insights I needed ahead of the meeting. I certainly couldn't call Heather—there was no way I could tell her I was even considering not moving to New York. Plus, I may have been getting ahead of myself with all that. I needed to get to Auckland first.

IT WAS MY favorite bach ever: more warm cookies, apple cider, and fresh eggs with a welcome note on arrival. The interior, warm and contemporary, was mixed with farm elements and all-glass windows. The view inspired me like nothing I'd ever seen. I sat outside on the patio, which overlooked a sheep field with green grass that rolled over the hilltop edge, dropping out of sight to the ocean below. I could see miles and miles of shoreline beneath me—I felt on top of the world and part of the sky as it blended with bold and colorful clouds announcing morning and night.

I'd signed up for another trip the next day. I'd be headed out on a sailboat to explore the coves and beaches of the national park. The short tours had been delightful, meeting other travelers and locals alike, and offering such a wealth of information and experiences. And meeting The GM had awoken the other side of me—the single side. It was time to bring back... you know it—Tanya!

Ding, ding, ding, chimed Tanya as I turned on the app.

"I missed you, too, my friend. But our time apart was essential—trust me," I said. "But now, let's find ourselves a... warrior. I feel like a warrior myself. Someone who's been through some battles and is coming out on the other side. I want to connect with someone who has passion and opinions—someone who isn't afraid to do the work, to show up for life, and take a long look in the mirror. Yes, Tanya, my heart is calling out with warrior energy."

But before I committed to scrolling, my heart was also calling out for my parents. I called the landline of my childhood home: the line that connected a receiver to my mom's hand and the farmland, delivering sound waves from the other side of the world. I've had that number memorized since I was at least four and have called countless times for salvation or celebration.

"Hi, Mom," I said, feeling a little nervous. Maybe something had gone wrong—maybe someone had gotten hurt or sick, or they were finally upset with me for being so drastically disconnected.

"Oh my, oh my, oh my—let me get your father!" yelled my mom. I'm sure the neighbors, over a mile away, heard her.

"Hi, SCOM," Dad said a few moments later.

"Hiiiiiiiii," I squealed, so excited I couldn't hide it. They didn't seem upset, but my nerves were still buzzing with anticipation. Maybe I missed them way more than I'd allowed myself to admit. Maybe this entire journey was scaring me, and the idea of sharing what I'd been going through out loud would make it even more real. Could I speak what had been going on?

"How are you?!" they said in unison.

"I am so good. I am," was all I could say. "But before I get into everything, how are you? How is home?" I needed a minute to figure out what to say or where to start.

Luckily, Mom jumped in. "We are status quo. I'm focusing on horse clients, and your father is flying—just trying to distract ourselves from the 'what-ifs' of what might be going on with you."

"Which is hard. But we check emails every day and follow the red dot on my phone," added my dad.

"You know we don't travel like you do, Whitney, so I have no idea what your daily life is like. But I keep Googling images of where you've been and imagine you smiling," my mom said.

"Google 'sheep farm in Nelson, New Zealand.' That's where I am right now. I'll email you a picture."

"It says they have more sheep than people," my mom read a moment later.

"And endless wineries, mountains, and beaches. I'm in love," I added.

"That doesn't sound half bad," my dad said. "How was India?"

After that, the questions continued until they ran out of breath. I realized answering their questions allowed me to avoid anything I wasn't ready to say. After twenty minutes of quick-fire, friendly interrogation, I finally said it: "I want to move here."

"Nelson?"

"New Zealand."

"What?"

"Yes, it feels right. Signs keep lining up, and—I don't know, I can't describe it, but I think it's the right thing to do."

Silence.

"What about New York?" my dad finally said.

"Are you still coming home for the holidays?" my mom asked, trying to redirect reality to bring me home. "Are you making it for Thanksgiving or Christmas?"

I decided it would be better to keep things streamlined for them, instead of sharing that I still had one foot in the New York camp. I would know how I felt after the interview, but at that moment, I wasn't collecting votes. "New York will still be there later in life. Plus, it's going into winter there, and I feel like I'm in sync with spring. Who knows how long I'll stay here, but I don't think I should leave."

"So you're not coming back anymore?"

"I'm not sure. I miss you guys! Trust me, I do—I think about you all the time. But financially, it isn't the easiest to fly back and forth."

"I think you should get out of New Zealand to make choices about New Zealand," my dad suggested.

"That's true," I agreed. "I actually have a trip to Thailand booked, so I'll be going there and can get my head wrapped around what's next. Don't worry, I already reached out to a jewelry store and started researching visa requirements."

"You're serious…" My mom's voice trailed off, and I imagined her trying not to cry. At least until they were off the phone.

"One hundred percent. I'm working on a plan—you'll see. I even know someone in Auckland that I'll hopefully connect with next week." I was referring to Jane, a friend I had made in Panama a few years ago on a yoga retreat. I'd emailed her from Queenstown to see if she'd be around to get together; I hadn't heard back yet, but I was confident we'd sort something out.

"Whitney… New Zealand? Are you *really* okay? This feels dramatic. And you said yourself, it isn't easy to fly back and forth—we'll *never* see you," Mom continued. The truth was that anywhere away from the farm was too far for her.

"If it's meant to be, it'll be. I'll figure it out, Mom, I promise. In a few days, I'll take the ferry to the North Island and drive up to the city. It's all up to fate, so we'll see what happens when I visit the jewelry store."

"You sound happy. You sound good, SCOM," my dad said.

"Thank you. I am. There's so much to tell you about everywhere and everyone I've met—I'll call you again with more details when I have more time."

"We love you," they said a few times in unison.

"I love you, too."

Talking to them—finally hearing their voices after over two months of silence—was wonderfully overwhelming. We usually spoke once a week, so the consistent lack of communication had felt like years. The phone call set off a ripple of emotion, and I couldn't help but wrap my arms around myself. You never quite get over wanting or needing your parents' approval and support; I was so lucky to have both. But I could also feel their hesitation, longing, and concern through the phone. I wasn't a parent, but I could imagine that seeing your child seemingly lost—both spiritually and literally, traipsing around the world—would send your natural instinct to protect them into a tailspin. I was sorry my actions were causing them to have to battle their instincts.

But even during my batshit crazy year, I knew without a doubt that they still had my back. Once I was ready, I wanted to sit down with them and share my internal revelations. I wanted to discuss these ideas, learn from their evolutions and setbacks, and get to know them as individuals, not just my parents. I trusted our relationship as a safe space and saw that exploring it was essential to understanding *me* more.

But first, I had to get my mind around my future. I saw a plan shifting in the sand, even if it wasn't ready to be solid.

HE WAS WALKING toward me; I could tell because there was no one else around, and he was walking like a man on a mission. I had arrived in Takapuna, a beach town just north of Auckland, a few hours before—just enough time to get checked in, unpack, and shower before my dessert date. I didn't like dessert, but time was precious and I was dying to meet this man. Tanya had matched us up five days ago, and we'd been chatting ever since—there had been significantly more dialogue than with any other match so far, and it had been enlightening. I called in warrior energy, wanting to meet someone with passion and determination, and he was an Olympian. He had competed in windsurfing races his entire life—he was now a coach as well, but as a competitor, his career included world championships, New Zealand titles, and even going to the London Olympics.

More like a Greek God, I thought to myself.

Seeing him in person, I had no idea how I was going to react; I think I'd been nervous since we'd matched. He was interesting and direct through text—he certainly knew his own mind. My intuition could tell that he was going to be a challenge, which was exactly what I wanted. My mind longed to converse with someone who had been through some stormy seas in life, and my spirit wanted to be around passion.

I was standing alone, under my hotel awning, and it was nearing nine at night. It was a calm evening. The stars were out, with a few clouds hiding them from view. According to my GPS, we were a short walk from the beach. He said he was local and knew a few restaurants that would be open for a quick bite and beverage.

"Hi, Whitney," he said, stepping into the light from the shadows.

"Hi," I said as he politely pulled me in for a kiss on the cheek. No hesitation, no lingering. The charisma of confident people tends to be either infectious or intimidating—I felt both.

"Thank you for walking over to meet me," I said.

"Happy to. Takapuna is a very safe place, but it's always better to accompany a lady at night. Are you ready to head to the restaurant?"

"Absolutely. I'm grateful to walk a bit after so many hours in the car today," I said.

"What's the commute from Nelson, including the Cook Strait Ferry?"

"Two hours to Picton, where the ferry departs. A three-and-a-half-hour trip on the water, then another eight hours to Auckland. So I traveled for around fourteen hours today," I said.

"Wow, Americans *are* crazy. What a drive," he said, shaking his head.

Laughing, I replied, "Yes. Long road trips are in our blood."

"Well, dessert is on me. You must be exhausted." He gave me a little smile.

"Thank you," I said, returning the gesture.

When we sat down at the table, I realized he was more distracting to look at than I'd imagined. Walking in the darkness, his frame was protective and strong, but seeing him in the light, I realized he was boyishly cute and ruggedly handsome at the same time. There was a depth, or darkness, about him that intrigued me, like Brad Pitt's Tristan in *Legends of the Fall*.

Conversation was quick and efficient, centering around athletic adventures. I was hanging on every word he shared about competitive windsurfing, training regimens, competitions, international dynamics, and coaching. I knew this world, and I knew the support role, too. It felt natural. He was equally curious about my life in the mountains, traveling, volunteering and gemology.

After dessert, which I actually ate, we went for a walk on the beach. The waves were peaceful, and we took a rocky footpath along the beachside community. My impression of Takapuna was amazing already; I loved the walkability and quaint downtown. Plus, being right on the beach and only fifteen minutes north of Auckland? It couldn't get any better, and I imagined myself apartment searching here.

"Would you like to come back to my place?" he asked, as we stopped along the trail.

"Yes, but I'm not going to," I said, just as confidently. "I'd love to see you again, though, if you're interested."

"I know you aren't in town for very long—how about I play tour guide tomorrow and show you around a bit?"

"I'd love that. I was hoping to get over to the West Coast to check out the black sand beaches. Is it worth it?"

"It is. We'll go to Bethells Beach—I know a great place for lunch along the way. I'll escort you home, then." He was very methodical, very matter of fact.

We started to walk back into town as it began to rain, softly at first. Then the sky opened up as if King Triton was raising the waves to the heavens, and we ran along the rocky path, quickly darting under the first tree for shelter. Wiping our soaking faces off and laughing, we looked at each other.

He gave me a look that clearly said, *Want me?*

And I answered, *Yes, please.*

We kissed until a clap of lightning jolted our bodies apart.

"Now you have to come to my place," he whispered into my ear.

"And how would that help us right now?" Water poured in every direction beyond the tree.

"It's right there," he said, pointing to a first-floor, ocean-facing condo not a hundred feet away.

"Oh, how convenient." I rolled my eyes and shoved his chest. *Whoa, muscles.*

"It's not my fault. It's the rain." He shrugged. "I guess you're meant to come with me tonight." It was almost as if he and the weather were in cahoots.

I wanted to go, I was just trying to hold out—trying to wait, to be harder to get this time. But he was right: the rain had destined us to take shelter together, at least for a little while.

"Lead the way."

I WAS IMPRESSED with my willpower. It was not easy to stay out of his bedroom. We dried off, made out, and cuddled until the rain stopped. Then he chivalrously walked me back to my apartment. The next few days found us together almost nonstop—laughing, learning, exploring, and yes, having sex. *Amazing* sex. He was an endurance athlete after all, and I loved the invitation to keep up. As with anything in life, there was a time to wait and a time to dive in—only we knew what was right for ourselves in that moment.

Mornings started with checking out new organic cafés, which usually led to walking on a beautiful beach, as they always seemed to be only a few minutes away. In the afternoons, I'd find a hike to explore, be it a cliff line jaunt or a lush trail to a waterfall.

I was falling in love with New Zealand more and more every day. The country and communities were wild and connected to nature in a way that spoke to my soul. The traditions of the Māori people were still alive and respected. The Haka, for instance—a ceremonial war dance calling upon their ancestors for strength and to represent a tribe's pride, strength, and unity—was performed before everything from professional rugby matches to wedding celebrations or special sessions of parliament.

And I was finally embracing being bad at something. Typically, I'm afraid of that—the perfectionist in me avoids even the possibility of failure. But I was obsessed with stand-up paddleboarding on the ocean; I had experience SUPing down rivers in Colorado and doing yoga on lakes, but the ocean was an entirely different dance. The powerful currents and vast expansiveness were intimidating, but the joy of surfing a wave was motivation enough to dive in. Although, I was *horrible* at it: I fell off, flailed about, swam to catch my board, then came up coughing and gasping for air. It was humbling. And it felt wonderful—it was liberating to be a beginner again, unafraid to try something new. I was also grateful for my body. If my spirit chose this body on purpose, knowing what it was meant to experience and accomplish in this lifetime, I appreciated the selection. Even after months of inactivity, my muscles fired right up, and my natural ability to adapt helped me navigate this new physical challenge.

Plus, The Olympian was a solid coach, always ready with advice. Seeing him was another metaphorical carrot stick: strong arms, solid chest, with perfect athletic grace maneuvering about the water. Don't get me started about his abs, leading down to the tops of his trunks—in this instance, reality was better than imagination.

After a few days of living the Kiwi life, my visit with Eberly had arrived. I could mix-and-match my way to a professional outfit, but I felt like wearing something different, so I purchased with purpose and wore a smart set—a fitted, deep blue, single-button suit with a white silk tank top underneath, a bold gold necklace and bracelet to compliment my rings, my scarf from Paris, and my red Dorothy stilettos. Thank goodness I was fearlessly embracing my loan for funding—it takes money to make money, right? I wanted to look the part.

The Olympian offered to drive me so I didn't have to handle parking, and we were headed there now. I was getting anxious—I wanted this.

"What do you think of fate versus destiny?" I asked to distract myself as we drove over the Auckland Harbor Bridge. Countless sailboats floated in the bay below.

"I believe in free will. Your life is what you make it." It was an appropriate answer from a hardworking and accomplished athlete. His results weren't handed to him.

"I believe in free will as well. And that's part of the big picture," I added.

"How do you see the big picture then?" he asked.

"Well, I think of destiny as the ultimate result, like what you're destined to *be*—a king, for instance. But fate is the present moment; it's *how* you get to be king that is mainly determined by choice, or one's free will."

"So, it's part of fate that we met, but that doesn't mean we're destined to be together."

As I laughed, I agreed with him. "Exactly."

"I've only ever wanted to sail—actually, I've only wanted to be the best sailor. Either way, the wind and ocean talk to me. It's the only communication I understand."

"It's courageous of you to follow your passion and relentlessly fight for your dreams."

"It's a lonely road, but it's mine," he said, looking out the window as we traversed the roads into the city.

Auckland has a beautiful skyline of prominent buildings, as well as the famous Sky Tower, where you can bungee jump off the rooftop. Driving into the concrete maze, I felt inspired by the same progressive energy as I had been in New York, and imagined myself finding a network of professionals here, having workday lunches and meeting up for happy hour.

I saw the store up ahead: classy entrance, dark colors, gold accents, with a locked and guarded door flanked by glass window displays. "Thank you for the ride, driver. Shall I text you when I'm ready for pickup?"

"Oh, you think this is a round-trip ride? Nah, it's just one way, missy." What a trickster.

"Cute. But considering you're driving *my* rental car, I think I'll be seeing you shortly, handsome."

"Good luck, kiddo. Go for gold."

"Thanks, Coach."

THE VISIT WENT great. In Eberly, it felt fabulous to be dressed up, surrounded by glass cases and the fine pieces I knew so well. The conversation easily escalated from a meet and greet into a full interview, and I quickly found myself proudly giving examples from my tenure with Framebridge. There was an opportunity to not only work in sales but also continue my path, creating strategic partnerships and unique events for Eberly's clients. After that, I changed my itinerary to stay in Takapuna instead of heading north to the Bay of Islands. Optimistic that I'd be living here soon, I figured the jaunt north could wait—I wanted to just *be* here while I was here, before I flew to Thailand in a few days.

I found a yoga studio around the corner from my hotel and went to my first kundalini class. Shit balls, did it do a number on me; it was an electric mix of science and spirit designed to activate your seven chakras. I looked in the mirror after an hour of holding specific poses, chanting mantras, and getting lost in a recipe of breathwork. My eyes were white—bright white and clear. It was amazing and effective, almost like an energetic medicine; I was hooked. During the class, I wanted to laugh, cry, scream, and sleep.

Speaking with the studio owner afterward, I asked about a necklace she had for sale. "It's a jade carving," she told me. "The symbol represents the wind—a sacred element to the Māori people."

"The color is vivid. It reminds me of tsavorite or emerald. The carvings are beautiful, too—such detail." It made me think of the fabled Emerald Tablet, where the secrets of alchemy are carved into a single stone, representing a portal to the soul of the world: a unifying force that leads all things to their destiny. *Was the legendary text from Hermes carved in jade?* I wondered.

"When a specific symbol calls your name, they say to follow it. It looks like you're already a friend of ideas like that, though," she said, pointing to my Pleiades tattoo. "Is that the Southern Cross?"

"No, it's the Seven Sisters. The maidens whom Orion is chasing through the sky. His belt points right to them."

"Ahhh, the sisters of the north. Well, the Southern Cross is very similar. Made from young, bright blue stars that are referred to as the sisters of the south. Pleiades' counterpart."

"What?" I did a double-take.

"Mmmmhmm," she nodded.

"That's incredible. So it's an astrological reflection, in a way." I tilted my head in her direction, still looking at the jade.

"You could say that. Maybe you have a counterpart here, in this part of the world." She had no idea what her words were relaying right now. "And you got the tattoo on your left arm, which holds the energy of your bloodline—your ancestors."

Maybe that energy healer years back was on to something. Maybe I am connected to the Pleiadians. I made a mental note to investigate further.

"Thank you for telling me all this. What an enlightening visit it's been," I said as I walked towards the register with the wind carving.

"I hope to see you again. You're welcome in for class or jewelry anytime."

"I'm hopeful I'll be in for a membership."

I would love for this to be my regular studio, I thought, leaving the store.

I now had the final piece of my tattoo puzzle. Lifting my chin and gazing straight ahead with new clarity, there was a skip in my step as I veered toward the beach. I had fallen asleep so many months ago with a dream and woken up with a purpose. And now, everything I'd gotten tattooed in blind faith made sense. *Fortis Fortuna Adiuvat*, Fortune Favors the Bold, represented my approach towards life, reminding me to take risks and embrace change. Manifest Magic represented the fact that we are active participants in life, we co-create our reality. Radiate Light was a beacon for connectedness, for spirit, for grace. And now, I realized the Pleiades constellation symbolized the traveler in me and was the ultimate, undeniable sign that New Zealand was to be my home. New Zealand was the inverse of my previous life, and the balance I needed: I would be leaving the mountains in Vail for the beach in Auckland. It also provided the city experience that drew me to New York.

The tattoos had not only helped me remember part of myself, they were also guiding me toward my future. It was like the wisdom was part of my DNA now, the ink a conscious memento of the journey it took to remember.

Driving to the airport for my departure to Thailand, I couldn't help but feel resistance. I loved it in New Zealand and had completely visualized life here. The idea of being offered a position with Eberly had begun to take root in my mind, not just as a professional opportunity, but as a symbolic reclamation. Perhaps, in some poetic twist, carving out a respected name for myself in the industry from this idyllic corner of the world would serve as the ultimate "f you" to Framebridge. I could summon that ambition; I was willing to do the work.

Sailing around Phuket had sounded fun and all, but it felt wrong to be flying away from a place that was strongly calling me to stay. However, my trip had been paid in full, and spending my money was one thing—wasting it was another. And as my dad had suggested, I should get out of New Zealand to think clearly about it. There had to be a reason I'd planned Thailand, and I was going to go through with the itinerary to find out what awaited me there.

Page number five of my passport was now stamped and complete, marking another testament of transformation. Given everything that had unfolded, I could hardly wait to see what lay ahead. Parting ways with The Olympian had been more pragmatic than passionate: a gentle closing rather than a dramatic goodbye. His farewell also subtly called me back. "Safe travels, blondie. I'll think of you every time it rains." I hadn't been looking for serious, but maybe serious had found me. Our connection felt familiar—grounded in a shared rhythm—and being with a competitive athlete felt normal. There was no commitment, since hope hinged on the job offer, but lovely potential.

At the airport newsstand, I reached for a bottle of water and a magazine when the cashier looked up and said, almost offhandedly, "I love your watch, it's beautiful." Her comment struck something in me. Without hesitation, I knew it belonged to her—continuing my pattern of letting go and choosing lightness, I removed the watch and held it out.

She hesitated, startled. "Oh no, I couldn't."

"Miss," I said gently, "this watch meant the world to me once. But I know, without a doubt, that it's meant for a new life now. It's no longer mine. So, either you accept it, or I toss it in that trash bin as I walk out the door." I gestured toward the nearby can.

She took the watch.

I walked away feeling unbound, like an energetic handcuff had been removed. Maybe tasting a new future had helped me release another relic from the past. Feeling decisive and free, I was ready for the twenty-hour overnight journey skimming above Australia, Indonesia, and Malaysia—it was time to detach from the world. With a quiet goodbye to New Zealand, I would soar at 35,000 feet above and awaken with a new welcome to page number six.

MY FIRST DAY in Phuket was a mix of anxiety and relaxation, rain and sunshine. I checked into a gorgeous hotel for the twenty-four hours before our sail, and the property came complete with multiple restaurants, swim-up bars, private beaches, water sports, a full-service spa, and a welcome ride in a golf cart. Lush jungle vegetation draped every doorway, and the terraced layout boasted magnificent views of the sea where smaller islands dotted the horizon. Smells of open-fire cooking, fresh spices, and tropical beverages wafted over the breeze. The idea of a massage sent my head spinning. Although splurging on this hotel for the night seemed well worth it, I decided to avoid the spa. In between spurts of warm, downpouring rain, I moved from stand-up paddling at the beach to napping in a cabana, then to my room to repack for the sail, and then to the lobby with my laptop, all in pursuit of distraction.

Because this was a group tour, I had nothing to arrange. After three weeks of planning everything in New Zealand, the lack of responsibility was welcome, but it also left space for my consciousness to fixate on the future—a future I was starting to actively plot again. I wasn't just traveling anymore.

It was dark now; evening had arrived, and I didn't plan to leave my hotel room until the morning when I was to join the catamaran crew. My mind spun as fast as my feet paced around the room. I hadn't heard from Eberly yet, and the job was all I could think about. After the departure tomorrow morning, I wouldn't have cell service or Wi-Fi for an entire week. What if they emailed and I couldn't reply? A whole week of not knowing seemed like torture.

My laptop was open on the bed, and I paced, refreshing my email, waiting for an update. Working for the store would give me financial security again, provide a visa for residency, and appease my family with a stable reason to move. I would be in an atmosphere where I could contribute, thrive by bringing my experience to the team, and start building a community in Auckland.

Plus, it would allow me to wrap up this incredible journey as a bona fide triumph. Six pages filled with discovery, and the seventh—the last page of the ex-Mrs. chapter—would be a celebration. With income in sight, I could choose a seventh and final destination, and spend the rest of my budget freely. All of these details made it possible to shove down the feelings I had felt in India—that something else called to me, that my career in jewelry was over. No, right now was about redemption: redemption for the shame of being laid off.

I had been doing it alone, and I had done *a lot*. I had gone from planner to spontaneous, embraced a plethora of diverse desires, gone from dependent to independent, and even started working on my internal relationship with myself. I had departed my status quo life and left everything familiar to get to know Whitney. And now the possibility of this job was a dream scenario that would allow me to get back on top and facilitate an official move halfway around the world.

On the other hand, if they didn't offer me a job, I'd be screwed. I could kiss moving to the Southern Hemisphere goodbye and would have to get seriously scrappy to make Manhattan work, or succumb to living in Vail for the next winter season, working a temp job and crashing in Jeannine's loft. Besides logistics, what would I be left with emotionally? The question scared me, sending shivers down my spine.

Manhattan could still make sense, I debated internally, more as a defense mechanism than anything. And maybe it was the right decision. It certainly wasn't a bad option, and I should have been simultaneously sending resumes there and following up on the apartment leads Heather was forwarding my way. How could I have put all my eggs into one basket? *I should know better than that by now,* I chastised myself. *I used to be a responsible, forward-thinking adult.* An immediate and intense cloak of doubt settled in; it felt heavy, damp, and cold, and I even started to shake. What was I going to do if I didn't get an offer? Tangible panic continued to creep in as I realized that I was almost dependent on it.

Ding. Email.

Hi Whitney,

We would be delighted to have you officially join the Eberly team. The details of your employment can be found in an official offer letter attached to this email. I know you're traveling at the moment, and there would be many details to sort out. So, enjoy the week, and please respond when you're back.

Best,
Owner

Oh my goodness. Oh, wow. It's going to happen—like, really happen. I made it happen. Holy shit, I'm moving to New Zealand! YES! I jumped up and down, silently pumping happy fists into the air and swirling about. I wanted to call everyone I knew and share the exciting news, but it was the middle of the night for Americans. I burst with joy, and that cloak of doubt immediately melted on the hotel room floor. Yes, I would take the job. I didn't care that I'd be doing something I'd done before or that I thought I was done with. This was the golden ticket to unlock the next stage of my life, and I'd eat a piece of humble pie to get it. Do you know who'd be excited? I sheepishly smiled to myself. Oh yes, I'd call The Olympian. My heart leapt at the idea of telling him the good news and feeling his shared enthusiasm from a world away. But after dialing, I hit voicemail.

I spun around and immediately drafted a reply to Eberly:

Hi Owner,

Thank you for giving me the time to consider. However, I accept. There are indeed details to sort, but I will make it happen. I look forward to joining the team in January and will be in touch to officially start the paperwork at the end of the week.

Best,
Whitney

Just before hitting send, I paused. I leaned back and realized I needed to take a *deep* breath and let this settle before jumping through the computer at them. My body buzzed, which felt incredible—everything was in sync, and I was feeling motivated and energized for the future again. *My* future. A future I was creating with passion and courage.

I wanted to celebrate. Thinking only of champagne, I bounced up and went into the bathroom to freshen up my makeup. "Hello there, magician," I said into the mirror, "Nice work." Then I beelined it to the hotel bar.

"CHAMPAGNE, PLEASE," I ordered.

"And what are we celebrating?" inquired a friendly couple a few seats down the tiki-style counter. She wore an off-the-shoulder, floor-length, crisp blue linen dress, and her curly blonde hair rested easily atop her shoulders. His ivory button-up was open one button too low, and brown leather flip-flops lay discarded under his chair.

"A new lease on life!"

"We'll drink to that—tell us everything." They were in their fifties, both entrepreneurs in tech and health, and traveling for a quick week away from their teenage children back in Australia. After giving them the CliffsNotes version of my journey, I ended with, "And now I'm back. Back into having an income, *maybe* starting a new relationship, and proving to everyone at home that I'm not crazy."

"Crazy gets such a bad rap," the wife laughed.

"Manifesting does, too," he added, twitching his toes. "I don't subscribe to the idea."

How can you not? I wondered. *It's just energy.* I asked him to explain further.

"Well, affirmations, positive thinking, and whatnot are cool— but where the rhetoric falls short for me is when bad things happen."

Interesting. After a sip of his slushy drink, he went on, "People like to take credit for their successes, but they faint at the slightest responsibility when things fall apart. Like when you lost your husband, house, and job all in twenty-four hours—no offense, but you didn't lose them. You created that."

"I did *not* manifest those twenty-four hours of hell," I quickly rebutted. "There were so many external circumstances influencing those outcomes."

"Sure, but there are always outside influences. It goes both ways. If you manifest the good things—sorry, girl—you manifest the bad, too." He seemed to be enjoying this.

"I think what my husband is trying to say," the woman said, "is to not be afraid of the failures or deflect blame."

"I agree it's just as important to know how to lose. But this is bigger than that." I was happy to share my recent insights with them. "Manifesting builds from emotion, and that requires intention for power. I didn't intend to create this life crisis—I didn't intend to hurt anyone, for that matter."

"Manifesting may build from emotion, sure, but it builds from *honest* emotion. And if underneath it all, your heart was craving freedom as you say—diverse experiences and to go at it alone—then that's the beacon your subconscious sent out. It obviously became your reality, just not in a way you liked."

Finishing my champagne and suddenly very uncomfortable in my seat and in their company, I ordered another glass to go.

"Well, yikes." They were strangers, and I decided being polite wasn't my priority right now. "I was just celebrating my first win in ages, and now you're saying I'm responsible for my own break-down. I'm just trying to figure it out, like anyone else would. Like I said, I didn't intend to hurt anyone." Why couldn't they see the difference and how far I'd come?

"People use good intentions as a scapegoat for accountability," he said. Everyone stayed silent after. "Our ego takes control, and we use good intentions as a free pass."

She quickly added, "But you're right, you deserve to celebrate as well, of course you do. And we're sorry." She patted his leg, encouraging him to nod in agreement. He readjusted in his seat. "This conversation just hits a nerve with us because there's a lot of propaganda out there which we feel tells our children to manifest their lives, instead of rolling up their sleeves to earn them, you know?"

I've done my fair share of earning what I have, lady. I've worked my ass off for all of it and am finally putting myself first, I thought, looking the other direction.

"Cool. Fair enough." I said, turning back to them. And then I was saved by the bell: The Olympian was calling me back. *Yes, something to reverse the mood here,* I thought, as I excused myself to answer.

"Hello," I answered, excited again.

"Hi, how's Thailand?" I immediately pictured his strong hand holding the phone near the jawline I'd been falling for—it sounded like he was at the beach.

"Wonderful. I mean, it was humid and a little rainy today, but I can't complain."

"If you did, no one would listen anyway." He was always direct; I could get used to that. I smiled at the idea of getting used to him in general.

"Good point. How's New Zealand? Does it miss me already?"

"Us Kiwis are just fine, thank you, with or without the blonde American—if you can imagine it," he teased.

"Well, you better get used to having one more American around." I was grinning like a clown again now—job and this handsome hunk? Yes, to both. Even my cheeks flushed.

"Oh, yeah? Did you get an offer?" I could hear an announcer call out over a loudspeaker in the back.

"I did."

"Congratulations. That must feel great—what are you going to say?" His tone was serious, almost flat.

"Yes, of course."

"Really? I have to admit, I'm surprised," it sounded like he finally leaned into the conversation.

"Why is that surprising?" I was so confused. He'd driven me to the meeting. He knew how important this was.

"I assumed your job search here was more testing to figure out what you wanted to do in New York. Like a practice round," he said. Was he serious? "New York has much more professional potential and suits your grand return—New Zealand is like a continued escape."

"No, moving to New Zealand is my priority, and a job is essential for that. This is perfect."

"I guess I don't know you that well, but it feels like this job would be putting a lioness in a cage. Taking it would be a cop out."

"A cage? A cage of possibility, maybe," I said, trying to remain lighthearted.

"Of course, of course. I'm happy for you—you're making it all happen. You should be proud."

"Thank you," I said, feeling depleted, but determined this was a good thing. "I'm not sure when I'll start, but my guess is it'll be after the holiday rush. They'll want me to train in January when there's slower floor traffic."

"Retail seasons—something I'm happy to avoid. Well, congrats again. I need to head back inside for the awards." Ah, he was at the afterparty for the weekly SUP races.

"Wait, aren't you curious when I'll be back to move in and get settled? It would be nice to meet up again." My head was spinning. He was technically being supportive, but it felt so cold.

"Maybe, we'll see. I mean, I hope you're not moving here for me—you know I'll be traveling all next year with the team, leaving at the end of January, and I don't plan to rearrange my schedule." He was getting colder as my cheeks were getting redder, only this time, with anger.

"I'm not moving to New Zealand for you," I said, trying to sound nonchalant. "But I thought, you know, an Olympian to help move boxes wouldn't be horrible."

"Of course, yeah. I mean, once you get here and are settled, if you need a hand with anything, let me know. I'll be happy to point you in the right direction."

"How kind of you."

"Always. Congrats again and have a great week. Hopefully you're sailing with a seasoned captain—the water can be tricky."

"I'm sure we are. Hope to talk soon."

"Bye-bye."

"Bye."

Hanging up the phone, I was stunned. And thoroughly confused—so many of his comments had thrown me off kilter. A lioness in a cage? Moving to New Zealand for him? Point me in the right direction? He was as polite as he would be to a stranger in the grocery store asking where the butter was.

I went back to my seat at the bar on autopilot, already forgetting the unnerving conversation I'd had with the couple. I now had additional disheartening information to process and was restless beyond explanation.

They asked if I was okay, referencing our conversation and unaware of what had transpired on the phone. Against my better judgment, I explained what happened.

"I agree with him about the job," said the husband.

Of course you do, I thought.

"You did just tell us that in India, you decided to never work in jewelry again. Now you are."

"But I *have to*, for a visa and income. And moving there matters more to me than being defiant about a career change."

"It's also good he kind of cut you off," she added. "Maybe it's not my place, but it sounds like staying single would be wise."

You're not my mother, I thought. *Don't pretend to know what my heart needs.*

"He didn't have to act so indifferent. He didn't have to do an abrupt 180 like that."

"Would you rather have him lead you on and then leave in January? I give him credit for being up front right away." Direct, huh? I *thought* I liked that about him—turned out Australians were just as unfiltered as Kiwis. "Well, I'm sure you've done that once or twice in life, too."

"Done what?"

"Flipped your attitude, opinion, or changed your mind. And when you did, I'm sure someone or something was on the other end of that change."

"Whew! You both like to throw mirrors up in people's faces, don't you? Well, I hope you've spent as much time examining yourselves as you have so rudely pointing out all my flaws." Abruptly standing to leave, I grabbed my glass. I had never been so rude to anyone in my life. "I'm going back up to my room to digest the rest of this." They nodded. Feeling my politeness kick back in, I added, "It was lovely to meet you, though, I think," waving as I walked away.

BACK IN THE safety and solitude of my room, I fumed. What had just happened? I felt horrible. On so many levels. Of course I wasn't moving to New Zealand for The Olympian—we'd just met. I decided to move before I met him. I had the job interview lined up before I met him. I called my parents and declared my love for the country and desire to join its citizens before I met him. How narcissistic to think it was for him, and then how detached he had become at the mere idea of me being on the same continent. Well, the writing on the wall was clear with that one.

But a lioness in a cage? Why did he make that comment? Professional opportunities aren't cages, and not all of us could play for a living—the offer was an amazing answer. So what if I wasn't passionate about the work anymore? I wasn't putting myself in a cage.

I'd been following the energy, pushing every boundary I could find, changing my perspective, and listening to my intuition. This was the universe sending that courage and optimism back with potential. It was providing an unobstructed door to a new future. I was fucking grateful right now, and all I had to do was walk through. I'd created this opportunity; they weren't even listing open positions. My inner vision aligned with outer action, and now it had become reality. Plus, I was seriously lucky to join Eberly—they seemed like kind people, and it was a respected, established business on the rise. And they wanted *me* to join them. Of course I was saying yes. What an honor it would be to work there. With renewed conviction, I opened my laptop and hit send on my acceptance email, not even allowing time for a proofread. Done. Decision made. I accepted the job.

I continued pacing, pushing my laptop away and The Olympian out of my mind, and began to rehash the conversation at the bar around manifestation—there was something I thought I was beginning to understand. That man said my subconscious was another inner faculty to consider when I thought about fault for my life blowing up. He was insinuating that I wanted all the upheaval to happen. With his logic, I was responsible for losing my husband, house, and job. But if I broke it down, I didn't want to lose my job. I didn't *desire* that, as you desire things you want to manifest. Maybe I was okay with leaving my house and had settled with my divorce by then, but what had really unhinged my life had been getting laid off. Consciously, I had been yearning for different and freedom, yes, but I had wanted it to be balanced with the stability of my career.

But what if my subconscious heard *freedom* and assumed that applied to all areas of life? *Complete freedom.* In that case, removing the final anchor of identity would have been mandatory. What if my conscious and subconscious weren't in alignment? What if those deeper beliefs contradicted my conscious intention? Which frequency triumphed?

Well, the subconscious is the powerful force that drives the whole process, and doesn't have the luxury of debating what was good or bad. It simply follows your true desires and acts to keep you on the path of your highest good. In that case, what we consider the bad or ugly parts of our lives are simply situations that materialized in a way we don't like. But they might be necessary to remove an obstacle or create an opportunity for us to learn from, to keep us on said path. What if my higher self had known from the beginning that losing everything was the only way to give me the true experience I craved? Then it would have conspired with the universe to remove anything hindering that outcome.

Shit balls. Maybe it *was* my fault—all my fault. Did I have to be accountable for where I had wound up? Had I ruined everything I'd built? If I didn't understand what I'd done, how could I trust the choices I was making now to decide where I went from here? How did I know if taking the job, or even moving, was what I truly wanted, or just a situation I had created? How could I discern the right next step?

No, it couldn't be that way. Even if my job was meant to be taken away, it didn't have to happen the way it did. They had cut me off—I wasn't responsible for that. After ten years of loyalty and hard work, they had ended it, just like that. Without even a proper goodbye, my career was over. They had flipped a switch—just like The Olympian. He had gone from being kind, supportive, and encouraging to distant, cold, and uninterested in a single moment. Abrupt change. There were switches flipping all around me—flip flop, flippity fucking flop.

I stopped, frozen.

I had flipped a switch.

That's what I had said to Heather about my marriage: that it was like a switch flipped in me when I saw the undeposited check lying on my kitchen counter. I caught my reflection pacing by the full-length mirror in my hotel room. I stared directly into my hollow eyes, seeing myself as if through my ex's eyes again. I had done it to him. Flipping that switch had cut him off and severed my commitment to our marriage. My reflection shattered into the thousands of images that had haunted me in the Hall of Mirrors in India, all pointing judgmental fingers right back in my face.

You did it first, they taunted.

Karma.

My breath stopped, as if someone had physically punched me in the gut; my jaw dropped open and my eyes quickly filled with self-loathing tears. My legs started to wobble and my chest caved inward as my body crumbled to the floor. I grabbed the shaggy carpet in my sweating, shaking hands and gripped it as hard as I would to stay on top of a bull at the rodeo. The fog of my thoughts cleared as my brain caught up to what my heart had just admitted, and I thought again, *that's how my ex-husband must have felt*. Except way, way worse. It wasn't a job; it was a marriage. I wasn't a boss; I was his wife. And we hadn't just met—our souls were bonded with over a decade of love. From his perspective, I had just flipped a switch. A switch we never came back from.

To him, in a single moment in time, I'd gone from 110 percent love and loyalty to neutral, indifferent, and off. I'd stopped doing the things he knew and loved about me. I'd stopped being interested in his adventures or putting my efforts into building our life together. I had always been the one in our relationship to guide the romance and ensure communication, but that dwindled as well. I had been searching so intensely for meaning, evolution, and freedom as an individual that it manifested outside our relationship because I hadn't been mature enough to separate the two. I hadn't respected him enough to let him see the unraveling. I hadn't respected our marriage enough anymore to wait. When a man called me infinitely interesting, I hadn't forgotten it, I hadn't walked away, I had turned back for more. I had broken my vows.

When I'd flipped the switch, my ex hadn't been aware of my internal struggle over the years, during which I'd been subconsciously creating space around my heart to protect it if he didn't come home from a day in the backcountry. A buffer for the unbearable pain I'd endure if he died. And he also hadn't been in the loop that I was deeply codependent, trying to be responsible for his happiness while inadvertently sabotaging my own. And I hadn't yet expressed how his coping mechanism for survivor's guilt was not only numbing his life and stunting his potential but also shutting me out, one drag of a joint at a time. He hadn't known because I hadn't known. I'd just tucked it all down, buried in denial, until it burst.

I saw the check again, lying dormant on our cold kitchen counter, and I knew in that instant that our marriage was over, but I hadn't been able to admit it—that would mean immediate failure. Instead, we had gone through the obligatory, societally accepted steps to divorce, and every one of them had hurt. We had uncovered much of this through therapy, but from his perspective, his wife—his best friend—had done a 180 in a single moment. What a sucker punch. No one deserves that.

How fucking unfair for him. How selfish and immature of me. I saw the parallels in my actions to those I resented most in others, and it seemed I was the wicked witch in my fairytale disaster. I heard the man from the bar echoing in my mind: *people use good intentions as a scapegoat for accountability.*

I saw the hypocritical cracks in my life and realized they all radiated from one central point: me. I was the one who had pulled the carpet out from under my own feet.

Losing my house had been a result of my actions. Losing my husband, my inactions. Losing my job—yup, me again.

I hadn't been ready to embrace my fate out east when the promotion had been offered. And when I'd said no, I had unknowingly set off a trajectory that derailed my career and propelled me towards being laid off. Throughout all of it, I had been too insecure to be vulnerable or honest with myself. My egotistical fear of failure and need for perfection had blinded me. How could I not have seen this before?

I crumbled.

The hotel room contained my sorrow and swirled with waves of rage. I banged my head against the wooden vanity while I remained limp on the floor. I looked to the right, my suitcase open and opinionless on the ground, indifferent to my emotions. I looked to the left, my laptop open on the bed, cursor waiting for action. I looked up, praying for forgiveness, and, finally, sat up, shut my eyes, wrapped my arms around my knees, and rocked. I rocked, attempting to soothe myself, until I realized *I still don't understand what I did or what I'm doing. Where I live or whether I have a job won't change that.* Nothing made sense. I cried myself to sleep, no longer celebrating new possibilities, but only feeling the bitter pain I had caused. It finally caught me.

WAKING UP IN the morning, I didn't feel any better. All the excitement I had felt, all the momentum and expansion I thought was beginning, was gone. My heart whispered to remain grateful for the present, and I was. After all, I was about to embark on my first overnight sailing adventure, charting a course through the exotic and breathtaking islands of the Andaman Sea. I knew I was fortunate. And yet, I couldn't seem to shake the oppressive weight that had settled over me like a lead vest in my sleep.

On paper, I had everything I'd asked for: a promising new job, a stable income, and the possibility of a place to call home. But I was still not happy. What in the ever-loving hell was wrong with me? After mentally branding myself with a scarlet letter and dubbing myself the wicked witch of all Oz, I concluded that my intuitive channels were blocked, my internal compass scrambled. If I were destined for a breakdown, at least it would unfold in paradise.

But the universe wasn't quite done toying with me. Our first group encounter only made matters worse; my skin nearly crawled when I spotted, of all people, the same couple from the bar standing at our rendezvous point. In the haze of my self-absorbed escapade, I'd never bothered to ask what their plans were for the week away from their children. Surprise! They were now a cabin down, and I had zero chance of peace. I had little doubt they'd be ready to highlight my next round of flaws. I would steer clear for now. Avoidance seemed the wisest strategy. Lowering my chin, I bypassed them and made my way toward a few unfamiliar faces—a few women who appeared to be traveling alone, gathered at the far end of the dock.

During introductions, we learned the catamaran officially housed four solo travelers: me, a girl from California, and another from Switzerland—my new roommates—as well as a funny but sarcastic man in his sixties, the dramatic duo from the bar, and a newlywed couple from the UK. That brought our passenger count to eight. We were joined by a four-person crew: our French captain in his forties, two grinning local chefs, and one youthful first mate. We were soon to be severed from the digital world, each of us permitted only a small, dry weekender bag of essentials. Our luggage and our Wi-Fi would be left behind on the dock, as we stepped into a simpler, saltier existence.

The stunning Lagoon 52 catamaran offered both interior and exterior lounge areas, a fully equipped kitchen, a diving platform, a dinghy, dual mainsails, and, perhaps most unexpectedly, ample pockets for privacy, despite our close quarters. Our days ahead promised a tapestry of island explorations, starlit evenings, bonfires on the sand, hikes through lush forest trails, and immersive visits to local villages. Food and drink would flow without restriction, with the chefs proudly introducing us to a menu of fresh, local cuisine. The bar operated on an honor system—a gesture of trust that added to the vessel's relaxed atmosphere.

It was midafternoon, we were an hour away from Phuket, and I had a cold beer in my hand. The sky was bright and clear, with our weekly forecast showing no sign of rain. So far, the random directional beacon of "sunshine in the forecast" had panned out; I'd experienced light rain a few times, but it had been welcomed. The showers in Queensland had brought me to the vineyards, and the charged thunderstorm in Takapuna had led to hiding under that fateful tree for steamy shelter. Other than that, almost every day on this multi-month-long journey around the world had been filled with sunshine—externally, at least.

I still have page number seven to plan, I remembered as I rocked in the netted hammock on the front of the boat. *Maybe the fresh breeze and gentle sea spray will wash away my guilt, and my imagination can hone in on a final country to visit.* But the tormenting tagline—*how do I know what I want?*—crept right back in. I decided to distract myself by tuning into the group's chatter instead.

"Elections seem like a scam. No one makes up their own mind anymore," one of the newlyweds was saying.

"And your generation forgets they even have a mind of their own. It's like you want to experience the social media version of life and consider yourselves woke without going out and learning the hard lessons," added the man in his sixties.

"Yeah, everyone wants to post a pic at the end of an IRON-MAN, but they think they can grab a special token from a video game and skip miles sixteen through ninety-eight," replied the other newlywed.

Interesting analogy, I thought. "The power of inception is so important," I added. "We can be told what we should do, but until you live it and it matters to you, it won't stick."

"But there's a recipe to life, right? Rules you grew up with and expectations to meet. Comparing yourself to the Jones's, as you Americans say," said the newlyweds, nodding.

"*Pff*, but you don't subscribe to the whole," replied the man. "You need to see societal expectations for what they are—a bullet list of ideas, not all or nothing rules. And you can't use them as excuses for your happy or unhappy life."

"Well, I followed the rules and then totally fucked up my life," I huffed, suddenly with no shame in talking about my catastrophe. "I'm recently divorced, homeless, and nearly broke. But," I quickly added, making sure to avoid eye contact with the couple from the bar, "I have a plan to fix it all, finally, and just accepted a new job."

"Lunch is ready," the chef called from the stern of the ship, protecting me from being barraged with opinions. We all hungrily headed to the lounge; I was happy to avoid exposing myself further, and my tummy was equally excited for our first meal aboard.

"Congrats," the girl from California said as we navigated the ropes and ladders to the back. "Seems like you're finding your way to a new life."

"More like stumbling."

"I'm divorced as well," she offered. "Do you miss your ex?"

"No. Well, I miss the friendship, but mostly embrace moving on. How about you?" I awkwardly added, "I still feel him with me sometimes. Does that sound weird?"

"My ex was an abusive asshole. I hate him. What do you mean you still feel him with you?"

"It's like some memories still connect us. I'll get very angry during points of stress and all of a sudden I'll *see* him. It's like I can feel what he's feeling."

"Maybe your soul contract isn't over."

"My what?" I looked back at her.

"Souls come down with agreements in this lifetime. Maybe you haven't learned what you need to yet. So strong emotions keep coming up, giving you the chance to see what you've been missing."

It certainly seemed like I had more to learn, I thought, as she continued. "Your reaction sheds light on what you've yet to process. The intense energy you feel is about you, not him." Pointing the finger at myself instead of others seemed to be a theme. "Plus," she went on, "if he is radiating out anger, that's *his* anger. It will reach you, sure, because there's no real distance, but you have a choice to absorb it or not."

"What do you mean, no real distance? I haven't seen him in months." We were nearing the lounge and walking slowly, a pace behind the others.

"Nonlocality. The idea that distant objects can be connected in ways that defy classical physics. It would be quantum entanglement in this situation, because particles of your being have mixed. It theorizes that they'll never completely separate—there is no unmixing."

"So, I'm stuck with the feeling of him forever?"

"No, like I said: it's your choice to absorb the energy and emotions you sense or not. I find that whenever I'm trying to move forward, it's impossible until I face the past and clear it. I'm not talking about thinking about who or what I'm leaving. I'm talking about complete clarity on who *I* was—my role in my own life."

"Starting to think about that one, yeah," I admitted, looking down at my hands after we took our seats at the end of the table. "I'm starting to see things from his perspective."

After a brief pause, she said, "Don't settle for partial truth. You're denying the true depth of the experience if you don't dive into your darkness, too. Your dragon." As she settled her napkin and positioned her water bottle, she continued, "We all fuck up, it's inevitable. But you only grow if you own up to your actions."

"What does that look like? And, I have to ask, where is all this advice coming from? Are you a psychologist, or something? Involved in AA?"

"Fair question," she laughed. "And no. I've learned a lot about myself and life during recent ayahuasca retreats. The medicine called to me after my divorce, and I've gone down some big rabbit holes of realization and research."

I hadn't thought about Aya since leaving Colorado.

"All I know is that when I decided my old life wasn't working anymore," she continued, "it took me ages to grasp that before I could transmute anything. I had to embrace my shadow self."

"Shadow self?"

"The sides of you that you hide. Or are ashamed of. The dragon."

"So, I need to slay my inner dragon?"

"I don't think of it like that. For me, I'm just getting to know mine. She's a bit bitchy and hesitant to open up, but we're getting acquainted, nonetheless. Aya helps with the dialogue." She rolled her eyes.

"Thank you, I think," I said, rising from the table.

"Lunch is almost ready," she reminded me. "Where are you going?"

"Don't wait for me, I'll be back," I said, and went below deck to be alone. The sea was calm, but I didn't seem to be getting a break from personal blows. My heart was starting to race, and, even though I didn't *want* to dive into these thoughts right now, I knew I couldn't idly join small talk. Like a moth to a flame, I beelined it to the tiny mirror in our tiny private bathroom to let the echoes of my mind consume me.

"I NEED A therapist," I whined to the mirror, half-laughing, half-desperate. Yesterday's revelations had hit like a freight train— an undeniable reckoning that I alone was responsible for the messes in my life. Not knowing how to integrate that truth was daunting enough, but the looming idea of diving headlong into my own shadow? That felt like a cosmic joke. My spirit was in knots, tangled in questions that had no clear beginning or end. *I suppose it's all connected,* I thought. *Everything is. If I was so absorbed in having my life put together that I missed the glaring signs that it was falling apart before, how do I step outside the situation now to make choices from a wiser perspective?* My frantic eyes just stared back at me in the coffin of a bathroom.

I already said yes to the job. It's the safe choice. And I need something safe right now, I thought, gripping the sink. But the guilt lingered like a bruise. *Should I call my ex? Would it matter to him at this point? And what about this shadow of mine? How exactly am I supposed to face it?*

The questions didn't let up. *What's even concealed in my shadow? A shadow surely contains more than just characteristics of myself that I find undesirable to society. Maybe it holds the truths I've long avoided—failures, harm I've caused, the corners I cut.* Perhaps I had once believed I was above dealing with the consequences, too immersed in ambition to notice the collateral damage. Was that who I'd become? A self-important perfectionist obsessed with achievement? And now, to that list, I'd have to add selfish, lazy, indulgent, and morally ambiguous. I slid my head into my hands, unable to look at my reflection any longer.

Had I always been like this? Or had I learned in childhood that survival meant avoiding accountability? Maybe decades of people-pleasing and sidestepping judgment had trained me to deceive even myself. And here I was, looping back into the very patterns that cracked me open in the first place.

Rising frustration and antagonizing thoughts jockeyed for attention in my psyche: *fancy job, attracted to an athlete (even if my connection with The Olympian is dead in the water), and desperately wanting to prove something to people back home. This is all ego, clawing its way back into the driver's seat.* Even my UTI and speeding ticket were signs from the universe to slow the fuck down. How quickly I had gone from trusting that I needed to create my own moral compass to being blinded by the crowns of the past.

This is truly a web of my own making, I thought.

I let out a gush of hot air, fogging the mirror. And then I took another deep breath. My head spun. It was all so overwhelming.

Every mirror I came across had been creating a black hole of unprocessed traumas and limiting beliefs, all of which I had no tools to navigate.

Forget that. I stood straight and ran the cold water. *I'm not all horrible. My spirit may be finally showing me the gamut of all my facets, and I have a lot to learn. But like anything else, it's not all or nothing.* I thought back to my recent behaviors. Maybe not every facet of my shadow was something to banish—maybe there were parts I liked. I liked the woman who emerged in France, sensual, unfiltered, and free. Maybe I was a bit of an epicurean: selfish with money, extravagant on occasion, and fond of my voice after a few drinks. I liked lying around all day doing nothing. I liked being alone. Maybe I found forced politeness or constant social performance exhausting. If these were my shadows, maybe they weren't flaws to fix, but truths to integrate.

I need to forge ahead. I know I have so much to be grateful for, I thought. I was not going to be able to think my way out of this. I concluded I should shut off my obsessive brain, compartmentalize for now, and deal with this existential crisis later.

I was famished, and didn't want to miss our first lunch at sea. So I refreshed my makeup, put on a bikini, and went above deck, into the light—literally and figuratively. After all, we didn't have cell service. I couldn't call anyone to vent or repent.

A FEW DAYS later, we were bound for Ko Phi Phi Le, the iconic island made famous by the film *The Beach*. What thrilled me most wasn't the destination itself, but the journey to get there: after diving from the catamaran into the blue sea, we would swim toward a rocky outcrop where a narrow staircase climbed up the cliffside. From there, we'd hike through a tangle of jungle pathways and rickety bridges, emerging at last into a tiny village before reaching the beach. That final reveal—the towering pinions rising proudly on either side of the cove—was said to be unforgettable. We'd have time to swim, unwind, and mingle with other travelers once we arrived.

After the first day at sea, I hadn't completely shaken my doubt or self-loathing, but I had managed to join the group and embrace the adventure. To my surprise, the group dynamics had remained lighthearted, and I'd found myself laughing more often than I expected. I had still made it a goal to strategically avoid the couple from the bar, which was hard to do on a small boat, but I was proud of my stealth maneuvers thus far. I totally loved my roommates; they were both seasoned and curious travelers, and the three of us had found a quick camaraderie.

Our days so far had been filled with swimming and snorkeling in crystalline waters, stand-up paddleboarding, yoga, and even the occasional impromptu photoshoot. We had explored hidden coves and remote islands, all punctuated by the chefs' exquisite meals, which exceeded every expectation. Thailand had been welcoming at every turn, and the hospitality of our crew was second to none.

Now, I reclined on a beanbag chair atop the deck, the sea breeze rustling the pages of my 5-Year Plan workbook. Its cover was sun-faded and its contents largely untouched: no fresh goals, insights, or revelations to record. I realized, with a faint twinge of guilt, that I'd spent my entire time in New Zealand without even opening it. Chapter 7, "Questions to Uncover Your True Self," was still blank. All it had taken was the distraction of adrenaline activities and men, and I had put a noticeable pause on my internal quest. Now the endeavor would take a completely different shape to include my shadow and incorporate my subconscious. *Hypocrite and undedicated need to be added to the list,* I thought, rolling my eyes and looking out to the ocean.

"What's everyone's favorite quote?" the girl from Switzerland asked the group.

I shared the quote that reconnected me with my intuition, telling me to leave my marriage. I explained that my grandmama had given it to me and how it had partially reframed my philosophy on life. "I wonder why your grandmama gave you that quote," someone chimed in. "It seems a bit odd, when you think of the plethora of choices out there."

Good question. I'd only thought about what it meant to me—I hadn't considered why she chose *that* one. Maybe it had meant something to her? Had she done the thing she thought she couldn't? Or was the opposite true—had she not done the thing she wanted? I closed my eyes and tried to surrender internally. I tried to feel the light I felt in India, to embrace a hug from home that I thought I could summon. Nothing. I didn't have the answer. But I couldn't help but think it was bigger than me, and that the advice was multigenerational—maybe I was healing something that would heal others. I wished more than anything that she was still here to ask.

Well, Grandmama, I whispered, keeping my eyes closed and face towards the sun, *it seems the thing I cannot do right now is simply figure myself out. I feel like I'm on a rollercoaster, and I'd appreciate a break. Please help; send me advice and I'll listen. At least I'll try.*

TO ME, THE sexiest thing in nature is moonlight on water. The silent movement of silvery, glistening light dancing with the cool, silky surface of wild waves is perfection: a connection, a relationship between the worlds above and below. If I could bottle it up as a perfume, it would be my signature scent.

I wonder what we look like from up there, I thought, as the catamaran gently rocked back and forth with the waves, the silhouettes of nearby islands rising tall from the water's surface. Dangling my feet off the railing, I leaned back on my hands with my head tilted towards the sky, and wondered if we left an energetic trail of light as we lived our lives. If I put a spotlight on the earth to mark every place I ever went, and at the end of my life connected all the spots like a constellation, it would create a spherical ornament: a 3D, energetic fingerprint of sorts. Something unique to each person and each lifetime.

What would my fingerprint show? Would the light burn brighter to highlight the explosions that redirected my path along the way? Or would it lay out the years and choices evenly, without judgment? I imagined my energetic fingerprint would show a different frequency from my last few months, maybe with a few spirals and zigzags hidden in there like hieroglyphics.

But right now, as I sat alone on deck during our last night at sea, my fingerprint was hovering, waiting for me to make my next move and continue creating the story of my life. That night was the last night I'd find myself in between lives: the last night of traveling without a plan. Because tomorrow, when we returned to cell service and expectation, my journey would move forward in a solid direction. It was time to let the world know I'd taken the job with Eberly and would move to New Zealand in January.

"Penny for your thoughts?" chimed our captain, topping the staircase to the deck.

I was surprised to see him. He'd kept quiet at dinners and during shore excursions, making sure we were safe and enjoying ourselves, of course, but elusive nonetheless. I shared my musings.

"Your energetic fingerprint? What's that?" I told him the theory I'd just made up, and he seemed to subscribe. "Besides that, I'm thinking of plans I need to make. I'm moving to New Zealand, but no one knows yet."

"That's big news. Congratulations."

"Thanks. It's perfect. I have a job lined up which will provide me with everything I need to get started—a visa, income, and a network. Plus, I'll get to finish this crazy trip I'm on, filling the pages of my passport with a final stamp of celebration. Maybe Japan, or Singapore, or… have any ideas?"

"I'd say yes to all of those places. You seem to have it all figured out," he said in his slight French accent. His tanned skin seemed to be a color that never faded—it was part of who he was, like the sun. He had thick brown hair, usually kept in a low ponytail, and always wore an official captain shirt with clean shorts, with either bare feet or loafers.

"Well, I don't know. It's a solid plan," I said, then paused. "But my gut isn't behind it, and my heart wants to run from it."

"Run from what?" His question lingered for a moment, the sound of water lapping our boat distracting me.

"The job," I stated, turning to face him, "I'm uniquely qualified, and it's a wonderful opportunity. But I made a promise to myself, and taking the job would break it." I'd even prayed about it.

"A promise not to work?"

"No, just not in jewelry again. A month ago, I was one hundred percent sure I was destined for something else." I shook my head. "Taking it is still clearly the sensible option. Which I already did, anyway, so it's a bit of a moot point."

"Just because it makes sense doesn't make it right," he said, lightly tapping his feet against the side of the boat.

"Yeah, my goal was to avoid retracing steps, but at the first chance I started cementing the past into the future." I rolled my eyes at myself in the darkness. "I've been so happy on this journey, not knowing what's next."

"Sounds like you're at a real point of cognitive dissonance."

It was true: my actions certainly contradicted my beliefs. "I just have this yearning to reinvent myself. But my bank account is something I'm desperate to right-size."

"Never trust a desperate person's actions," he said. "Especially your own."

Decent rule to follow. For the quiet type, he was full of advice—he looked confident giving it, too, as he leaned back on his elbows, kindly holding space for me. I asked if he had a personal story to go with that one, and he told me about his own journey of awakening, leaving an esteemed culinary career to be a brave pirate. He had been destined for freedom, but had stumbled more than once along the way.

"I'm not just financially desperate, though. I've started to see that I've been denying accountability for a lot in my life. I'm worried I don't know myself well enough right now to make choices about anything."

"Decisions should be a split-second type of thing," he continued, "you can only make choices based on the information you have in that moment."

"Sure," I half nodded, "and roads not taken still go somewhere."

"Maybe you need to right some wrongs or clear the air. But forgive yourself so you can move on."

"Forgive myself? I've barely started to understand what I've done."

"It'll take time. But what's more important? To accept the job and report back to the safety zone? There's no shame in that; it's a valid option. Or is it better to say no to anything that keeps you as the past version of yourself?"

"I mean, my heart says the latter, but my bank account and my head are screaming for security."

"Okay, then. For conversation's sake, is it literally down to the last one hundred dollars or whatever to eat?"

"No, if I know I'll have an income again, I can spend the small amount I have left to cover my seventh trip and get me home to regroup and move in January."

"What if you didn't take the job?"

"I would need to fly home immediately. There isn't enough money left to continue traveling and then get situated in a new city."

"How does *that* feel in your body?"

"Even worse, because then I don't accomplish the one thing I know for sure... that I'm meant to live in New Zealand."

"Ah, so that's the siren song?"

"Yes. That's why I was so motivated to get a job lined up and make it happen."

"If you trust yourself to move home and figure out a job, why not trust yourself to get to New Zealand and do the same?"

"The lack of friends, visas, or network will make it harder."

"But possible?"

I sighed. "Anything is possible."

"Hmmm... how would it feel if you went home, did what you needed to, and used the final funds to get back to New Zealand, so you had a chance to figure it out?"

I was quiet for a spell. "Scary. My hair is standing up," I said, raising my arms. "I almost feel like laughing. You know, a nervous, holy shit, panicky kind of laugh? I never thought of saying no and going anyway."

"Does it feel like freedom?"

"So much so. But I'd have to return to the US right away, rush everything, and pray I can make it happen in time."

"Why the rush?"

"Because without this job, I couldn't get an essential skills visa. My events background isn't unique; it isn't considered a special skill. I'd have to get a working student visa and, funny enough, I turn too old to qualify for that in about a month. Plus, I'd have to double down on myself and use the rest of the loan I have, with no way of knowing how I'd pay it back. And then use credit cards to survive."

"But could it work?"

"It's possible..."

"I see. Don't you owe it to yourself to go for it? At least then you'd be living in coherence with your only honest goal and not compromising yourself with an agenda that isn't in alignment."

This catamaran journey wasn't only rocking with the waves, it was rocking my world. Like a message from the mystics I now knew, I was meant to go to New Zealand without a plan.

"You're completely right—I can't move halfway around the world to hit repeat, even if it's easily justifiable. Even if it would be comparatively easy. I didn't come this far to only come this far. And if I want to build an authentic me, a new path forward, I need to make sure each brick fits. Oh, shit, I can't take the job. Oh, shit... but I still *have* to go." I let this sink in for a moment as the wind started to pick up. The captain looked at the flags, clocking the atmospheric change: things were starting to move. "This means I need to fly home right after we get back, and I won't accomplish my goal of filling all the pages in my passport with stamps. I'd have to leave the last page blank."

"How fitting. The final entry is a heroic early return, only to turn around and leave again, going after what you truly want. Not a failure at all, just a change."

Not a failure, just a change. I like that.

"It feels like this is the first time I'm being tested with a truly critical decision. I have to choose to say no to something great, choose to leave an amazing offer on the table, and say yes to the unknown. I have to jump *again*, into a trust fall with the universe."

"We never really know if we're evolving until moments like this. You've got courage. And I know what it takes to hunt for a destination unlocked."

"Unlocked. I had a pen from a hotel in Panama that said, 'Destination Unlocked.' I always liked that pen." And the retreat I got it on was my first solo trip ever—the trip where I started questioning everything in my life. This felt right. Just an hour ago, I was completely convinced I'd take the job, and now I knew I couldn't. "You permitted me to not have it all figured out. You reminded me to trust one simple fact. Again."

It felt as though he wanted to hug me, but his professionalism held him back.

"How do you feel?" he asked.

"Nervous," I said. "It won't be easy, but it'll be worth it."

He smiled. "And free?"

"A new level of free. Freedom with sovereignty."

"Keep going. The details will align," he replied, as he started maneuvering to rise from our seat along the railing.

"How do I thank you?" I asked with urgency as he headed down the ladder.

"When you see a kindred spirit pondering similar questions, do the same."

Alone again, I looked up at the night sky and let out a *long* breath I must have been holding the entire conversation.

What just happened? Did I dream that, or was he some sort of angel? I asked myself. Closing my eyes, I imagined myself up in the stars again, looking down on our boat. What is it to be human? Being here, in this exact time and space, in this body, is a miracle in and of itself. Each one of us individually weaving our energetic fingerprints, eternally overlapping to experience the interconnectedness of all things.

I guess I'd just made life a little more straightforward for myself. *Steph was right: Fuck Yes and No Less. I see it works for more than just clothes. Fuck yes, I'm moving to New Zealand. And it feels like the most human thing of all to not have it figured out.* Still sitting on the side of the boat, I became my six-year-old self again, who whispered, *I'm thinking. And then I will be brave.*

"Good advice, kid," I said aloud. "But I think I'll adjust it to 'feel and be brave.'"

And then I jumped off the side of the boat and in a new direction.

The cold water rushed my senses and cleansed the past. Immersed in the underwater silence, I felt the oxygen in my blood radiate through my body while my spirit swirled around me with joy. I lingered for a few moments in the darkness. I lingered to integrate with more than I knew and welcome what was left to learn, respecting both the light and the dark within me.

Finally, I came up for air and, after a float, swam back to the boat. As I climbed the ladder towards the railing and my towel, I heard a faint song coming from below deck: U2's "Where the Streets Have No Name." My heart immediately filled with love and connection to home, to my mom. I closed my eyes and could smell the sand in the indoor riding arena kicked up by the dancing hooves of her Arabian horse. I could see my mom riding gracefully, proudly, smiling as they went through her dressage routine choreographed to this song. Watching her ride, I could feel the freedom singing straight out of her soul. I knew my dad was similarly liberated when he was surrounded by endless horizons in the cockpit.

If we're lucky, we all find our unique experience of internal freedom. And this song was a sign that I was becoming connected with mine, even if I didn't know what it was yet.

I STARED OUT the oval window from my economy seat, 35,000 feet above the Pacific Ocean. Physically detached from the world but overflowing with connection to it, I took a sip of red wine and nestled in for the twelve-hour flight from Thailand to Wisconsin. Two days ago, we had docked back in Phuket. Departure from the catamaran had entailed sincere hugs all around, and I had even humbly thanked the couple from the bar for their harsh advice, to which they'd wished me well. Everyone had exchanged contact details and promised to stay in touch; my roommate from California had invited me to visit her in San Francisco, mentioning that I should join her next year at an event called Burning Man. But even if I didn't see anyone again, it was perfect as it was: the sail had provided me with an isolation bubble and cast of characters I needed to avoid repeating momentous mistakes moving forward.

The captain had offered his apartment in Phuket for me to extend my stay and think things through while he took off on another tour, but I had kindly declined, and stayed instead in a convenient hotel right by the airport. I'd booked a flight back to the Midwest for the next day. My parents had been thrilled I was on my way home, yet confused that I refused to divulge further plans—plans I concluded would be better delivered in person.

I had also sent an awkward and apologetic email to Eberly rescinding my acceptance of their offer. It had taken longer to hit send than when my hasty celebration delayed my initial acceptance, the embarrassment of my indecision mounting. I hoped that in the future I'd know myself better to avoid the residual negative impact. But not three minutes later, the first critical piece of fate had fallen into place to inspire me to keep going: I'd received an email from Jane, my friend who lives in Auckland, who was thrilled that I was thinking about moving and had provided the first open door to make it happen.

An open door to stay in her new home.

She and her fiancé were going on holiday for three weeks over Christmas and New Year, and she had invited me to use their beautiful home and car as a base of exploration while taking care of their adorable puppy Luna. What a gift—divine timing and critical assistance. I now trusted, without a doubt, the quote from Paulo Coelho: "When you want something, all the universe conspires in helping you to achieve it." My immediate response was *yes*. Yes, with everything in and around me, this was right. But I had to keep in mind that without the working student visa, I could only stay six months without the right to work, which I couldn't afford. With the visa, I could stay a year *and* work. The visa was non-negotiable.

The rest needed to come together like a zipper to work. The problem was that essential elements were flying in from all different directions. I was simply radiating out an ask, had a belief in the result, and was receptive to the journey. The tapestry would unveil itself one free, spontaneous, and separate thread at a time; but I would also need to get my type A, uber-organized self to hustle to do my part in supporting this alignment. That meant, upon landing, that I'd need to arrange my divorce papers, new passport, medical check, and luggage to allow for as much wiggle room as possible within my ten-day window in the US. Whew.

I sat back in my seat and loosened the belt, settling into the fact that this flight was the final leg of my spontaneous, solo adventure of following serendipitous signs and weather forecasts to fill the blank pages in my passport.

What had I just lived? I shook my head and flexed my shoulders to get comfortable. Pages one through three led me to France, Switzerland, and Italy. Then, to cover pages four through six, a reframing of intention led to group tours in India and Thailand, which sandwiched a life-changing visit to New Zealand. What would fill the seventh and final page?

Nothing.

I released the feeling of failure from not filling all seven pages with foreign destinations, and replaced it instead with self-acceptance: the journey was perfect the way it unfolded, even if it wasn't the way I imagined it. I wasn't ending early or leaving it incomplete, I was adjusting the course due to new desires and new information. I was flowing like the river back in Vail, full of faith and flexibility; I was making decisions for me and only me instead of letting outside judgements or old emotions shackle my route ahead.

The seventh and forever blank page actually held everything: it held my surrender, my love, my pain, my courage, and now my conviction to start again. My final choice was made of free will to change—not in the future, but now. To end it now. To begin again, now. I would leave it blank and let go. I wasn't in between lives, I was showing up for *my* life. All of it.

No one has the right to tell you how much time is necessary for evolution, or healing, or to gain wisdom, because of how long it took them. *We* decide. And I couldn't keep looking at my past as something to fix—I had to respect it for what it was, the reality and entirety of it, and say thank you for the magic, thank you for the lessons, but I choose to let it go. Nothing needed to be fixed.

Living a spherical life means embracing it all: diversified external experiences, internal evolution, good memories, *and* bad mistakes. But beyond that, it's about feeding your passion, loving the wild, respecting your shadow, facing your fears, having the courage to apologize, and above all, the courage to hope. I realized that all of it left an imprint on our energetic bodies, but the difference between feeling that emotion and becoming emotional was the attachment to the story. And if I saw myself as a spirit embracing being human, my entire outlook changed.

Sinking further into my seat and enjoying my wine, soft tears returned to my lashes. I could release my attachment to my story—I wasn't angry that I had been laid off anymore. I was filled with pure gratitude for the decade-long career I had enjoyed with Framebridge and the incredible experiences I had while working there. It wasn't their fault I wasn't ready when it ended; it was just business. And it was time I released my resentment so I could fully appreciate that chapter of my life. That's the vibration I wanted to carry with me: gratitude for them and for my work there.

I wasn't a failure because I didn't own a home anymore or have a buttoned-up life on paper. I was raw and stripping down to the bare bones to rebuild an authentic life in alignment with my higher self, and that would take time. It was freeing, not to know everything all at once. It was liberating to wait for life to surprise me while trusting the quiet confidence that I was capable of figuring it out when it did. Society would continue as it had, and my only responsibility was to be honest with myself.

Now closing my eyes and dropping into my heartbeat, I tuned out everything in the plane besides the rhythm of the beat itself. My love. My former marriage, my ex-husband. He wasn't the problem; he had his own problems, but he wasn't mine, nor was our marriage. I was the problem. I had fallen in love so young, and so fully, that I hadn't known where he ended and I began—I had only focused on fixing him instead of seeing me. My self-worth had rested on his approval, and my identity had become dependent on his. I hadn't been fully respecting him, because I hadn't been respecting myself.

There were no words to describe the space that had been left after walking away from that love. But clinging to past emotions, holding an old connection, and retracing the pain, blame, and fear was no longer what I chose to do. Life had created the conditions that made it impossible to stay together because we were destined to part. Just as we had been destined to love, our souls had known it was temporary and that's why it had been so intense. As tears fully streamed down my cheeks, I whispered out loud, "I thank you for the love, and I release you."

I released my ex, so his energy could be free to find love again. I released my anger, so it no longer shadowed the beauty of what was. I released my codependent connection to a human I had been sure I could never be without. I released my guilt and accepted that things were the way they were meant to be. I cut the cord to free my soul. I cut the cord to free it all.

It was time to fully remember the love, for all of it. To completely move forward, I needed not only to acknowledge the pain but also to honor the joy. The happy memories, too, deserved to be seen, respected, and consciously released. If I were to trust myself in the future, I first had to extend grace to the version of myself who had lived, chosen, and loved in the past. I wanted to immerse myself in the brightest memories, to feel their warmth fully, to allow the emotional resonance to flood me without resistance. Only by surrendering to their impact could I truly alchemize the energy and clear space for what was to come—I would honor and release so that the loop was closed. So, tucked in the window seat, I lost myself in memories for hours. I remembered the love.

Breathing slowly, the life I had lived was incredible. The journey to fill my passport was incredible; I had been so lucky. I opened my lips slightly to exhale. I was also so lucky to begin again. So, echoing the advice I gave to every first-year mountain climber joining my fundraising events in Colorado, I asked myself, "How did you reach the summit or accomplish the goal? One step at a time."

For my move to New Zealand to materialize, fate certainly needed to play a role—so did two governments, my ability to juggle productivity around the holidays, and a whole lot of shipping, transportation, and packing logistics. But for that moment in the plane, I needed to rest. Sleep was the most productive thing, I confirmed to myself as I dropped the window cover.

Would it work?

My heart said *yes*; my brain said *we shall see*.

I envisioned my energy shooting across the sky in that airplane like a shooting star. I reminded myself that I was bulletproof, but not like I had thought before I left: strong and steadfast in my convictions and impermeable to others' opinions or judgments. Now, I was bulletproof because I simply saw myself as light. Since bullets couldn't hit light, I didn't need to worry about the proverbial shots.

WISCONSIN IN DECEMBER is full of warm fires, icy roads, Packer football games, and family time. Even landing at the Chicago airport made me feel welcomed—welcomed with the smell of melted cheese, which reminded me of baseball games, movie theaters, and potlucks. Just hours later that day, I was cozied up with sixteen family members in my parents' living room, sipping pre-dinner cocktails with festive spices and garnishes, playing with my nieces, and catching up.

My aunts and uncles all wore relaxed but elegant winter garments, festive Santa socks, and silk shirts or wool sweaters. My brother and his family—his wife and two daughters—wore adorable matching pajamas. Seeing my niece's uninhibited joy was a pure reminder that someday I wanted to be blessed with children.

My extended family is irreplaceable; they are close, supportive, challenging, and… well, family. For us, that has meant always being there for each other, no matter what. They may subtly suggest a "better" way to do something, recommended by someone "smarter" (how to cut an avocado, for instance, as advised by *Cooks Illustrated*) or investigate a project you're working on to make sure it's practical and efficient (like, say, analyzing the steps needed to build a wooden deck). But ultimately, they will help you get whatever needs getting done, done—with love in their heart.

There is healthy competition, comparison, and expectation, too; since I was the first to get divorced, the questions and concerns over the past year were plentiful. Now, announcing a move to New Zealand was one thing, but the fact that I was moving without a plan was an entirely different ballgame.

"How could that be *right*?" they wondered.

"What is *right*, anyway?" I asked back.

They came at me from a place of compassion, but it was jarring to explain myself again after so many months of solo choices. "Whitney, you've always had a plan. Why this?"

"I know, right. It's a massive divergence for me," I said to my fellow Capricorns as their inquisition ruffled my metaphorical feathers. Even as an alpine ski racer, the practice of looking a few gates ahead was ingrained in my psyche.

"I'm excited to think about professional reinvention; I just don't know what my options are until I get there."

And I know I'm capable of figuring it out, I added just to myself.

"You do have a portfolio career," my cousin, who was now going to school in Paris, said.

"I trust this. I'm sure it's the right decision," I added, trying not to fall back into the habit of overexplaining.

"You said the same thing about getting married at twenty-four," poked my father.

Ugh, are we really going to bring up my divorce? Like a proof point of my inept ability to make big choices? I stopped myself. *Don't get worked up, Whitney. He didn't live it.*

I softly responded, "True. And I was right."

That got the attention of others in the room.

"Getting married to whom and when I did was perfect," I said, and relished using the word that haunted my childhood with new purpose. "What we had was beautiful; our love was amazing. I'm scared I may never know a love like that again. But I'm sure as shit grateful I did."

Dating had been fun, but nothing compared to a decade of love with your best friend.

"None of you can imagine how it hurts to leave someone you *still* love but know you have to. None of you can imagine how lonely it is to embrace the world without your best friend as you try to figure out who you are. And none of you can imagine how exhausting it is to feel the need to explain it to other people to make sure *they* are okay." That last comment made a few listeners adjust their seats and sit straighter. It also reminded me it wasn't my job to make sure others were okay with who I am.

After a brief moment, my mom said, "You raise your children with confidence and courage to create their own lives, and then they do." She shrugged her shoulders and smiled.

"But in reality, you are a bridesmaid in two weddings next year, one in Italy and one in Mexico. The commute from New Zealand isn't short or cheap," challenged my youngest uncle. I hoped this wasn't the start of a full laundry list of risks or negative outlooks about the move.

"Aw, come on, we're a family of pilots," I said to lighten the room. My oldest uncle is a retired pilot for United Airlines, and my youngest is an active Captain for Delta. "I'm sure one of you could just pop down and pick me up." That inspired a bit of laughter, which turned the spotlight elsewhere and ignited separate conversations. I overheard the evening's menu, a few recipes, university recaps, and travel plans all being shared—processing the beat of the conversations was welcomed, and I melted into the normalcy of it.

Putting my wine down instead of drinking it, I tried to relax my nerves further.

Love, I reminded myself. *They have nothing but love for me, and how I react to their questions is my choice. I don't have to get frustrated or defensive. We have different points of view, that's all.*

I cuddled up in a corner spot on the couch and glanced out the window. It was a clear and cold winter evening with only a dusting of snow blanketing the frozen earth—just enough to hear the grass crunch under your step. I imagined the horses staying warm in the barn, eating hay with tiny icicles on their whiskers from their steamy breath.

This family, this home, taught me to soar and explore, while grounding me with deep roots, nourished by generations of love and hard work—a foundation to which I could always return. The home I associated with the farm was unlike any other I had known or would ever know; it was woven into my blood and bones. Yet I came to understand there is another true home within—the one we carry in our hearts. Nothing can replace the power of physical presence, but when distance stretches like lifetimes between us, knowing we can summon the strength of that connection is transcendent. Ether cords are eternal—we can simply choose to amplify or soften their current.

"MY HEATHER!" I sang as I answered the phone, jumping into my same spot on the couch the next day.

"Hello, my Whitney. How are you?"

"Utterly exhausted, and wonderful," I laughed.

"I have all evening reserved for you. Because even though it's been just over three months since you were here for my engagement party, it feels like a lifetime since I've heard your voice. Catch me up on everything: your travels, your plans, how soon you'll become my neighbor..." and with that, we launched into a two-hour-long conversation, laughing, crying, and challenging each other. My extended family members weren't the only ones questioning the details.

"To recap your twenty-two-step crazy plan to make this happen, you have to repack your life in Vail, go to the courthouse for official divorce documents and mail them in for a name change and new passport, return to New Zealand before Christmas, and get a working holiday student visa approved, which all has to happen before your thirty-first birthday on January 8th? That's only in twenty-eight days—with a slew of major holidays in between."

"Yeah, a few things have to work out well," I agreed.

"You have bare bone funds, only a temporary place to stay, and no employment commitments once you get there. What if it doesn't work, Whit?"

"Back to Jeannine's loft, I guess. Assuming I'd be broke, Manhattan won't be an option." And I'd cry into my pillow every night from the paralyzing knowledge of what could have been.

"Whitney, you're the woman who builds a company from scratch just to help family and reinvents herself at the same job to remain loyal but still innovate. A seasonal temp position—or goodness knows what else is available in New Zealand—doesn't seem dignified enough for your potential. Please reconsider this. You could stay in Wisconsin while you look—*seriously* look this time—for work in Manhattan, and with your community here, you could design a temporary relocation plan." She took a breath. "You deserved your time away, no one's questioning that. And your journey was incredible. But maybe it's good to respect it for what it was and leave it at that. Refocus now as you had planned, reignite the momentum, and fulfill those dreams of hosting events and making a name for yourself in the most influential city in the world."

"I love you, Heather, and your points are all valid. Trust me, I'm tempted to make those choices and stay stateside. I'm petrified that this will turn out to be a disaster and I'll dig myself into a real hole that'll take years to climb out from. But catastrophe isn't guaranteed; it's only one possibility. There's another possibility: that I'll be wildly successful." I wondered what that would even look like. But I continued, "The only guaranteed failure would be not trying at all. And even though I'm riddled with anxiety, my trust in this path outweighs that very real and legitimate fear of it. I must try—it's the only way I can look myself in the eye."

"Okay, then. Why is New Zealand so special?"

"Why not?" was my quick answer, but I followed with, "I could list the tangible reasons, but the truth is, I just know."

"It's not that I don't believe in you, I just worry for you. But you do seem very optimistic for someone facing so much uncertainty."

"Proactive attunement, my friend. I'm consciously deciding what energy I want to bring to this situation and thus doing my part to create the reality."

"I guess we'll see how it goes for you."

"So, will you come visit?"

"Me? Wait, you will still make it to Italy for my wedding, won't you?"

"One hundred percent, no question about it. Even if I have to get a job with the airline itself to fly there, I will get there."

"Weirdly enough, I know you will. If anyone can pull this off—all of it—it's you. I am happy you've found conviction and purpose again, at least."

"You'll always be my unofficial advisor, my Heather, and such an amazing friend. Once I get there and the dust has settled, you'll be my first call to write my new resume, update LinkedIn, and sort job listings."

"Speaking of, you can't just disconnect again. Let's keep normal communication open this time."

"I'm back. I'm online, in more ways than one; social media and messaging included."

"I've missed you. I love you."

"I love you, too." Our conversation ended, as did our plan to live in the same city. But my Heather would always be part of the home in my heart, no matter where we were in the world.

AFTER ANOTHER EVENING of laughter, hugs, and stories with my extended family—and one wild night out on the town with Steph, who roared with laughter at my dating tales—I finally had a quiet evening alone with my parents. We huddled in front of the fire with a puzzle out on the live edge oak coffee table made by my great-grandfather.

"You know, SCOM, when people asked about you while you were gone, the general sentiment was, 'Poor Whitney, to be going through such a hard time and being so lost.' But I'd tell them, 'I don't think she sees it that way.' I know it wasn't easy, but you did it—for you."

"Thank you, Dad," I said. "It means the world to me that you see it that way." After surviving my recent hardships, I sensed a shift. Their regard for me was widening, not as their child, but as an adult.

"Last summer, when everything was fresh, it was really difficult for us to understand the deeper reasons why it was all happening. But seeing you believe in your convictions, we knew we just had to trust you."

"I know my actions go against every piece of advice you have. Thank you for stepping away from that, and for seeing *me* in the middle of all this drastic change," I said, choking up.

"Throughout life, you learn to pick your battles," he said, grabbing the tissues himself. "All that matters is how proud of you we are. I know without a doubt it's hard to do what you're doing."

Seeing my dad tear up was something new. Growing up, he had been more of the solemn and strong type, but recently, he'd been embracing a slice of vulnerability.

"You've inspired me to embrace change as well, in my own way," my mom said.

"Do tell?"

"I created new Pandora stations! I found musicians from all the countries you visited and have been playing the music to imagine being there with you."

"That's amazing, Mom."

"You've always taken decisive action," my dad said. "Do you remember when you were in seventh grade and quit playing the trumpet in band?"

"Yes."

"You were very good. And being in band is a family tradition. But you quit because you knew, even though you were capable of succeeding, that it wasn't meant for you. Strong discernment is a powerful gift, and you've always known what's meant for you and what isn't."

"That's a great reminder. Although I'm not clear yet on when I got disconnected from that gift, it feels like I've reawakened more than just a few habits from childhood."

"I know when you stopped listening to yourself," my mom said.

"You do?"

"Two pivotal moments come to mind. The first was when you started dating—you were like a chameleon, a shapeshifter, fitting in with every age, or group, or type of boyfriend. But you seemed to do so at the loss of your own uniqueness. And then, do you remember the big party your freshman year that was reported to the school for serving alcohol? And everyone attending had to miss sporting events and whatnot?"

"Yes, but I didn't miss anything because my boyfriend said I was with him—that I wasn't at the party."

"Yes. But you were, you know you were. And it was the first time in your life you lied about something and completely dodged all accountability for your actions."

My breath left me. "And I've been doing it in various ways since," I said. "I even started skipping school after that."

"Whitney, you're an honorable person, but that moment changed you. If you've noticed a pattern from it—especially a subconscious one—dive into it to understand more."

"Thanks, Mom. I plan to."

"Someday you'll turn lead to gold, my girl," my mom said, completing the puzzle.

"So, no job, no house, and no partner. Sounds like you're starting the next journey just as you did the last," my dad said.

"Exactly," I said. "So! Let's not dwell on it." I added with a wink and continued, "Let's get some fresh air! I feel... inspired. Like we need to ride."

Talking to them about everything the past few days had been enlightening and heartwarming, but I was ready to run; it was time to balance all the mental activity with a little physical movement.

"The snow has been falling all day and there's about six inches of soft powder in the fields," my dad, the pilot weatherman, said.

"You know what that means," smiled my mom.

"Of course I do! Repeat of my sixteenth birthday ride?" I said, ready to get my warm clothes and riding boots on. Memories of riding my horse at night with pillows of soft snow spraying up around us as we silently ran across the hillside were motivating me to move. There is magic in snow: its fragility and strength, an entire world held in every snowflake.

"I'll get the horses ready to be saddled and meet you both in the barn," said my mom as she walked over to hug my dad. Their love was unconditional, unspoken, and kind.

With that, we were off to fly through the hayfields that have been a part of our family for over 180 years, on the backs of strong horses, the winter air lacing our laughing lungs. Generations, seasons, and species, all flowing together. We are eternally connected. We are irrevocably free.

"JEANNINE!" I SCREAMED as we hugged in the Denver airport pickup area a few days later.

"Oh my *god*, welcome back!" she squealed.

"Shit balls," I said pulling away from her. "It's been a ride, my friend."

"And I want to know everything—don't leave any bits out. We have the whole two-hour drive to Vail, and I want your voice to be hoarse after telling me everything."

"Well, that's graphic. Okay, weirdo."

"Shut up and start talking."

"Glory, it's cold here."

"December in Colorado—don't be so surprised, you Kiwi."

"I'm not a Kiwi yet. It's going to be an Amazing Race Special Edition if I even get to leave again in a week, combined with covert, high-stakes roulette to see if I can have a shot at being a Kiwi."

"Damn."

"But first, I have five days in Vail."

"Right. And catch me up; I need to hear about the men. Dish— was Tanya helpful after I left?"

Starting with The Guide and ending with The Olympian, I told her everything. "Isn't it incredible how some people can be so influential in your life, but you only know them for a blip in time?" I learned so much about myself through those experiences.

"Unique friendships for sure. And on that note, *my* spreadsheet is officially retired."

"Do tell! Who is the devil that deleted the docket?"

She told me all about her new boyfriend—how they met, the overlapping friends they shared, and, of course, upcoming holiday plans.

"Speaking of holiday parties, how's the annual Framebridge soiree coming together?" The event was always my favorite of the year.

Despite my reassurance that I had found contentment in my early retirement from the industry, she treaded lightly with the details.

"I emailed Mr. Framebridge," I told her.

"Why? What did you say?"

"Happy holidays, that I hoped they had a great year. Made a joke about parties past and told him I missed the crew but was happy to hear of their continued success."

"And?"

"He responded the same day—very kind and supportive." It instilled a sense of softer closure.

As the Jeep and our conversation rolled along, so did our elevation from sea level. When we neared the Valley I loved so dearly, I felt a pang of grief; even though I was excited for what was to come, leaving still held such sorrow. Life would continue here—officially—without me.

We talked about the upcoming going-away party my friends were hosting for me and the logistics around Jeannine's purchase of my Jeep. Eliminating those payments was going to help my balance sheet, and I finally had the courage to ask her for a favor.

"Anything," she replied.

Quietly looking down at my hands and caressing a few of my rings, I said, "I want you to sell my rings."

She almost flipped the car, and I did a double-take out my window to make sure we were still within the lanes.

"Excuse me, *what*?"

"I know, I know. They've been my magic. But I realized they aren't—like Rose at the end of *Titanic*, it's time to throw them back to the ocean."

"Babe, some things are meant to be heirlooms. Why don't you just think about it?"

"I'm going to leave them with you. If they don't sell, they don't sell. But I have to try—plus, it would give me more liquidity."

"I understand," she said quietly. "I'll let you know the offer."

"Thank you." For the first time, I noticed there was soft music playing through the speakers. Tom Petty—one of my favorites.

"Are you going to call your ex? I don't think he's in town, is he?"

"I don't know, he may be in Wisconsin for Christmas. But I do plan to call him."

"Know what you're going to say?"

"Not exactly, but I think I should create space for anything that comes up. I'd say I'm sorry."

"Sorry for what? Would you change anything?"

"No." My Mrs. chapter felt sealed; I felt whole. "But within a breakup, there's certain healing that can only happen between those two people. And maybe if he knew the things I understand now, or if I took responsibility for my part in it all, maybe it would help him, too."

"Are you trying to take care of him again? His healing is his journey. Maybe you shouldn't muddle the two."

"True. And maybe codependent people need to heal independently. Ultimately, it's up to him if he'll answer my call or not, no matter what I have to say. I'll just hold the space."

"Well, alright then, enough about boys. Tell me about everything else."

I took a deep breath before diving into a monologue of memories. Having this time with Jeannine during our drive up to Vail was so special—a gift of uninterrupted time with someone who knew me almost as well as I knew myself. A drive filled to the brim with deep conversations as we passed the silhouettes of the majestic mountains out my window.

"You went for it, Whitney. You did what you set out to do and then some. And you inspired me to do the same! After Switzerland, I knew I had to mix it up, too, so I took a weekend off to shop in Denver, got dressed up for fancy dinners, and even had a spa day. I balanced the masculine and feminine," she said, reminding me that had also been when she'd met her new boyfriend.

You go, girl, I thought. "How'd it feel?"

"Way overdue. Balance is something we all need, but it's not always easy to consciously create."

"And it evolves. We need different things at different times in our lives; it's just up to us to continually ask questions and not be afraid to make changes." I continued, "My subconscious manifested the changes I craved, only they were just delivered as a bomb of pain instead of a slower, more systematic evolution."

"What do you mean you manifested the bomb?" I explained that I understood now how universal laws are always on and always honest. Like gravity: whether you believe it or not, it's always active.

"Okay, blonde Buddha, where can I get more of this ageless wisdom?"

"You laugh! But I've found that embracing my inner knowing feels like a real superpower. Like I'm communicating to a guardian angel on my shoulder."

"So, let me get this straight," she said, sounding serious now. "Tinder-ing around the world is the quickest path to enlightenment?"

We both laughed.

"One hundred percent. Only way to do it," I said with a flirty shrug.

"You seem happy, that's for sure." It was true: I was quietly, powerfully, and uniquely happy.

"I think I've had a permanent mindset change and thus a frequency shift. It's just physics. I feel the same, but different."

"Does your tattoo make sense now?" she asked with enthusiasm, and I told her the stories of reliving and remembering their truths.

There wasn't a minute of silence during the drive home, and I was overflowing with gratitude for friendship. Jeannine, Steph, Heather—all of my friends had been incredibly supportive. They asked the hard questions, provided a place to crash, snuck a twenty-dollar bill in my pocket, and both literally and energetically cheered me on throughout the past few years. Unconditional love connects us anywhere in the world, and my soul was safe with them. My failures, growth, and hope all had a sacred place to just be.

BACK IN VAIL, I was face-to-face with a life gone by. I knew the view from each of the mountain peaks I had flown over to arrive here, and from the landscape to the people at the grocery store, being back in town was intimate. But even though my return sent my emotions on a rollercoaster ride, I was finally learning how to raise my hands up and go with the flow. Every trailhead, river landing, café, and mountain peak spoke to me like a page from my photo albums, whispering inside jokes and marking secret spots. Beyond sadness, I felt respect.

Oddly enough, as well as I knew this valley, it felt like I was seeing everything for the *first* time. Vuja De: the opposite of déjà vu, meaning looking at something I've seen a hundred times, but with new eyes and a new heart. A heart that remembers the past but is fresh with perspective and free from needing to cling to it.

Over the course of a few days, I repacked my belongings into suitcases and storage boxes. The kit would make an REI salesperson proud, loaded with gear for both fun and survival in all seasons. This stuff still needed to rest; it didn't need to come with me. Where I was headed, I hoped to appreciate the mountain vistas for their beauty and presence without scheming the quickest route up. Or down—I wanted to enjoy the flow that came from going down an open ski run instead of the pressure of bearing down gate after gate in a race. But because I knew my love of this lifestyle was real, I kept that gear tucked away for a sporty resurgence in another chapter. Not knowing when or where that would be was a suspense the packing tape would have to hold. Contrary to that last time I had spent sorting these belongings, my cheeks were dry—there were no tears. This time, I was filled with hope for the future and faith in the current leading me there.

It was an oddly cold Colorado day with a cloudy, grey sky; Jeannine was at work, and I was running errands in *her* Jeep. Music played through the speakers while I sang my way around town—I had gone to the courthouse in the morning to acquire a certified original copy of my divorce decree, coupled it with an original copy of my birth certificate and passport name change request form, and was ready to leave it in the metal drop box.

With a FedEx overnight envelope in hand, I took one last flip through the pages of my passport, full of stamps and stories. These pages held the secrets of an awakening I didn't even know I needed. They unlocked a destination inside that now felt like home—a destination of freedom, of sovereignty. It was another piece of me, that passport, stitching together years of adventures in its binding, a world entrance ticket that showed I had gone out and gotten after it, filling all but *one* of its pages. The wind was blowing, and it was cold. But the weather wasn't staying my hand—my heart was.

It was significantly harder than I thought it would be to put my passport in the packet and seal it up. What if there was a storm coming in and someone couldn't pick this up tomorrow? What if they lost it? What if I never got it back and couldn't remember what it represented? Shaking my head and wiggling my toes, I mustered the courage for what was next, and dropped it in the slot.

Just as I had honored the mountains with a silent mantra when I'd left so many months before, my heart saluted the journey now: *thank you for more, thank you for less. Thank you for presence. I'll take care of the rest.*

Done.

My prep list was done.

Fingers crossed, fate would escort all of the moving pieces on efficient journeys so that I *could* keep going. And triple fingers crossed, my new passport would be delivered to my hotel at the airport before my flight. It had one day to be delivered to the rush center in Denver, one day to process, and one day to ship. I was cutting it down to the wire. In this situation, time was very real.

THERE WAS A certain liberation to surrendering to an unknown fate. And then there was the crazy-making side when I realized I was entering the final push; I had spent the night at the Denver airport's Westin, so my luggage and I were there and ready to go. I had one day left to travel to New Zealand, and if I didn't make it, I would have invested all that time, energy, and cash for nothing. It was almost too painful—and possibly unwise—to think about. In the ultimate optimistic move, I set an appointment for a health checkup in Auckland for December 22nd, the last day the office was open before the holidays and the day after I arrived.

I tried to ignore my nerves as I stood next to the check-in counter; I had been standing there for the last ninety minutes, waiting. Waiting for the FedEx driver to deliver my package. Now, my newly minted, maiden-name-carrying passport, needed to arrive in the next thirty-six minutes for me to make the international baggage drop cut-off time. There was just one big problem: airport traffic.

The FedEx driver had already circled the Westin Airport drop-off zone three times and just texted that he'd be another few minutes. Without my passport, I would be staying in Vail with no plan B.

I explained my situation at check-in. They wouldn't let me drop my bags until it was sorted, so I had been standing next to the final counter of the airline's area, anxious sweat curling my freshly blow-dried hair.

To pile on the anxiety, I didn't even have a confirmed seat on the flight. My youngest uncle had gifted me a standby ticket to help with cash flow, but all of the flights that week were oversold, and the best chance I had at getting a seat was on the flight I was rushing towards that left in two hours. I was dead last on the list, but I had a chance. FedEx needed to deliver my passport, like, now.

"Ma'am? We can check you in for another ten minutes; after that, I'm afraid you won't be able to check any bags."

"Thank you—the package should be here any minute. Really, I swear they're close."

I maneuvered my two large, checked suitcases, my carry-on, and my laptop bag a few feet closer. *Oh, God, please don't make me go back to Vail. Please don't. I cannot.*

"Whitney?" I heard a breathy voice call out from a man in uniform.

"Yes. That's me—I'll sign for it," I said, nearly grabbing the machine from him and ripping the envelope open.

"Good luck to you."

"You have no idea… thank you, sir."

This was step number one.

I zipped through check-in and bag drop, then ran to the far security screening area to skip the long lines, rushed through the train doors to head to terminal three, and finally got to my gate, completing step number two.

Then I had to sit and wait.

Again.

I watched every passenger board the flight to LA as I clung to my standby ticket, praying they would call my name and swap it out for a confirmed seat.

Waiting, waiting, waiting.

I wasn't used to flying standby and it certainly added to an intense day, but the price was unbeatable. I looked around the gate area as the seats emptied and watched the overhead screens as seat details got added behind other names on the standby list, one by one.

"Whitney?" called the agent.

"Yes," I said, nearly jumping out of my skin. "That's me."

"We have a seat available. Here is your new boarding pass— good luck to you."

"Thank you. I'll need some more of that."

Sitting down in my middle seat near the back of the plane, it was all I could do to keep it together. I started to cry.

Step number three, done—I'd at least make it to LA. From there, I needed to get a seat on my flight to Auckland: step four. After arriving in New Zealand, I'd begin a whole new list of things to arrange for my visa, housing, and so forth; but first, I just had to get there. Just like climbing a mountain: *one step at a time, one step closer.*

I didn't have my normal window seat where I could gaze at the clouds, hide my face, and release it all. *But who cares, I guess? So a few strangers see me cry?* I couldn't stop it anymore, anyway. Silent tears full of teetertottering emotion dropped from my eyes, and I thought of my ride to the airport the night before. The shuttle van had picked me up, and I'd packed my suitcases in the back and taken a seat in front, listening to music while other passengers came and went. It was a playlist of greatest hits, and I didn't fight it; I dropped in. I had purposely played songs from my wedding, and songs I had once danced to live. I'd found musical memories of laughter and love during that drive, and had welcomed them all. Driving to the airport before I left on my journey a few months before, I had been with Jeannine and my ex—what a difference time can make. What a difference a few choices can make.

It's crazy to be fighting so hard when you don't even know what you're fighting for, I thought to myself now. *I don't know what life will look like or if I'll even want to stay. But I guess I'm fighting for the chance; I'm fighting for the freedom to follow my heart. And that is worth the risk.*

WALKING OFF THAT airplane, I felt like Tom Cruise in *Top Gun* when he landed on the Navy carrier that final time, theme song and all. The stakes in our situations were different, but I felt the urge to celebrate the same. I had a three-hour layover in LA and found a quiet bar to settle into. I wasn't nervous about getting a seat on the flight to Auckland—the employee system showed thirty seats available, and I was number three on the standby list. The odds were in my favor.

Holding my new passport, I flipped through the pages. *All* blank. Completely unstamped and open. That alone made me feel like the next phase of life had officially arrived. But the big sign of freedom was my name: Whitney Joy *Swenson.* The name on my birth certificate, the name etched into the universe when my spirit chose to dive down to walk this human experience in this body, the name I'd begin again with. *Hello, Ms. Swenson,* I thought. *It's nice to see you again.* I pulled out a new journal.

I put pen to paper in its blank pages: *I'm here. Alone and on my way. I had to leave it all to get quiet enough to listen, to tune into my intuition. I had to leave it all to create the space to remember. And now I've left it all to start again. Not by default or denial, but by choice. From sex clubs to prayer chambers, skydiving to kundalini, I showed up—for me, as me. Embracing life as a spherical human be-ing. I may not have complete clarity on what defines me, but I know my eyes are open and I accept the risk it takes to walk into the unknown, again.*

My philosopher's soul believes in the magic within and around me, void of external definition. I belong here, just as I am. We all belong here, and we all deserve to be free. Every person on the planet is capable of utilizing the latent power within; if you are conscious, you are connected.

Ring, Ring. My phone interrupted my thoughts: it was my oldest uncle.

"Hi, Whitney. How's LAX?"

"Bursting with people and somehow quiet at the same time. I love airports."

"I know the feeling." As a career captain for United, he certainly did.

"Well, you're going to be in them a whole lot more if you'd like."

"What do you mean?" Maybe he'd gotten me a job with corporate? They had an office in Auckland.

"I know you're traveling on a Delta standby ticket, so that got me thinking that I should check to see if I have any active benefits anymore. I thought they all ended when I retired, but it turns out I still have a few passes."

"*Amazing.* Oh, wow." If both of my uncles were able to give me tickets, I'd be able to get to both international weddings next year.

"I don't have tickets, though, I have passes. Which means I can only give it to one family member every six months. But when you have it, you can travel unlimited."

"*What?*"

"Yep. You'll be a pass rider, so you can travel anywhere we fly, whenever there's a seat open."

"*Wow!* This is crazy."

"Well, thank you for inspiring me to check. This also means I have a pass again, so it's helpful for everyone."

"Thank you *so* much for letting me use one. Thank you."

"We wish you the best and can't wait to see you on your next trip home. I'm happy to help in this small way."

"Thank you. I love you."

"I love you, too. Enjoy the flight, and I'll email you your flying credentials."

Holy shit. I was a pass rider now? I couldn't have even imagined this—manifesting without attachment to results ended up being better than I could have ever expected. I had promised my mom I'd figure out a way to get back and forth, but this? This was way beyond. It was all syncing up; all the signs said *keep going.*

"Would you like another?" asked the bartender.

"Yes, I'd love another one of the same," I replied. It was time to double down and trust what I wanted, drinks included.

Over the radio, Brooks and Dunn's "The Dance" drifted softly. *Musicians are like tuning forks for the world,* I thought, *healing bits and pieces with specific frequencies.* People talk about using the Fibonacci sequence to create harmony and structure, but maybe the soul of the earth is a country song. They say a lot, but keep it simple. *I'm eternally grateful for the dance.*

"Here you go," said the bartender, handing me a second Negroni. Inspired by Sicily, Negronis had become one of my favorite souvenirs from the journey. The best souvenirs, to me, aren't bought in stores or airports, but are elements of real experiences that transport me back through time and space. I sipped my drink and fell back into my mind, tuning everything else out.

Like Dorothy in the Wizard of Oz and with my red stilettos, I wrote, *I'm walking the yellow brick road. However, we aren't victims of random circumstance but co-creators of reality; when I met the wizard, I realized I was the wizard. I'm also both the good and bad witches, the lioness, the tin man, and the scarecrow. We all are. Our spirits are like the light reflected from a faceted gemstone with different holograms of characters evolving and transforming with the rays of the sun. We all have so many beautiful facets to explore, even if we may not like everything we see.*

I understand now that my triggers reflected what I had yet to face in myself. But I want to give my shadow a handshake, not cast it in the role of a villain. I can still be compassionate and embrace my inner rebel. I can still be honest and rile up my innate challenger.

Ring, ring, interrupted my thoughts again.

It was him—everything stopped.

I had left my ex a message a few days earlier, and he was calling me back. I sat up as panic set in. *Do I answer? I should answer. We should talk; it could help. I know I need to answer.* As I watched his name flash on the display, everything stayed frozen—an invisible cord stilled my hand. I just stared at my phone. For the first time, I didn't want to talk to him. But deeper than that, I didn't *need* to talk to him. I didn't need him to be proud of me. In that joyous, glorious moment of embracing my ultimate freedoms and personal power, I didn't need him to validate it. For the first time, I didn't need him to validate me. I sat back, hands in my lap. No, I wouldn't answer. I didn't answer. I could call him back any other time, but not right now—this moment was for me.

Tears of self-love and respect pooled in my lashes, and, reaching for my wallet to pay for my drinks, I noticed my naked fingers. Everything is connected, and there are so many layers to saying goodbye. In that moment, I saw my rings left on the kitchen table at Jeannine's and saw my ex hanging up his phone. The energy binding us all together was undeniable, but I was stronger. I let them all go.

When I opened my wallet, I saw the corner of something sticking out from a side pocket. My lottery ticket and Cards Against Humanity card! Seeing the duo made me burst out laughing. Smiling to myself, I thought, *They have served me well. I'll keep the lottery ticket, since I'm still holding out hope for my career to surprise me.* But I joyfully left the game card with my receipt.

It was time to pass on its magical influence. Its message was a part of me now; no need for the physical reminder. My mind and heart were in complete coherence: *I'm a mother fucking sorcerer. And so are you*, I whispered to the world.

HOME. BAREFOOT WITH warm waves from the Pacific Ocean tickling my toes on the Takapuna beach shore, there are beautiful rose bushes blooming and the air is fragrant with possibility. My visa has been approved, with no contingency on qualifying special skills, and my belongings are all settled into a long-term rental just a hundred feet away. It's January eighth, my birthday, and I'm a young thirty-one. I have an interview tomorrow with a local business owner who operates an executive event and luxury tour company; I've never worked on the corporate side of things, but I'm excited to see if he has a part-time opening for someone with my skill set. And in a few weeks, I'll join Alec and Anne at their wedding reception— what a surprise. I can't wait to catch up and hug her growing belly.

Looking at the horizon, I take in my new view: just in front of me, I can make out the gorgeous silhouette of Rangitoto, a dormant volcano just offshore, with a bright red and white lighthouse in front of it. To my right, there is a wide, open beach leading to cliffs to hike around with more beach after that. To my left are cafés and shops and a welcoming park. On the ocean, a group of stand-up paddle-boarders are warming up for the town race. But for once, I have no desire to compete at anything. I have nothing to prove. No, there's a quiet in me—a calm. I can just be me.

Beyond Rangitoto is Waiheke, a whole island of wine. As inviting as that sounds, wine tasting excursions will have to wait—I spent the remainder of my loan in the US and am now solely surviving on credit cards. I allocated the bulk of them to rent and food for the next two months, a small amount for a yoga membership to continue kundalini, and, in a final Hail Mary to fate and investing in myself, I spent the last available credit in my name on tuition for life and executive coaching certifications, hypnotherapy, and NLP classes. I find myself holding far more questions than when I first embarked on this journey, and I feel an urgent need to better understand who I am. There is a lot of work to do. But now, I am ready to face my reflection.

I haven't spoken to my ex-husband yet, but maybe that's for the best. I know we'll connect again if we're meant to. And if not, there's also a peace in not having closure—to just let it be. He is on his path, and I am on mine. What I *will* do is promise not to carry my harmful patterns forward, work at being a better partner, choose to step into uncomfortable conversations, be vulnerable and humble, and strive to find home within myself so I'm not searching for someone else to complete me.

I think back to the diplomatic suite in Sicily: if I were there with influential people around the board table who could make anything happen, what would I pitch? Right now—nothing. I would ask questions: what drives them? What challenges or achievements have directed their lives, and what do they recommend for someone reinventing themselves? What are they confused or curious about? What does the world need right now?

Filling the seven blank pages of my old passport was a powerful awakening —a catalyst for change, inquisition into self, and evolution. Yet I am only beginning the real quest: to discover my own personal legend, stepping into alignment with my soul-driven purpose. I am just starting to glimpse the wisdom of the mystics, to see how the five dimensions of reality interweave to shape our existence. And my exposure to extrasensory experiences, spiritual laws, and metaphysics has been but a blink in the vast expanse of possibility. I am just beginning.

So here I am, grounding once more in a distant land. My energy is interconnected, radiating outward in fractal patterns both deep into the Earth—drawing strength and wisdom from ancient soils—and high beyond the stars, where I sense the shimmer of cosmic energy above, reminding me that I belong to both the tangible and the infinite.

I am here, I hear my soul say. *I am here to live, to create, to begin again.* I am ready to embrace yet another blank page. For I trust that it is in the unknown chapters that the magic unfolds.

This lioness is free.

EPILOGUE:
DECEMBER 2022

THE LATE AFTERNOON sun slants through the window, bathing my bedroom in a soft, golden glow. I stand before the full-length mirror, my silhouette reshaped by the unmistakable curve of my pregnant belly. My hands cradle the gentle swell, attuned to the silent, sacred presence within. I could never have predicted this moment—living in Austin, Texas, married once more, and expecting my first child, six years after I spent my thirty-first birthday on Takapuna Beach.

As I trace soft circles around my belly, light catches my wedding ring and dances around the room like luminescent fireflies. I smile, recalling what has shaped me since that day. A relentless thirst for evolution called in mentors, medicine journeys, and a knotty, long, dark night of the soul. I built a robust portfolio career and created financial freedom. Romantically, I called in my king because I finally stepped into my own sovereignty. My connection to the unseen remains ever-present: I am a student of the mystics, of energy, of cosmic intelligence, and I strive to integrate this human experience with higher realms of consciousness.

I gaze at my reflection, not with critique or comparison, but with quiet reverence and deep gratitude. This life is a tapestry woven from unexpected turns, raw endings, and breathtaking, bold beginnings. It seems almost impossible to fathom the distance I've traveled—not merely around the world, but within myself. My journey has been stitched together by moments of wild abandon, unlikely connections, and profound stillness.

This body—once climbing mountain ridges, swimming through tides of heartbreak and jumping out of airplanes—now carries the most sacred terrain of all: the feet of another soul who will one day walk through the world, exploring its edges, and stretching the boundaries of what is possible.

Closing my eyes, I imagine our hearts beating in unison—soft, low, resonant—and joining the eternal song of humanity. The hum is ancient and sacred.

To my little one: I am honored that my own heartbeat will be the first rhythm you ever come to know. I picture your tiny hand curled around my finger on the day you're born and smile, knowing we are all connected: my hand with my mother's, hers before that and further back still, through generations untold.

But evolution lies in our willingness to reinvent ourselves, over and over again. Change is necessary; do not fear it. I wish for you the courage it takes to honor your free will. My child, I want you to know the power of showing up—fully, honestly, and unapologetically—for your own life. Release the need to conform to someone else's idea of what "success" should look like. You are a co-creator of your own reality, and you hold limitless magic inside, just by be-ing. You activate that power by being *you*. By embracing your unique vibrancy.

The future is yours to shape. Dream boldly. Be true. Love freely. So that when your dust goes back to the stars your spirit will shake its head, saying, *Well, that was surprising, and raw, and wildly fun.*

I meet my gaze in the mirror: blue eyes stare back as everything else dissolves into a blur. They swell with warm, luminous, and loving tears. I see your movement in the reflection and whisper:

My dear sweet child, I promise you…
I will make mistakes. I am not perfect, nor do I expect you to be.
Life is raw and messy, but it is also beautiful and thrilling.
I promise you: I will stand by you, tall and proud, to face whatever fate brings us.

I promise you that I will love you.
Thank you for choosing me. Thank you for choosing now.
My dear sweet child...
Life won't be easy, but it'll be worth it.

Now, the page is truly blank, waiting for the ink of *your* story.
The best is yet to come.

Thank you for your presence and attention in reading *Seven Blank Pages*. If these words moved you—whether with resonance, reflection, or even challenge—I would be deeply grateful if you'd share your experience in an Amazon review. Your voice helps guide future readers to this story.

This is only the beginning. There is so much more to explore. Visit www.whitneyjoy.com to dive deeper:

Book Club Questions
Journal Prompts
Newsletter
Podcasts & Events
Quizzes and more

Together, let's keep turning the page.

whitney@whitneyjoy.com
@whitneyjoywrites

Magnetic: Where Courage Meets Magic
Awakening the Freedom Already Inside You